THE PENGUIN SPORTS LIBRARY

BUTTERCUPS AND STRONG BOYS

William Plummer is a senior writer for *People* magazine. He is the author of *The Holy Goof: A Life of Neal
Cassady*. He lives in Montclair, New Jersey.

Buttercups and STRONG BOYS

A SOJOURN AT THE GOLDEN GLOVES

WILLIAM PLUMMER

PENGUIN BOOKS

PENGUIN BOOKS
Published by the Penguin Group
Viking Penguin, a division of Penguin Books USA Inc.,
40 West 23rd Street, New York, New York 10010, U.S.A.
Penguin Books Ltd, 27 Wrights Lane, London W8 5TZ, England
Penguin Books Australia Ltd, Ringwood, Victoria, Australia
Penguin Books Canada Ltd, 2801 John Street,
Markham, Ontario, Canada L3R 1B4
Penguin Books (N.Z.) Ltd, 182–190 Wairau Road,
Auckland 10, New Zealand

Penguin Books Ltd, Registered Offices:
Harmondsworth, Middlesex, England

First published in the United States of America by Viking Penguin,
a division of Penguin Books USA Inc., 1989
Published in Penguin Books 1990

1   3   5   7   9   10   8   6   4   2

LIBRARY OF CONGRESS CATALOGING IN PUBLICATION DATA
Plummer, William, 1945–
Buttercups and strong boys: a sojourn at the Golden Gloves/
William Plummer.
p.   cm.
Reprint. Originally published: New York, N.Y., U.S.A.: Viking,
1989.
ISBN 0 14 00.8899 7
1. Boxing—United States.   2. Golden Gloves Tournament.
I. Title.
GV1125.P58   1990
796.8'3'0973—dc20   89–38515

Printed in the United States of America
Set in Times Roman

*For Nicky and Deg
and in memory of Kid*

Reader, have you ever seen a fight?
If not, you have a pleasure to come . . .
WILLIAM HAZLITT

When one has not had a good father,
one must create one.
FRIEDRICH NIETZSCHE

Author's Note

I owe some people for this book. Most of them are mentioned in the text. In addition, I want to thank the folks at Madison Square Garden and the public relations staff at the *Daily News* for letting me into the building each night during the Golden Gloves tournament. I want to thank them for allowing me to mingle with the fighters and the officials and, especially, for never asking me what I planned to write. I want to thank Tommy Hanrahan, Dr. Max Novich, Bert Randolph Sugar, Ron Arias, Peter Carlson, Pat Ryan and Jeanette Leardi for reading my manuscript and saving me from errors of fact and interpretation, as well as for shoring up my morale. I want to thank Reid Boates and Gerald Howard for one-twoing this book into print, and Molly, as always, for working in my corner.

A word on the composition of this book: It is the product of three years of hanging around the Rosarios' gym tamped down, for the purpose of dramatic unity, into one, the 1982–83 Golden Gloves season. The people in these pages are real and so are their actions. In many cases, however, I have changed their names and more salient details to protect their privacy. I have changed nothing about Mickey and Negra Rosario, who, I trust, as you read this, are still up there in Spanish Harlem, holding out a candle to the Children of the Night.

The Cast at Casa Rosario

Mickey Rosario: Once known and feared throughout Harlem as "Little Mickey," the former gang-leader-turned-boxing-trainer was the gym's first cause and, in many cases, a kid's last hope.

Negra Rosario: The trainer's weirder half, she was a Puerto Rican spiritist who worked the corners with her husband and all but spooked the other side into submission.

Refugio: Redeemed from a life of sloth by boxing, he was Mickey's assistant trainer; he was also, by dint of being a santero-in-the-works, Negra's chosen nemesis.

Chino Number One: A Don Ho look-alike from the South Bronx with a dazzling smile and a penchant for eating right hands, he was probably the toughest kid in the building.

Chino Number Two: A sullen piece of goods who felt the world was against him, he resembled Chino Number One in nickname only, which had to do with almond-shaped eyes.

Reggie Jones: The two Chinos' compadre in the welterweight follies, he was something of a "moustache" fighter—which is to say, he was fine until the boxing gave way to fighting.

Ariel: A genial prince of Africa by way of the Caribbean and Flatbush Avenue, he was bound for medical school and probably shouldn't have been donning the mufflers at all.

Smooth: A one-time dervish with the Rocksteady Crew and a former Golden Gloves champ, he quit on the stool two years ago and was now out to re-cover himself with glory.

Milton Street: A self-styled badass and enemy of society who was of late trying to blend with the Caucasian mainstream, he worried that he was a fraud and hooked, hooked, and hooked.

Johnny Luna: The gifted but star-crossed son of one of Panama's greatest fighters, he made his bed in the gym and carried himself like Prometheus.

Cuba: To most of us, a dark and distasteful enigma just off the boat from Mariel, he was, to Mickey, a lost and demented child, an almost certain tragedy in the making.

Luke: A bull of a youngster from Trinidad, he was torn between his parents' pacific beliefs and his own pugilistic ambitions.

Cuchillo: A knife-scarred rube from the sticks of Puerto Rico who could have taught Con Ed about energy, he was unfazeable in the ring, assuming you could get him into it.

Tiburón: A barrio fashion plate in his lime green and tangerine attire, he was the most experienced fighter in the gym and, as I found out, no mean con man, to boot.

Nelson: The greenest of rookies with just a month or so in the gym, he was Refugio's dark horse for a pair of golden gloves and the focus of Negra's midnight suspicions.

Jackson: The resident strong boy with a refined sense of self, he went to college and worked with retarded kids and punched with the oomph of a mine cave-in.

BUTTERCUPS AND STRONG BOYS

Chapter 1

IT'S WAR THEN, RIGHT, FELLOWS?

We gathered amid the heavy bags near the entrance to the gym, where Negra lay curled in pain over a table. A short tobacco-colored woman with bright black eyes and a two-inch scar starting at her hairline and melting into the bridge of her nose, Negra was Mickey the trainer's wife. The divot in her brow was a souvenir of a childhood spent in the South Bronx. It recalled a quarrel with an older girl that concluded with Negra being pushed into the sharp outside corner of a tenement. The scar was acutely sensitive to fluctuations in the atmosphere and gave her the ability to predict cold weather.

Remarkable as this was, it really seemed little more than a parlor trick compared to the rest of what she called her "powers." At the moment, for example, her entire being was scrolled around another and more ominous pressure front that was apparently gathering speed in her gut. She seemed to be querying her abdomen with fingers that moved like moles beneath the dark lawn of her jacket, kneading her entrails through layers of flesh and fabric for ripples of occult intelligence.

In a word, one she did not much care for, Negra Rosario was a "spiritist." She did not like the word because it suggested she had a choice in the matter and was . . . what? Daffy in the extreme. Or worse, one of those upwardly mobile, more-gringo-than-thou Nuyorican women playing at folk religion. She'd seen them in the botanicas, or spiritist drugstores, which dot the barrio like a rash of K Marts. Invariably, these women were rigged for slumming, got up just short of Carmen Miranda and stuffing their Vuitton bags with incense and *despojos de amor*. The latter were prebottled baths meant to entice a man. They were also a dead giveaway, for no spiritist worth her salt would stoop to ready-made magic. Not when she could so easily toil and trouble up her own. (Recipe from the *Spiritist's Cookbook:* Boil five yellow roses and *paraiso*—Costa Rica nightshade—in a vat of water. Add cinnamon, cloves, and honey. Now stand naked in the shower and pour the mess over your head. Repeat five days running, then take to the street and ambush the would-be lover with desire the moment the poor fool chances downwind of you.)

To Negra's mind, there was nothing the least bit quaint or picturesque about the pains that routinely wracked her body. Where Joan of Arc had her voices, and Santa Teresa her ecstasies, Negra, alas, had her cramps. Not to mention her fevers, chills, bouts with numbness in the arms and legs, or the times it seemed the population of Ponce was camping in her mouth. In each case, some "thing," some etherous delegate from the Spirit World, was trying to get in touch with her. Sending her cryptic telegrams coded in pain, which she, in turn, was at pains to unscramble. Perhaps it meant to warn her, this thing, of the latest Judas Iscariot idling on her horizon. Perhaps the imp merely wished to tempt her with the day's number in the Lotto. Perhaps, and this was to be hoped for, it brought balm for her nerves over the evening's fight card.

Negra had questions. She *always* had questions. But tonight was not just any night. Tonight she and Mickey had three young warriors making their debuts in the New York Golden Gloves. Would they, she wondered, return home from battle unscathed? Flush with both victory and good health? A lesser but still real concern: Would she and Mickey continue as an enchanted combination in the netherworld of New York City boxing?

Negra was a sort of psychic wind chime, a soft touch for any bugbear blowing through the neighborhood. She was the familiar of certain saints, whose names she would not disclose, lest they lose their bloom. She was practiced in the use of herbs and candles to ward off evil and purchase the saints' goodwill. Above all, apparently whether she wished to or not, she held open house to the footloose dead.

A few nights earlier, lying in bed with Mickey, she had watched a large black man dressed in green boxing trunks climb from her husband's body, come round to her side of the mattress, and plop down beside her, stretching full out, as if to measure her for a future habitation. She passed a sleepless night and approached her husband in the morning.

"Let me tell you something I see last night," she said. But Mickey quickly interposed.

"Don't start with me, woman!"

Years ago, in a moment of pique, he had taken all her particolored plaster and wooden and plastic saints, which she kept in seemingly casual array in her son Ralphie's room, and he dumped them in the incinerator. Negra sulked, raked him with her eyes, withheld her Delphic services. She stopped putting *oraciones,* or special supplications, in the socks of his fighters. She even stopped praying for her husband. From that day forward nothing seemed to go right. His kids lost fights they shouldn't have. Mickey himself was stabbed on the way home from Roosevelt Hospital, where he worked as a $200-a-week storeroom clerk, delivering I.V.s to the docs, flowers and tropical birds to the patients. Ralphie, their youngest, was a baby at the time, and Negra was sitting with him and his older brother, Mike, Jr. in their five-room apartment in the project on 121st Street. An equal-opportunity fabulist, as likely to rehearse the saga of the Sorcerer's Apprentice as the birth of *Juracan* (the Taino Indian god of the winds), Negra had spotted little green elves in the four corners of the room and was just beginning to stretch a tale about them, when, suddenly, she felt Mickey's pain. *Felt?* The pain was so real and palpable it nearly blew her off one of the vinyl-seated chairs belonging to the dinette set.

"I hope you father hurry up and get home soon," she said, even as the object of her concern lay in a pool of blood mere blocks away. "Because I think I going to faint. I feel like they have just ripped my chest."

Mickey was wiser now, if only that he knew there were things he did not know. (Still more things, that is, since he always had a healthy sense of his own ignorance.) He let her place the apothecary scales on the shelf behind his desk in his office at the gym. The scales signified that he was a Libra and concerned with the balance of right and wrong in the world. (Or, as Negra would say, that "he like to start arguments, so he could settle them.") He let her put the statue of Saint Jude, the patron of gamblers, on another shelf and even took her part when Cuba, a shadowy, sometimes rival spiritist in the gym, started dunking it in the glass of water customarily placed at its feet, I guess as a sort of reflecting pool. Mickey also wore without complaint the tiny gold medal of Saint Lazaro she gave him. That was not Lazarus the Stiff who was retrieved for a celebrated curtain call, but the other fellow, Lazarus the Leper, also known as Babalu, the voodoo god briefly given mainstream currency by Desi Arnaz's sappy Ricky Ricardo. (Remember, "Babalu, Babalu-Aye! Babalu, Babalu-Aye!"?) An emaciated coot dappled with bleeding sores, or so he was depicted in the statuary, Saint Lazarus was the champion of the mentally and physically infirm and of pets and children.

At forty-six, Mickey was in good repair. He was maybe ten pounds heavier than he was in the days when, as a flyweight, he faced a steady stream of bantam- and featherweight fighters for little more than carfare. No matter. According to Negra, Mickey partook of Saint Lazarus' aura. The truth was the trainer did have a way with children, and the mangy curs of the barrio did seem to sense something special in him. I'd seen packs of them approach him out on the street and, totally unbidden, proceed to sniff and lick his feet, their tails likely, at any moment, to copter them into the air. "Come on, Saint Lazaro," Negra would say on these occasions, her eyes ablaze with the pride of prophecy. "Come on and tear yourself from your admirers."

These days Mickey merely snickered when the boys in the gym said that Negra had "a special radio" whose signal was not of this world. With only a habitual trace of irony, he called her his "secret weapon." And, indeed, she was. Negra worked the corners with her husband at the Felt Forum, Ridgewood Grove, Atlantic City, wherever his kids were booked to fight. She was an adept with a bucket and a boreal wind to the opposing camp. Her mere presence at ringside, dark and brooding and volatile, was enough to spook many of the other trainers in the City. Especially the Cubanos. More especially still, the freshly arrived and strangely skittish Marielitos.

Negra was, in short, Mickey's edge. But he would ignore her and her sibylline throes just now. For he had men's business in front of him: three young fighters poking up like stalks of asparagus amid the heavy bags, their minds filled with green thoughts about the Golden Gloves.

"You got some idea what's going to happen."

Mickey was speaking to Reggie Jones, whose purple turtleneck seemed to flush out the highlights in his glitterblack skin. Like fellow boxers Chino Number One and Chino Number Two, Reggie was twentyish, a tall, slender welterweight. He was last year's Connecticut Golden Gloves champion in the 147-pound class. Which is to say, he was an experienced kid and, things being equal, should have been listed in the Open Division of the New York Gloves. But Mickey, always attuned to the main chance, managed to insinuate him among the supposedly rank beginners in the Novice Division. He counted on Big City chauvinism: He knew that nobody in New York would deign to know from Connecticut. Which one was Connecticut, anyway? The one that looked like a key?

"You got less idea what's going to happen," he said to Chino Number One, who'd been in the gym, off and on, since he was ten. Chino Number One was actually at least as seasoned as Reggie. But his experience was gathered beneath the rose, mostly in the clandestine entertainments called "smokers," held weekly in obscure little boxing clubs throughout the five boroughs. Chino Number One, like Mickey himself, whom he idolized and emulated, fell largely outside the purview of the so-called legitimate boxing establishment.

"And you got no idea at all," he said, turning to Chino Number Two, the only true Novice in the lot.

The two Chinos did not resemble one another. Rather they dovetailed in some third entity: the Latino's notion of the "Chinaman," which, I gathered, had mostly to do with almond-shaped eyes. Both young men had dark, almost Indian complexions. Both had jet black hair that went back in waves and fairly angular features. Chino Number One actually did look passingly Polynesian. One friend who'd caught the drift called him "Don Ho" after the Hawaiian crooner with the lovely hula hands. Chino's many female boosters, however, gazed into his lavish smile and claimed they saw the TV hunk Erik Estrada reflected there. Chino Number Two was more *tipico*. Terracotta in color and not a little sullen, he might have easily been dressed in sackcloth and pictured cutting sugar cane on one of those black and Day-Glo plates sold in the kiosks of Old San Juan: *Recuerdos de Puerto Rico*. At the moment, Chino Number Two was wearing a white terry cloth robe and sweating profusely. He was not a natural welterweight, or "47-pounder," as boxing people say, but walked around at about 165. Even though in the preliminary rounds the kids were allowed to be as much as ten pounds over the limit, Chino Number Two still went through something to make the weight.

"Now, let me tell you from the get-go," Mickey continued, "there ain't nothing out there that's going to outshine you. There should be no diarrhea attack. Sure, you got nerves. You human, ain't you? But you got the good condition. You don't give a hell what you see in front of you. I tell you right now you going to see some big, ugly black fellows. You going to see some scrawny-looking Ricans. You going to see some white fellows that don't leave well enough alone. And the coaches, all big, bad, you know. And they got them pretty shirts and jackets." The trainer laughed. The kids smiled.

"But listen to me. And, really, I hate to say this, but it got to come out my mouth." Mickey paused and looked significantly at each kid in turn. Then he set out once more on the adventure that speaking in English had always been for him, ever since grammar school, when he was plunked down among the cold people in this cold land, when his thoughts would spin ahead of his ability to lathe them into shape with this strange tongue, when the words would cower behind his lips, then charge out like a cavalry of bumper cars. Causing the white kids to laugh at him. Causing his hand to fly out in bewildered retributive violence. "Now, correct me if I'm right," he said. "But you on a *destroy mission!*

"Another thing. There's a whole lot of people I don't like there. Out of one hundred percent of the people, ninety-nine and three-quarters I don't like. I don't trust. But that don't mean you got to aggravate with them. Don't worry if you see me arguing or cursing somebody. I can handle myself. I don't need you. You don't need me. So just sit and relax and stay to each other. And whatever you do is more or less to talk and brag on you buddies. Like, 'That Chino there, Number One, he's a hell of a puncher.' Or, 'Hey, that Reggie Jones, watch out for him.' You pushing each other. Really, what you doing is selling each other out. That's what it come down to.

"It may be only one of you fights. Maybe one or two gets byes. Maybe all three fight. Once the bout is made, if it's a white kid from Rockaway, the crowd going to go, 'Woooo!' They mention you name, there going to be silence. Maybe boos. Once the official call you to the center of the ring, you go out there with confidence. With the eyes I can tell I'm going to beat you. I just look at you. I just put my eyes on you. The eyes can scare a man half to death.

"Okay? Time to shake. Look it here." The trainer balled his hands and showed them how to slap ten with gloves on. "*Pam!* Let you opponent know you ain't jivin'. Yuh! *Wap!* Let's go. Down on you knee and cross in the corner, if you religious. They announce you name, you take you bow and return to me and Negra. Once the bell ring, son, once you leave that corner, two seconds have gone. By the time you make contact, three or five seconds more have gone. So you really fighting a minute and fifty seconds a round. And they just three rounds. You hit the fellow, *Pam! Pam! Pam!* Every combination goes and don't get caught by a lucky punch. Because you get hit, it don't have to be a hard punch. Down you go, and that's it. They say in the amateur it don't mean nothing if you get put on you fanny. Don't believe this. In the eye of the judge, it look like you got whupped. So you come back to the corner and get you thing together. Work down, work up, work up and down, and move them hands. Because you fellows are known to be jab fighters, from left-right-left. You got to move that jab, because that's what you got best.

"Reggie, get you uppercuts and hooks and everything together, and don't be leaving that chin up in the air.

"Chino Number One, don't walk straight at the man, now. Some of these fellows going to come right to you. They might slap at you. But they going to quit, because you got too much right here." Mickey tapped his heart.

"Chino Number Two, you got to give that bastard fear from the get-go. You show him respect, believe me, I'm going to come back without a winner.

"It's up to you fellows to bring it home. We looking for the Finals, and I expect you to fight each other in the Semis. Unless of course you scared of each other." There was general laughter at the absurdity of this idea.

"Any questions? *Piensa bien,* think hard now."

"Show time," said Chino Number One.

"It's war then, right, fellows?"

We boarded the number six train at Lex and 110th, bound on an hour-and-a-half passage underground to Rockaway Beach, the easternmost extreme of the City's subway system and the site of the evening's entertainment.

The six, by the time we got on it, looked like something out of a World War Two movie. A troop train. As I leaned out the door, holding it for stragglers in that contagious uptown manner, I half expected to see Ann Sheridan and Betty Grable on the parapet tearfully waving us off to high deeds Over There. Instead, I was confronted with a conga line of Latinos, who were playing the cars like musical chairs. We had been preceded on the six by fighting coves from the Jerome, Apollo, and Fort Apache boxing clubs, three of your basic PR collectives out of the South Bronx, whose trainers were compadres of the Rosarios and were greeted accordingly.

At Union Square we were joined by a contingent from the Empire Sporting Club, which operated out of the venerable Gramercy Gym. A couple of doors down from the old Lüchow's Restaurant, Gramercy was started in the thirties by maverick fight manager Cus D'Amato and counted Rocky Graziano and Floyd Patterson among its more distinguished alumni. Come Saturdays, the word was that the Word itself was manifest in its precincts: Norman Mailer *et entourage* could be seen gamboling among the plug-uglies.

Just below City Hall the entire company disembarked in favor of the A train, which snaked down the west side of Manhattan from Washington Heights, collecting its own irregulars along the way. In the number was a batch of Dominicans from Artie Colon's Westside A. C., which operated out of a clammy tenement basement on the low end of Washington Heights.

"Platanos," said Mickey, as the Dominicans seeped into the car.

"Platanos?" I asked.

"Banana-heads." He raised his voice as the train pulled from the station and began the roar that defeated conversation.

I looked at him.

"Breakfast," he shouted, nodding toward Artie, a diminutive fellow with thick black frames on his glasses who made me think of the actor and TV shill Arnold Stang. Chunky! What a chunk of chocolate.

Put simply, *too* simply, the Dominicans ate bananas for breakfast. Habitually. Incorrigibly. Which was a barbaric practice to Puerto Ricans, who generally slice the fruit and cook it so that any piece might be draped across your fork like a soft clock in a Dali landscape, and serve it with rice and beans at least once a day, but never before noon.

The banana business was a dodge, of course. But an interesting one, with a smoldering subtext. The short of it was this: The Dominican made Mickey nervous. A certain kind of high-flown Cuban was bad enough, irritating, even to gringos with no stake in the Latino pecking order, for his air of fallen grandeur. "You ask a Cubano what he is in Cuba," Negra once said to me, "he tell you, 'Doctor, lawyer, accountant.' They ain't got no poor people there. You ask him where his money go, he say, 'Castro take it.' The Cubano got his nose so high into the air I think he going to drown sometime if it rain."

But the Dominican was different and *other*. Those were shadows nesting in his cheeks, there, below the moist slivers of broken glass that were his eyes. The Dominican was lean and hungry and slick. And with good reason: There were maybe half a million of him holed up in New York and every second one, it seemed, was here illegally. He had traveled by small boat and the evening star from Santo Domingo to San Juan and was often detected, even scuttled, en route. He had hidden at Stop Fifteen in Santurce amid the squalor of the Dominican ghetto, from which he eventually took the midnight flight to the Big City, where he had nothing but his fugitive wit and rapacity to recommend him. You could play the *platano*'s ribs like a vibraharp; of course, he'd be inventorying your pocket while you did. The Dominican was the sleek greyhound of survival, an appellative PRs in New York such as Mickey had heretofore reserved for themselves with the kind of pride only the lifelong hardcase can have in his lot.

"There's a change of hands now," shouted Mickey into my ear. "The Ricans got it too easy. There's a new breed coming up in the poverty line."

I could see a smile flicker at Mickey's lips. As ever, he was both amused and, deliciously, redemptively, I thought, self-amused.

We also hooked up on the A with a mixed lot of blacks and Latinos from the Times Square Gym, the third-floor walk-up on Forty-second Street, run by a former associate of Mickey's named Jimmy Glenn. Just in from Broadway, Times Square was directly across the street from a citadel of the cinematic and performing arts, which boasted, "New SEXtacular, SEXciting, SEXational LOVE Acts on Stage!" It was hemmed in by camera and check-cashing and tuxedo rental shops, by $2.98 steak joints, adult-books stalls, and raree-shows. It was frequented by both amateurs and pros—boxers, that is—and it served as a sometime refuge for the three-card-monte dudes as well as the "Check it out!" boys, who otherwise spent most of their time on the street, gesturing the fetid promise of a dance or "massage" through some doorway where the walls sweated.

The group from Bobby Gleason's was still more diverse. A dank, sinuous, lead paint–tattered establishment, buried amid the clothing racks and *schmata* salesmen of the garment district, Gleason's was probably the reigning professional spa in this the post-Stillman's era. It was to New York what the Main Street Gym was to L.A., or Johnny Tocco's to Vegas, a place where the top pros came to taper down before making a star turn in the Garden or the casino-hotels of Atlantic City. It was where three-time World Champion Wilfred Benitez played the ropes almost daily. Where that Hamlet of heavyweights, Gerry Cooney, honed sharp his hook when not sicklied-over with the pale cast of thought. Where half the heavy bags were held together

11

with silver duct tape and a prayer and where the ring birds, old pugs with mouths like tired button loops, peered down from a balcony upon the teeming floor. Gleason's was synonymous with Big-time Boxing, money ruled its roost; for my money it had no soul.

But there were soulful folk in it. Notably, the handler Hobey Chestnut, a languid black man with a prominent bay window and enough chains around his neck to pull a Diamond Rio from a glacier. Chestnut was a canny survivor who tended his own modest garden in the back lots of boxing. For years he had been handling Irish kids from Hell's Kitchen, dipping most especially into a rugged gang called "Westies" who shouldered the legacy of such storied neighborhood bullies as the gunsel "One Lung" Curran and the Attica-trained butcher Eddie Comiskey who emerged from stir to practice his cuts on human beings. Most of these Westies fought with their faces, almost as a religion. But they could be cajoled into keeping their gloves up, fitted with a semblance of a jab to preface the right hand, and brought along for ten, sometimes fifteen, crowd-pleasing fights, until they finally faced an authentic prospect and took the short course in reality.

Mickey detested the Hobey Chestnuts of the world, the small-timers who often fronted for tough guys and whose only and persistent hope was that one day the heavens might split open and some raw but discernible Rocco Marchegiano would descend from the blue and ask to put on the mufflers. "Flesh peddlers," Mickey called these fellows, and it was hard to argue with him. For while he was not right, I felt, about Hobey Chestnut in particular, he was no doubt right about the genre and he clearly had righteousness itself on his side. By this I mean, Mickey never made a cent off his several young pros, even though he both managed and trained them and was entitled to at least one-third of every purse. Never mind that these kids were basically four- and six-round fighters and made no more than $250 to $400 a go, which was scale at the Garden and better than most places, short of TV. The trainer would not have tapped into their earnings, in any case, unless they were substantial, say, a contender's wages in the tens of thousands. And of course he had no written contract with them. They were always free to walk, whenever. He considered them his sons.

Hobey Chestnut was one of our topics, Mickey's and mine. And we went around on him. At these differences of opinion Negra herself would rouse from meditation on her cramps to join in the educative effort.

"Bill," Mickey would say. "You been with us how long?"

A year or so.

"And you from here, right?" He'd make a sweeping gesture that would take in most of Harlem and subequatorial parts of the Bronx.

You know I'm not.

"But you learn you ABCs in the street, right? That's how come you know about us ghetto peoples?"

No again.

"Oh, then, you been around boxing a long time, that explain why you so familiar with these here Hobey Chestnut fellows?"

"Bill," Negra would break in, "let me tell you something. Mickey once have a kid named Modesto. We pick him off the street, we take him home with us, he sleep on our furnitures. Mickey take this Modesto and make him into a beautiful fighter. A heavyweight fighter. A beautiful heavyweight fighter that's Puerto Rican. Do you know what that mean? Do you know how much money somebody could make with that kid—*a Puerto Rican heavyweight that could fight?*

"Suddenly, after he win the Gloves, the kid got a father we never hear of before who seen his picture in the paper. This man who leave Modesto when he a baby he come and take Modesto away from us and give him to this other man he know down at the Solar Gym and, Bill, this other man is a flesh peddler. Let me tell you, this kid maybe could have been a champion of the world, but they use him and when they done they throw him away like garbage. His own father do this. Now, I think, Modesto is over there." Negra pointed toward Ward's

Island, which is about half a mile from the gym and in the middle of the East River. It's the site of a state mental hospital.

I could have argued that Hobey Chestnut was timber cut in a different part of the forest, that he was solicitous of his fighters and that, if anything, shrewdly undermatched them. That his kids, when they were finally winnowed out, simply regained their proper level, like water sluiced from an artificial lake. That they lapsed back to construction work maybe, or to pouring shots in one of those Ninth Avenue gin mills where the proprietors have a notorious soft spot for veterans of the Leather-pushing Trade. I could have said these things, but I didn't. I didn't argue at all.

There was little point in arguing with Mickey, who generally responded on such occasions not to sense, but to animus. Rather I countered parable with parable. I answered Negra's moral tale with one of my own, spun out of some of the gaudier threads of Hobey Chestnut's life, his love life, in fact, to which he'd made me privy during a companionable lull one evening at the Gloves and which, in its themes of reclamation and loss, bore glancing similarity to Negra's rendition of the Puerto Rican heavyweight.

Mickey knew what he knew. But he was not terminally doctrinaire, and for all his desire to be as shifty and ruthless as your local Dominican, he was as vulnerable as the rest of us housebroken gringos to real-life soap. Especially as I held back the more lurid details of Hobey Chestnut's misspent youth (how he used to, for example, hijack trucks under the auspices of the Bonanno family). Especially as I did not actually tell him Hobey's story, not directly anyway, but rather let him overhear it. Retailed it in front of him to a third party, thereby permitting him to take it in and sort it out at his leisure.

Even as I served up the story to said third party, I watched Mickey on the slant. I peered down into his eyes and could almost see the wheels whir into activity, the engines begin to fire, a new persuasion start to pick up steam. . . . And now, here he was, hanging by a strap on the A train, clapping Hobey

Chestnut's shoulder with his free hand in a universal gesture of *amistad,* as we hurtled through the dark beneath New York Bay and into the wilds of Brooklyn.

"How you doing?" I yelled at Hobey over the roar of the subway.

"Pretty fair," he allowed.

"Win tonight?" I nodded toward the kid at his side, who looked to be the usual bouquet of shamrocks.

"Better. Been on his ass like white on rice."

The twin spires of St. Rose of Lima, our journey's goal, pricked up among luxury beach-front apartments that turned their back on the ramshackle multifamily dwellings making up most of Rockaway and promenaded grandly along the Atlantic Ocean. Farther down the boardwalk, in better sync with the land's-end feel of the once-shanty Irish but now eclectically poor town, there loomed the white bones of a roller coaster against the speeding evening sky.

Looking down upon this scene from Rockaway station, I felt a chill along my spine. Maybe it was just the cold. Maybe. I looked over and thought I saw Mickey experience his own tremor. I noticed too that a number of the trainers and fighters who'd been on the train had paused beside us. They were wearing gaily colored windbreakers that bespoke participation in the Miller High Life Spanish Gloves, the Budweiser Empire Games, and so on, a latter-day, if sudsy equivalent perhaps to the Ancient Greeks' Pythian, Isthmian, and Nemean circuit. They were representatives of so many self-styled city-states within the City, so many insular tyrannies and oligarchies prone to petty jealousy and squabbling over such things as international junkets and youth-center funding. But here they were, gathered this night beneath the common banner of the City of New York and mesmerized by the funky landscape down below and what it portended.

For eight weeks running through the tag end of winter, some 1,200 ephebes aged sixteen to twenty-five from the greater New

York metropolitan area would wage approximately 500 contests, sometimes as many as 30 bouts a night five and six nights a week. They would do this, in many cases, merely to be able to say they'd been in the hunt for the Golden Gloves. They had entered on a dare. Or proverbial Americans on the cusp of manhood, they'd been curious to see what they were made of. These, by and large, were the so-called unattached fighters— which is to say, kids who had decided not to join a gym and place themselves under the tutelage of a trainer but determined to tough it out alone. All that was necessary, after all, to enter the Gloves was a sound constitution, fifteen bucks to join the local chapter of the American Boxing Federation, and literacy and coordination enough to fill out the sign-up coupons that started appearing long about November in the *Daily News,* the newspaper which originated the event in the twenties and continued to get behind it.

Club fighters, such as the ones who flanked me on the platform, entered the tournament for more considered reasons. They did so because for better than half a century the New York Golden Gloves has been the foremost domestic beauty contest in pugilism—because it is attended from the Quarter-finals on by a host of professional talent scouts, by managers, matchmakers, and promoters, most of whom will tell you they are looking for the next Ray Leonard. They probably are. But those with democratic sensibilities, and large platters to fill, also tend to keep an eye out for the latest bargains in beefcake: local hero-types who will sell tickets by the gross in the watering holes of Brooklyn and Queens, sturdy prelim boys to shore up the nation's undercard.

All told, 22 New York Golden Glovers had gone on as professionals to win world championships. More impressive still, between 1928 and 1976 a total of 141 fighters (including alternates) represented America in the modern-day Olympic games. Of these, some 25 percent had either competed in the New York Gloves or its annual intercity set-to with Chicago. According to Greek myth, the first Olympics was held before the invention of man and in honor of Zeus' victory over Cronus, his Titan father, who had the disagreeable habit of eating his own children. Apollo, they say, was a double victor that day. First, he burned wing-footed Hermes in the foot race; then he vanquished Ares the war god in boxing, which, your current-day enthusiast might say, was not unlike beating a Philadelphia fighter in his own building.

The New York tournament has its own cast of heroes and mythy stories, which are every bit as compelling, I think, and a sight more credible than those purveyed by Pausanias in his second-century *Guide to Greece,* in which main-eventers are forever being turned into wolves or installed among the stars. Every young fighter in the City knows, for example, that an underaged Walker Smith used the AAU (Amateur Athletic Union) card of a gym mate to enter the 1939 Golden Gloves. That he kept the gym mate's name, Ray Robinson, as his nom de guerre and added "Sugar," as he subsequently established himself as the sweetest fighter of the modern era.

Fewer know the story of Vito Antuofermo, who in the early seventies snuck into the tournament without his parents' permission. One night, following a victory, the future Middleweight Champion of the World peered across the ring to see his old man slipping through the ropes. Vito turned and ran to escape his father's wrath, only to discover that his father meant to embrace him—that Papa Antuofermo had known all along about his kid's secret project and was taking his own equally secret pleasure in it. From that night forward the man would carry the boy's gym bag to each fight, right up to the appointed day in 1979 when Vito took the championship belt from Hugo Corro of Argentina.

The bitter cold notwithstanding, we arrived at the church school gymnasium to find a sizable group of trainers and fighters queued up outside the door. Some of the kids had their scarfs tied under their chins and around their ears, others shadowboxed with the wind that cracked across the boardwalk. Mickey whisked us past this dim company, past the cop at the door and into the foyer, where the little silver-haired Fergus who monitored the ebb and flow of fistic personnel for the *Daily News,* and who clearly enjoyed keeping the evening's principals on ice out-of-doors, started to voice a protest around his nine-inch stogie. Then he saw who it was that was bolting the usual pleasantries.

"Rules is for other people. Hey, Rosario?"

Wordlessly, Mickey beamed into the building, even as Negra screwed an eye into the little shitheel that, had he been of her tribe, would have sent him scrambling for his *resguardo,* or anti-whammy kit—maybe a white drawstring purse filled with garlic, *yerbabuena* (peppermint), parsley, and camphor, which he would have taken to seven churches and dipped in seven different flavors of holy water and would now be clutching seven ways till sundown.

"Mick the Quick," said one of the glove handlers, as we hurried by, making for the elementary-school classrooms that served as dressing parlors. The fellow, a bearded Hispanic, was parked along the corridor, opening up boxes of fresh wine-colored twelve-ounce Everlast thumbless gloves. He was a sight to behold, a Grand Panjandrum of Buttons, measled from the waist up with lettered disks of the sort that used to say I LIKE IKE or IS THERE LIFE AFTER BIRTH? His said OFFICIAL in bold black letters against a white field, and FLOAT LIKE A BUTTERFLY/ STING LIKE A BEE (circa 1978), and I LOVE CHARLIE "WHITE LIGHTNING" BROWN, touting the latest hothouse prospect from the Windy City. Several contained snapshots: one was of the glove handler and Floyd Patterson arm in arm like Asshole Buddies from the Ark, another was of the glove handler and the missus and the four kids (all girls!) radiant in their Sunday best before a Christmas tree.

"Not Mick the Quick," said the trainer, pausing for a high five. "Mick the Slick. Quick and dumb ain't no good. Just get you in trouble faster."

The blackboard of the first-grade classroom was framed with

silhouettes: plump little Cupids taking aim at pink paper hearts beneath the legend, "Love Is in the Air." Before long it would be Valentine's Day, and the date was Palmer-perfect up in the corner of the blackboard itself. A poem about the snow by some lesser e.e. cummings petered down the adjoining wall. Above the door was a plaque bearing a "Peace Prayer":

> *Lord make me an instrument of Thy Peace*
> *Where there is hatred, let me sow love*
> *Where there is injury, pardon. . . .*

A few yards away, in tidy counterpoint to this sentiment, the fighters were crammed into desks built for six-year-olds, the sort where books and the like are stored beneath the seat and spill out at a touch or a hard look. The fighters' coaches hovered about them. One from Long Island was pouring a white liquid into a clear plastic mold: Wait seven minutes for the business to set up, then form it to your incisors. Presto! a custom-fit mouthguard. Another was painting the inner reaches of his kid's nostrils with Adrenalin, a purely preventive measure to stanch the flow of hypothetical blood. Still another caught my quizzical appraisal of the fighter beside him. "He don't look like much," said the trainer. "But, Lord, how he tear 'em up." The kid's hair was done in dreadlocks, each one garnished with a pink ribbon. You could have skated on his eyes.

As Mickey waited for Reggie and the two Chinos to strip down to weigh-in, he observed a black kid, dapper in Cossack hat and matching shearling coat, struggling with the hand wraps of a friend. The latter was a moon-faced white kid with quill-like bristles around his mouth, who seemed awed by the proceedings.

"Use some help?" asked Mickey.

"Why not?" said Cossack Hat. He essayed to be cool but was clearly relieved by the offer.

Wrapping a fighter's hands is an art, if not quite a science. The object is to turn the arm from shoulder to fingertip into a continuous instrument, which, when properly wielded, approximates a two-by-four coming through a ground-floor window. It must always be borne in mind, however, that said instrument is mortal and comes with movable parts. Proper bandaging provides stability for the twenty-six joints in the hand and serves to transmit and disperse the force of a blow. Which is to say, it sends the shock from a punch in a straight line from the hand back through the wrist to the arm and the shoulder, which are better equipped to take it. Should there be a fracture at some point in a fight, the bandaging ensures that the bones do not stray and cause real damage; in many cases, it permits the kid to continue fighting, since the pain usually won't set in until hours later. The Scylla and Charybdis of the undertaking are circulation and the wrist: rank amateurs tend to wrap the hand too tight, thereby cutting off the flow of blood and causing numbness from the elbow down; often they steer away from the wrist entirely, with the result that the hand does a half-gainer into the forearm, snapping the wrist like a celery stalk.

"How you feel?" asked Mickey. He was used to probing a kid's psyche, up to a point, while weaving his hands with the ten yards of Curity bandage provided each fighter by the tournament.

"Scared," blurted the kid.

It was an unanticipated rift of candor that cut through even the studied cool of Cossack Hat, causing him to take a sudden and unprecedented interest in the floorboards. The reaction of the surrounding trainers and fighters was more dramatic. Several started to get up and relocate, then appeared to reconsider and stay put. "Dag," said one, shaking his head. "Cripes o'mighty," said another. It was as if the moon-faced kid had emptied his bowels in front of them and mere proximity to the enormity would cause mass unmanning. Mickey ignored the to-do. He simply immersed himself in the task before him.

Typically, he begins by banding the wrist maybe six times around. Then he moves on to the hand proper, wrapping up to but not on the knuckles, making sure the fighter keeps his fingers spread so he has the slack to ball them in a fist once the job is done. Next, the trainer lays ten to fifteen lengths of bandage across the knuckles themselves, makes a couple of loops around the thumb, even as he crisscrosses the hand and wrist to bind the two together. He takes the remaining bandage back up to the wrist and brings it down in three individual strips, passing the strips between the fingers and tucking each on the other side in the wrap that accumulates on the palm. He lightly seals the finished product with the permitted couple lengths of tape. Any more than a couple is considered "loading up." Old-time fighters were known to lard their wraps with alum, which would cake with sweat and harden into something like plaster. In the pros, a boxing commission official will stop by to examine and initial each hand with a ball-point pen before the fighter slips on the gloves. In the amateurs it's strictly scout's honor.

"Scared, hell," said Mickey. "You ever fight before?"

"No."

"Hell, there's nothing to it." This said, the trainer turned, rolled his eyes in my direction, and went off to see to his own.

There would be no byes this night. All three kids would fight. Assuming, of course, that Chino Number Two could make the weight.

We coated him from head to toe with Vaseline, then swathed him in cut-up Hefty bags, which were as much a staple as gauze or Adrenalin in the beat-up aluminum suitcase Mickey portaged to every fight. The idea was to turn Chino Number Two into a walking sauna. To this end, we bound him at the joints with adhesive so that the resinous sheets would remain in place while he reapplied his street clothes: union suit, jeans, shirt, sweater, socks, shoes, topped off with Negra's puffy white down parka.

We took him across the hall to the boys room, where we stuffed a towel under the door and turned on the faucets in the sinks to promote humidity. Then we watched as he attempted to jump rope in the foreshortened space where all the fixtures were scaled for K-through-six.

"I don't know, man," said the object of our attentions. "When I leave my house I weighing one fifty-nine. I don't know where them three pounds coming from."

"You tell me," said Mickey. "I am going to believe what you tell me."

"I don't eat nothing, man. *Verdad,* is the truth."

"Who said anything about eating? You feeling guilty? Let's see them teeth." Mickey pulled on Chino Number Two's jaw. "Tell me that ain't food on them."

Chino Number Two crouched down to peer into the tiny mirror above the dollhouse sink that hit him at the knees. "*Joder!* Man, they always looking like that."

We left Chino Number Two to his rope in the boys room and made our way down the corridor to the school nurse's office, where Gloves officials were matching the fighters. Mickey wanted an early glimpse of Chino Number Two's opponent, who was, we learned, from Knight's Community Center, an indifferent gym in central Harlem. The plan was for me to stand at the door of the dressing parlor and sing out the kid's name and for Mickey to assess him on the hoof.

"Lopez," I shouted. And a short, nondescript Latino answered the call. "They want you upfront."

"Damn," said the kid. "Ain't one thing, is another." I tried to look sympathetic, as he disappeared down the hall in his go-aheads and bikini briefs.

Mickey waved his hand in dismissal. *Nada.* Piece of cake. But he nevertheless sent Negra to uncover the identity of the kid's trainer, generally the best index in the Gloves to a fighter's quality. Reggie, meanwhile, was sitting where Mickey left him fifteen minutes earlier. He had his Bible tucked in the belt of his white terry-cloth robe and appeared as serene and vacant as a spring day. Mickey began to wrap Reggie's hands. Pretty soon Chino Number One strode into the dressing precinct, whistling ostentatiously, his eyes dancing.

Ever the disciple, Chino Number One had carried the master's obliquity a step further. He had not simply managed to discover his opponent and survey him on the sly, but had actually introduced himself and set down to chat, elaborately admiring the kid's Carrera Porsche sunglasses, his shimmering Chams shirt, and high-laced Puma shoes, even while eliciting the name of his high school and unctuously agreeing that it was overbrimming with the chilliest peppers in the City.

"You meddle you words into the guy," he explained. "He get to like you a little. When it come time to fight, he don't want to so much."

Sometimes when he was especially pleased with himself, as he was now, Chino Number One would throw his head back in silent laughter and you could see each of his impossibly white upper teeth against the dark roof of his mouth. They looked like runway lights on an airstrip at night.

"Chino, you think about spitting ever so often?"

We were back in the boys room and Chino Number Two, who'd shed two pounds, still had one to go.

"Spit."

More sullen than ever, Chino Number Two jumped over to the sink and hawked dramatically, but could call up little. Most of his excess water had already drained along the Hefty bags to his shoes, which sounded like squeegees as they traversed the floor.

"Let's all blow on him," said Chino Number One.

"Best not," said Reggie. "He so skinny now, he could sail right out the building." Both kids were delighted with their gym mate's plight.

"My trouble is I trust you," said Mickey to the sodden fighter. "I got to tell you, son, it embarrass me, it embarrass the whole club, when you come in overweight. Anybody got to make pee-pee?"

The trainer had turned to the rest of us. "Serious, now." He started to laugh himself. Then, cupping his mouth with one hand, he grew confidential. "It psychology. He see us going, he can't help it, he got to do it himself."

The four of us bellied up to the urinal while Chino Number Two continued with his rope. We bent at the knees to clear the lintel and repeatedly flushed the works so to give Chino's bladder subliminal encouragement.

"Chino, you got to go yet?"

"Yeah, I got to go," he said, suddenly tossing aside his rope and racing to take a seat in one of the stalls. "But you ain't going to like what I got to do."

We quickly zipped up and exited.

As the Three Sisters and their earthly instrument, the local matchmaker, would have it, Chino Number Two was scheduled to be the first of Mickey's kids to come to scratch. The news, smacking as it did of a fatal conjunction of the stars, appeared to plunge the already beleaguered fighter still deeper into his usual planetary blues. Yet moments before he set foot in the ring, Fortune appeared to perk up some and smile upon him.

Which is to say, Negra was back from reconnoitering the enemy camp and burbling like a brook. Lopez's trainer turned out to be a Cubano, a Marielito, in fact, and highly suggestible. Merely by passing several times before him and fixing his lamps with her own burning coals, Negra had brought the fellow to such a pitch that he had cried out for everyone along the corridor to hear, *"No me cruce la piedra!"* It was the sort of thing you might say, a beat too late, to a black cat who'd strayed across your path.

"Oh boy!" Negra chortled, "do I got *his* character."

Chino Number Two broke from his chute like a Maura bull to daylight. Halfway across the ring he began to snap off a succession of jabs, and then another, in a display of apparent willingness that immediately put the crowd in his corner.

"Hey, Lopez," screamed a wag hard behind the press section. "Time to turn in your green card!"

"*Bzzzzz!*" intoned another, who'd taken creative note of Lopez's trunks, which featured black and yellow stripes banded horizontally. "Look, it's a friggin' bumblebee."

"Yeah, but he got no stinger!"

It scarcely mattered that each of Chino's jabs played out several inches short of Lopez's kisser. Or that he held his hands exaggeratedly high and weirdly close together, as if he were cuffed at the wrists or suspending a quantity of knitting between them which the opponent would kindly gather into a ball. Nor did it matter that Chino Number Two, when he did make contact, failed to turn his punches over, which is where the power is. Actually, Chino's open-glove blows did have some impact. They resulted in loud slaps that reverberated through the gymnasium, gathering many "Ooohs!" and "Ahs!" from the Saint Rose fancy along the way. The crowd, like most crowds, was a sum of frustrated desires and seething anxieties, a freelance grievance in search of an evening's advocate. In the first half-minute of the first round it thought it found one in Chino Number Two.

Alas, after the initial adrenal surge, Mickey's fighter regressed to form. Which is to say: Chino Number Two was what the old-timers, the curb brokers and gym lawyers who keep the lexicon, call an "agony fighter." To wit, you throw a punch, he ducks, and maybe hits you quick. You don't throw a punch, he doesn't throw one either. The "agony" is, of course, the audience's, especially when two such buttercups are matched in the ring. This is a fate that is usually headed off in the pros by thoughtful matchmakers who—unlike their straitlaced amateur counterparts, who are interested only in "fair competition"—generally have the fans' entertainment in mind.

In any case, it took both the crowd and Lopez himself the better part of the first stanza to realize that Chino Number Two was not going to lead, but rather was going to bob menacingly in place in the center of the ring or, for variety, skitter along the periphery, occasionally loosing that weirdly structured jab of his, which issued elbow-up and in two sections, somewhat like a gooseneck lamp. Only too familiar with the phenomenon, Mickey and Negra were halfway up the steps and already incurring the referee's warning for their corner talk.

"*Tu primero!*" screamed Negra. "You first, Chino!"

"*Mueve la mano, coño!* Move them hands!" yelled Mickey.

By the second episode, Lopez, with help from his Cuban trainer, who was hissing bravely at Negra from behind the opposing turnbuckle, had largely figured Chino out. The kid began to make bold sorties, disdaining the jab and milling overhand lefts and rights at Mickey's fighter, who backed straight into the ropes, flailing his own arms as he went. Chino was beet-eyed and seemingly on his last legs when he returned to his corner, trailing the always fickle crowd's abuse like clattering cans on a wedding vehicle.

Now, in recent weeks, Mickey and I had discussed what, ethically (my word, not his), could be said to pump up a fighter between rounds. I had recoiled from the last-ditch tactic employed by Gerry Cooney's manager in the title fight against Larry Holmes. "C'mon, Gerry. Do it for Tony," the fellow had said, alluding to Cooney's dead father. The latter, as the entire sporting public knew, had started Cooney off in their Long Island backyard maybe a dozen years earlier and was the crux of the kid's ongoing guilt and manufactured aspiration.

Mickey merely smiled at me. My naïveté was not just showing, it was pulsing in neon. "You want to know what this Rappaport fellow did wrong?"

"Yes, I do."

"He got caught."

Simple as that.

"Yes. He was stupid. He say the thing on TV, when they got them microphones in his corner. Look, you call this a sport, but we ain't playing here. We looking for a edge and we ain't so dainty about where we find it. You religious?"

"Me? Not so much."

"Me neither. But, believe me, if that kid in that corner is a Jew, I been bar mitzvah. If he praying to Allah, I'm going to get right down on the floor and pray with him. I bring up a kid's mother, I bring up his father, his uncle, his cat, his dog. Sometimes I bring them all together in one spot. Like what you call a sense."

"A 'sense'?"

"You know. When they all dead and they come back."

"A séance."

"Right. Listen, now, because I ain't going to tell you twice. Negra and me we got these kids for two, sometime ten years, when they go in the Gloves. We been through smokers with them. We lived with these kids, slept with them. We already know their motive. We know when they angry, when they ready to cry. We know who got heart and who don't got heart and who got too much heart for his own good. We know who need to be souped up to fight. Slapped in the face even. Embarrassed right there in the ring, for all the world to see. . . ."

Chino Number Two did not require public humiliation this night. Nor did Mickey feel the need, this time out, to bring up Chino Number Two's toddler son, who was living in the South Bronx with the teen-age girl Chino never quite got around to marrying, not far from his grandmother's project where the fighter himself abided. No, between rounds two and three Mickey needed to kindle but a single thought in the dry precincts of Chino's brain for him to come out smoking and win the last round, and therefore the fight, convincingly.

"*Está cansado*. Look how tired he is," said Mickey. He trained his fighter's gaze on the recumbent Lopez, who, in actuality, was on a roll and had to be a good deal fresher than Chino himself, but who, under the power of suggestion, seemed, even to me, to get as limp as yesterday's lettuce.

"Thank God," said Mickey. "You just getting you second wind."

*   *   *

Reggie Jones did not get off so easy. En route to his victory he took one upside the head from Mickey after both the first and second stanzas. Reggie was a stylish fighter, one of a handful in the gym who paid out his punches in meaningful sequence. Yet, unaccountably, he tended to welsh on his gift, to capitulate to pressure and brawl.

"Listen, son," said Mickey to Reggie prior to the final episode. "You got a nobody over there. This turkey's got nothing, *nothing!* You understand? You got to keep that right hand by you chest and move the left. Let's don't worry about knocking nobody out."

Chino Number One's fight, on the other hand, was over virtually before it started. For Mickey's kid no sooner touched right gloves with his opponent in the timeworn gesture of athletic civility than he came across with his left, causing the astonished opponent to go silly at the knees. When Chino Number One spun off the ropes, where his opponent's weight had propelled him, he sought to hit the kid again but could not find him. Then he looked down and discovered him puddled around the much admired high-laced Puma boxing shoes.

"You snuck him," I said to Chino, later, as he bent to hot-comb his hair before the tiny boys room mirror.

"The rule say, 'Protect yourself at all time,' " he responded, without losing a stroke. He turned and smiled that smile. "How I look?" Devastating.

What the kid from the high school with the chilliest peppers in the City had failed to notice about his newfound, "meddling" amigo was that Chino Number One was a southpaw. Which is to say, his considerable power was in his left hand, not in the right, which he extended pro forma at the tip-off. But, then, there was no way the kid could have picked up on Chino's sinistrality. For shortly before entering the ring, Mickey had instructed his fighter to warm up in orthodox fashion. Which is to say, right-handed. Strenuously, right under the kid's nose.

The kid never knew what hit him.

*   *   *

Mounting the stairs to the subway platform for the long hike back to the City, we came across the moon-faced fighter with the ratty moustache, who had been battered into quick submission by the Rastaman I'd encountered in the dressing parlor. If anything, it was even colder out, the winds more unruly, than when we'd arrived some five hours earlier. But the moon-faced kid was in his shirt sleeves. He was visibly upset. He kept walking away from Cossack Hat, who implored him to put on the pea jacket draped over his arm.

Mickey grabbed the kid as he went by. "What you see here?" he asked. Mickey took the kid's hand and forcibly straightened out each clenched finger in turn.

"I don't know. Five fingers."

"Right. And five more on you other hand. Listen, son, you got you health. You got you future." He paused and stared into the kid's pig-slit eyes. "Hell, you got you good looks."

The kid laughed. Cossack Hat laughed. We all laughed. I could make out the white bones of the roller coaster in the distance.

Chapter 2

KISSIN' HER YERSELF

I guess you could say that I owed Mushy for my friendship with Mickey and Negra. For he was the one who sent me to the Golden Gloves in the first place.

You could tell old Mush had been a fighter, although it wasn't so much the claw for a right hand that gave him away as it was the gaiety, which hung about him like cigar smoke at a vintage club fight. All old fighters, like tragic heroes, I told myself, were gay—which is to say, they were in love with their fates.

And the talk, especially it was the talk that betrayed him. Wonderfully hokey stuff that should have filled the bubbles of the old Joe Palooka comic strip, instead of the lame *Biff! Bam!* stuff that did. In the Book According to Mushy, the boxing arena was no mere site for fisticuffs. It was a mixing bowl. The ring was the square circle, and the fellows in it might be round-heels or ham-and-eggers, buttercups or strong boys. A good kid had rosin in his veins. He could douse your glims, maybe put you on Queer Street, solely with the aid of the boxer's best friend. Which is to say, he could blacken your eyes, even daze you, with the jab alone.

Mushy didn't go on about himself. That would have been bad form. But I gathered that back in the days when the Italian boys were calling themselves Dundee and the Jewish boys were swiping classic attitudes off Grecian urns and slicking their hair with brilliantine, back when young blacks, not even fighters really, were still being herded into battle royals for the delectation of fat cats at white men's clubs, Old Mush, well, he was a prelim kid, maybe even a prospect. He was Delancey Street's own "Fighting Newsboy." When I met him, he was hawking papers again. He had been for decades, out of a plyboard stand on the Great White Way.

Several times a month, en route to my editorial job on Sixth Avenue, I would stop to ask after the latest *Ring* or *Boxing Illustrated* and, naturally, to chat about the current crop of "punchilists." Mushy took it upon himself to enhance my reading bill of fare. For a dash of the exotic, there was Britain's *Boxing News,* filled with Welsh wallopers and Liverpudlian larrupers. Locally, he favored the *News World,* the daily paper put out by the Reverend Moon, which gave over two pages each Monday to doings at metropolitan mixing bowls. For sheer orneriness, there was someone named Malcolm "Flash" Gordon, whose *Tonight's Boxing Program* raked the weekly accumulation of muck generated by promoters "Dung" King and "Marsa" Bob Arum, a pair of pragmatists in the American grain said to be so sensitive to the human adventure they could hear a dollar bill drop on a shag rug. Flash was a piece of work, a plain speaker in that relentless way that some people are vegetarians and White Castle Restaurants are white. When Ray "Boom Boom" Mancini was matched with Duk Koo Kim, Flash curled his lip and sneered at the fight, referring to the South Korean as "Pe Suh Shit." It was a stroke of wit he so fancied he declined to give it up, even after the kid waged the battle of his young life and ended up losing it in the process. Flash never took a backward step.

One day, into February, Mushy was holding forth on bums and their importance to the sport. "How else a comer gonna get his experience if he don't fight bums? How else you gonna know blue chip from cow chip?" He was well along in his tour down Cauliflower Alley, idling, in fact, at that intersection where club fighters touch mitts with tomato cans, when he abruptly asked whether I'd ever attended New York's amateur classic, the Golden Gloves, which was a great place to see the bums and champions of tomorrow, the whole chain of being in embryo.

I knew about the Gloves, of course. Yet I had to answer that I'd not seen them, or any other live fight, for that matter. Though I'd read avidly in boxing literature, from *The Odyssey*—the Greeks were an ongoing, if undeveloped interest—to Leonard Gardner's *Fat City,* my most immediate experience of the "sweet science of bruising" was television.

"Television!" said Mushy. "You can't compare a real fight and TV!" He looked personally aggrieved, as if I had fouled the air in front of him.

"You know what Arthur Donovan said?" he asked, alluding to the referee who'd mediated between Dempsey and Tunney, among others.

I did not.

" 'It's like the difference between watchin' a dame get kissed and kissin' her yerself.' "

A few nights later, I puckered up and took the Broadway local down to Madison Square Garden's Felt Forum, the 5,000-seat arena wedged beneath the Garden proper. I called ahead and got press credentials, which gave me a ringside view and the privilege of descending to the bowels of the building where the fighters geared. I arrived late and, as it turned out, somewhat in luck. I had missed more than half of the evening's twenty-odd contests, but according to a pert, not-so-young thing who took results for *El Diario,* I was still in time for the seasonal debut of the "Dancing Bears."

The what? I asked.

"The novice heavyweights," she said.

They 'dance'?

"Stick around." She smiled. "You'll see."

At the New York Gloves the heavyweights, green or otherwise, are invariably made to tango on the tail end of the card.

These are the so-called walk-out bouts. But New York is a heavyweight town in most respects, and I noticed that few of the thousand-or-so spectators were seeking the exits. Clearly, a good portion of the crowd had more than a casual interest in the proceedings. A bevy of bottle-blondes just behind me was sporting black T-shirts bearing the legend NAPPY'S GIRLS. Nappy himself was apparently still to come, as his amply-lunged supporters were deep in conversation and primping before pocketbook mirrors. A second group, klatched boozily to my left, was not wearing any distinctive costume, although the men were partial to lumber apparel, thick wool shirts and steel-toed shoes. They were, however, univocal in their cheering, which was of the sort usually heard at football games. "Here we go, Jimbo, *here we go!* Here we go, Jimbo, *here we go!*"

Jimbo was obviously one of the huge steers presently before us, who, with the sound of clapper on steel, charged across the ring to collide belly first, much as the Tons-of-Fun Brothers used to do on Saturday mornings at the Rialto. The two young men, both with Slavic surnames and heads that might have stood freely in the sands of Easter Island, were extremely willing, but lacking in science. They tasked each other, mostly around the shoulders and in the kidneys, with horizon-sweeping hooks, which did little damage, but quickly had each man gasping from exertion and blushing all over his milky body. After several increasingly less titanic collisions, the pair gave up punching almost entirely, and except for a modicum of wrestling, clutched one another in a slew-footed pas de deux until the music finally gave out.

Somehow the judges met in a decision. Alas, they did not pick Jimbo but the other fellow—the one with the nautical scene imprinted high up on the meaty part of the arm.

The decision proved to be a blow of vastly greater proportion than any struck by either fighter in the previous quarter of an hour. It proved, in fact, to be insupportable to the choral group to my left. For some time, I'd noticed, several of the burliest basso profundos had been gathering at the bicycle rail that separated the freeloading press from the paying public. The announcement of the victor, by a fellow in a ruffled shirt whose name sounded like "pizza," precipitated the chorusers into action—actually sent several of them sailing over the press barrier and onto the ring apron, from whence they could more efficiently rain cries of "Bullshit!" onto the retreating officials.

Finally, after much commentary on the parentage and sexual specialties of the judges, after a flight of Frisbees improvised on the spot from drooling beer cups, and after a mustering of the rent-a-cops with their billy clubs rampant, order was restored. The Jimboists receded from the arena.

Yet Nature, as is well-known, abhors a vacuum. Even as the noise in the room returned to a comfortable hum, the pool of pulchritude immediately behind me began to swell to attention. "Nah-PEE! Nah-PEE! Nah-PEE!" A large square package, wrapped in pink with a silver bow at the middle, could be descried in the middle distance, chugging down the aisle toward the ring. The heralded Nappy, as my friend Mushy might say, was just moments away from his maiden do-si-do with Destiny.

I went back to the Felt Forum the very next night. And the following night, and the night after that, and three nights the next week, and the next, and so on, until the tournament moved upstairs for its finale in the Garden itself. I went with it. How could I not? I was smitten.

I felt as though I had entered another world, and I was eager to get to the Forum early each night to watch that world pass in review. I would post myself at the fighters' entrance, behind that officious little mick who monitored the traffic of fistic personnel with all the charm of Cerberus at the Infernal Gates. The fighters and their handlers would squeeze through the corrugated-steel doors in regulated trickles, where they were "carded" before being permitted to descend to the dressing rooms. The kids carried their American Boxing Federation I.D.s in shiny red folders, flimsy ABF issue which they quickly personalized as wallets. Inside, the folders had facing clear plastic panels, one of which, of course, harbored the ABF document, while the other offered a small window on their lives. Through it was visible all manner of keepsake and talisman, whatever was portable and totemically indispensable, including scapulars, locks of hair, prayers in gold leaf, pix of bimbos and bambinos. The ABF cards themselves were of interest. On the back were listed the date, location, opponent, and result of each of the kid's matches in sanctioned shows; on the front was vital information about height, weight, age, and up in the corner, in an effort to curb tribal use of the card, was stapled a thumbnail glossy of the perpetrator himself. These snaps were acquired, almost without exception it seemed, four for a buck and a half from photo booths in Times Square arcades. They had that telltale sepia sheen and melt-in-the-hand feel, and sometimes along the border you would see part of a head, the goofy fraction of a friend who at the last moment poked through the curtain and into Cyclops' gaze.

Hats. I'd never seen so many before, and in such variety. Not just watch caps and porkpies and snap-brims, that like. But berets, Connemaras, motorcycle and Mao and Beatle caps in cloth and leather, velours wafting the plume of the cavalier, knitted Inca deals with flaps, the occasional fez or boater or derby, even the modified turban, beneath which one might discover a domestic Muslim, or maybe just a young blood, his hair gooped with relaxing cream and stuffed inside a toque fashioned from one of sis's nylons. Above all, kids and handlers alike wore those cake-shaped baseball caps, "gim'me hats" they call them, that don't seem to get sold in the stores but are nonetheless ubiquitous and advertise everything from processed bat guano to the latest licks of Earth, Wind & Fire.

Kids came in carrying apples and pears in baggies, thermoses filled with Hawaiian Punch or homemade broth. They came with their pockets laden with chocolate bars, cookies, Ring Dings, Twinkies, Magic Mommy Brownies, a junk-food pantry of instant energy for the post-weigh-in repast. They shouldered a variety of bags, again talking a medley of gyms, tournaments, magazines, airlines, athletic companies. And across their arms, straight from the cleaners and still bearing the transparent wrapper, the better-heeled or more-veteran among them draped their robes. These tended to come in combos of black and silver, gold and royal blue, with here and there a glint of vermillion, sienna, and apricot. They were emblazoned across the back with a range of hopeful sobriquets, some claiming kinship with past masters and geographical areas, others pointing up wished-for or actual wrinkles of style. BROWN BOMBER II," said one. THE CONEY ISLAND CYCLONE, said another. MANNY "MANOS DE PIEDRA" PEREZ, HAVANA BON BON, "BATTLING" BOBBY BARTOLO, BABY SPINKS, SAMMY "TOO SWEET" CAMACHO, "IRISH" SEAN O'MALLEY, NEIL "THE EEL" EDWARDS, IRAN "THE BLADE" BARKLAY, "BICYCLE" BOB BOWEN, and so on.

Below stairs, along the dressing-room corridor, the Golden Gloves field command was the first door on the left. In one corner of the cramped, vaguely triangular room, a thin, laconic man named Bill Lemien attempted to weigh the fighters on the Garden's ancient Fairbanks scale. In another corner, the evening's pair of designated physicians were giving spot examinations to the kids who'd made weight. The real physicals having been administered back in December, they were checking now for broken bones, hernia, irregular heart beat, and sluggish reflexes, which might indicate drug use. Along the back of the room, Matt Cusack, the dean of New York amateur boxing, was busy making the fights, matching the kids by height and age as well as by weight. Age was critical, especially in the early rounds of the tournament where the disparity in skills and experience was the greatest. Wherever possible, the Gloves matchmakers tried not to pair boys of sixteen with men of twenty-five. They also tried to head off what they called "Mutt and Jeff fights," the feeling being that the taller kid had a distinct advantage over the shorter kid, who needed to get inside his opponent's guard to be effective and often couldn't within the three rounds afforded by amateur boxing.

Matt Cusack was a distinguished-looking gent with several

decades' tenure in the old AAU, who had twice shepherded the U.S. boxing team through the Olympics. In his blue blazer and rep tie, with his ivory hair carefully parted on the side, he looked an odd duck amid the preponderantly swarthy talent of the Gloves, as if he had wandered down from the New York Athletic Club out of a sense of noblesse oblige. Actually, Matt was a first-generation American whose father had come over during Teddy Roosevelt's reign to drive a carriage for a family of swells living in midtown Manhattan and ended up in a blue suit with brass buttons walking a beat. Matt apparently had a lively sense of humor as well as a storied fondness for charade. Not long ago, I was told, he had a massive light heavyweight on the scale, who, despite several efforts, just missed making the 178-pound limit. Time was short, drastic measures were in order, if the fellow were going to compete. Matt couldn't help but notice, as the kid dropped his shorts, that he was as endowed as Harvard and Yale put together.

"Tell me," he said to the trainer, pointing to the kid's member, which was monumental even at rest. "Does he fight with that?"

Naturally, the trainer was puzzled by the question. But taking in the matchmaker's elegant appearance and deadpan manner, he answered straightforwardly and in the negative.

"All right, then," said Matt. "Put it on the table. He'll make the weight yet." And he promptly reached for the cleaver kept on hand for just such a purpose.

The corridor outside the Gloves field command was a great paper dragon on Chinese New Year, with new sets of legs constantly filtering in and out through the half-dozen dressing rooms. As with Heraclitus' river, you could never step twice into the same corridor, for the people who had occupied it but a moment ago had since flowed on. It was not a place, in any case, for fighters, who merely passed through en route to the weigh-in or to the stairs and the ring itself and who otherwise holed up in the dressing rooms amid the congenial din of the ghetto-blasters. Rather, the corridor was meant for the trainers and seconds who lingered with an assortment of VIPs: city-based promoters and matchmakers, professional managers, salesmen for Tuf-Wear or Everlast, the occasional world champion and contender on the make, as well as numerous past stars of the tournament, many of whom had friends or gym mates in the Gloves and who were themselves in the pupae stage of pro careers. The trainers smoked, lined up for the pay phone, shuffled their kids' ABF I.D.s like bubblegum cards.

"You heard about Cha Cha?" the fellow next to me, sucking on his pipe, asked another padding down the hallway. Cha Cha Ciarcia, I quickly discovered, was a small-time promoter in the tristate area who had yet to cover his phone bill with his earnings in the business. He was someone even the characters thought a character. When asked, for instance, why he kept on promoting fights when all he did was lose money, Cha Cha would grow thoughtful and say, "I guess you could call it a sickness."

The story at hand was about one of Cha Cha's recent galas footed at the Rollerama in Brooklyn. "Seems," said the raconteur beside me, removing his Dr. Grabo, "half an hour before show time they couldn't find the round girl, which was always an important feature of the Chach's promotion. So he sent Skinny Vinnie upstairs to the bowling alley to find him another. Well, finally, this young guy comes up to Vinnie and tells him his sister's a looker and for twenty-five bucks she'd be tickled to carry the cards.

"Half an hour later this doll wearing a sequinned mini-skirt and a pound of war paint shows up. Says her brother sent her. Well, Vinnie he just heaves himself a sigh of relief, piles the round card on her, and points her toward the ring. Things are going along great. The morons at ringside are howling like crazy every time the doll bends over to get in or out of the ring. Vinnie himself tells Cha Cha, 'She ain't much in the mug, but get a load of them gams!'" And the Chach, your noted expert on womanflesh, naturally he agrees.

"Things are pushing to a close. It's the last round of the last fight and what's the doll do but reach up and damned if she don't pull off her hair! It's a wig. A few seconds later the horrible truth sinks in. 'She's a guy! She's a guy!' everybody starts to screaming.

"Hell, not only is she a guy, she's the same guy as told Skinny Vinnie he was going home for his sister. Poor ol' Cha Cha. He'd like to die, right there in the Rollerama. And so would all these morons who been staring up her skirt and carrying on all night, like she was Bo Derek.

"But wait, wait!" said the pipe smoker to his audience, which was near-obliterated with laughter. "The good part comes later. One of the deputy commissioners, who's there at the show, writes a letter to Commissioner Prenderville, saying as how the Chach should have his license revoked for 'employing transvestites.'"

It was only natural that I should see Negra first. There was no missing her, really. Negra was the first woman to work a corner in New York since lightweight champ Lou Jenkins had his best gal Katie flog a towel for him back in the forties. I remember being struck by how petite Negra was and how seemingly demure, standing tippy-toe in her white tassle moccasins, averting her gaze, as she reached one arm through the ropes to extend the elastic on her fighter's trunks so that he might renovate his lungs with oxygen. Then she opened her mouth to share a passing thought with the referee, and the illusion of her delicacy was shattered with the air around her.

Mickey was an easier make. The trainer put me in thrall pretty much the way he does every newcomer to the Golden Gloves. When I first saw him—I mean really *saw* him, for I must have been watching him for weeks before I actually saw him—he was perched on one knee between the redwood thighs of a heavyweight. It was that interval between rounds in which the one-minute angel must perform his prodigies of restoration, and Mickey was clearly beside himself, trembling with anger at his kid's performance. Finally, he punctuated a series of broad Mediterraneanate arm movements and furious remarks with a short open-face right hand to the cheek of the slumping fighter. It all but brought down the house. The crowd, I later realized, after paying repeated witness to the spectacle, had grown queerly still in freighted anticipation of what was known throughout the Gloves as Mickey's signature gesture. A gesture that was all the more astonishing because it invoked a tableau in which a gnat reared up to sting Gargantua and not only got away with it, but Gargantua promptly requited the attention by exploding from the corner to pound his foe to the canvas.

Who was this trainer? Where in the City had he carved his lair? And, how did he get away with this shit? Such were the questions I posed along the press loop.

I quickly learned that Mickey Rosario and his wife Negra had set up shop in east Harlem. Their gym was in Thomas Jefferson Park, the old Italian park on 112th and First Avenue. Their son Mike, Jr. was a three-time Gloves champion, and they had another one coming along who was said to make Mike look like a piker. Rosario was top-drawer, as amateur trainers go. He started Hector "Macho" Camacho and he guided the fledgling Billy Costello all the way through the amateurs, or, as Mush would say, the Simon Pures. . . . Only, well, he was a handful, something of a bad actor, maybe even a black eye to the game, what with slapping the kids and all.

Each year, it seemed, one of the local TV sportscasters would lay in wait for him. In one frame, this fellow, Werner Wolf, would show Rosario's fighter getting it from his opponent. In the next he would show Rosario himself greeting the kid with the flat of his hand. "You're having a tough night, right?" the sportscaster would say. "So you go back to your corner for a little sympathy, right? Wrong. *Whack!* Come on, gim'me a break! Even the kid's corner is hitting him!"

Worse still, said one of the officials, "You tell Rosario he's got to stop abusing his kids and he just stares at you. Like it's the O.K. Corral and he's waiting for you to draw first so he can gun you down."

Rosario looked, I thought, like pictures I'd seen of the young

Guglielmo Papaleo. Willie Pep, that is, the "Will o' the Wisp," featherweight king of the forties, one of the superior ring technicians of all time, who generally won his fights going away but still took a dollop of gratuitous pleasure from lacing, heeling, gouging his hapless opponents. There was no one feature in particular that sewed Rosario and Pep together. It was something in the play of tightly curled hair, somewhat jugged ears, thin, mobile countenance and eyes that changed like island weather.

I watched Mickey for days before attempting to approach him, watched him peacock along the ring apron before and after his kids' fights, pausing now and again to stretch in a fashion that was elaborately feline, to dangle histrionically over the ropes or lean out toward the crowd to chat with a friend or fan. It was instantly apparent that the trainer was energized by the public gaze, that he used it for photosynthesis. Yet it was equally clear that he was oblivious to all of us, that we, the audience, were somehow there at his sufferance, if not quite at his invitation. He was, I thought, like the waiter in the word-of-mouth bistro who is both utterly aware and sublimely indifferent to the clientele, who performs his snappy ceremonies for himself and only incidentally for the customer, whom he regards as something akin to elevator music. It was also clear that the trainer was steeped in his own private drama. In those instances when his kids lost, I watched him swoop down on the judges, demanding to see the scoring. I watched him slam down the card with a look that would purge the impurities from iron ore and a few choice words, whatever he could muster, I would later learn, to throw a scare into the officials for the next time a kid of his came across the proscenium.

One night, I looked on as Mickey endured what Mushy would call a "bottomless" performance by one of his fighters. The kid, a tall skinny Hispanic, was poised for flight from the outset. You could almost see his ears prick up, his eyes move from the front to the side of his head, as he turned from tiger to coney and made ready to show his heels at the snap of a jab. Afterwards, I followed the defeated company down to its dressing room and sat quietly in the corner, listening as the trainer spoke to the humiliated fighter.

"All I can do is provide you water and you mouthpiece," said Mickey. "You got to do the fighting youself, son. You want to make something of youself, don't you?"

"Yes," said the kid. He was standing against the wall amid a sea of gym bags. The wall was a shade of hospital green and the kid was still in his boxing togs, but he seemed naked.

"You know you got to work at it all you life."

"I keep thinking he going to tire."

"You can't think that way out there. You got to be a animal."

"He was aggressive."

"No, he wasn't. He was just walking forward."

"I hit him with some good body punches."

"You hit him with nothing," said Mickey, softly. "You were ten feet from him. Tell me, am I wrong?"

"No. You right, Mick. One hundred percent. I feel bad." The kid began to cry. "I want to win the fight for you, Mick."

"No, no, no!" said the trainer. "You do it for youself, son. You *numero uno*. You number two, three, and four. And five, six, seven, eight, nine, and ten too. You have feelings for me. That's nice. But you do it for you. You have anything left over, then you think of me. Maybe."

The trainer was quiet for a moment. "You want to quit?" The kid shifted nervously. "I don't want you to quit. The reason I coming down on you, see, life is not this way. You can't give things away, son. Not when you work so hard. Not when you come where you come from. You all by youself in this world. You know that now, I think. Because them six minutes up there in that ring they the loneliest six minutes you got in life."

"I guess I wasn't belief in myself."

"But how come *I* believe in you?"

"Well, when I got my second wind—"

"Wait now! We don't want no excuses. We got to be a man about this here."

"You right." The kid laughed, gingerly fingered his jaw. "That slap you give me, Mick, it harder than what he give me."

"Hey," said Mickey, smiling broadly. "We didn't lose nothing. We ain't busted up. We going home happy. I'm going to get you ready for the Nationals. Remember, Smooth got stopped a couple years ago and what happen to him?"

"He go back to the gym."

"And what happen at the gym?"

The kid was baffled. "You work him hard?"

"I embarrass him. I punch him, I kick him, I bite him. And what's he do the next year?"

"He win it all! He get the Gloves!"

"You want a week off?"

"I be there tomorrow."

"That's what I like to hear."

For upwards of an hour, I don't know how long, really, Mickey and I sat in the bowels of Madison Square Garden and exchanged the stories of our lives. Actually, it just seemed as though we did, so sure and immediate was our rapport. In point of fact, we talked almost exclusively about our beginnings and about the two men who bestrode them as the Colossus once did the harbor at Rhodes.

I went first with the idea of priming Mickey for his telling, but I found that I quickly got caught up in my own. I told Mickey about my coming of age in New Jersey in one of those lazy little dells with a river winding through it that serve as bedrooms for the Big City. I told him most especially about my grandfather, my mother's father, and my earliest beau ideal.

Tall, leonine, with a thicket of silver hair, my grandfather was a Captain of Industry, a millionaire in the custom-shoe business in the days when it meant something to be a millionaire. My grandfather bought a new Caddy in some daring pastel shade every other year and skippered it with vast one-handed ease. He had great hulking friends with names like Mac and Monte, latter-day satyrs whose voices clapped like thunder and with whom he drank deep and often and ended up imbibing a nonalcoholic elixir called "Near Beer," in penance, I have no doubt, for being himself with such a vengeance. "How ya doin', kid?" my grandfather would say whenever he saw me. At a loss for comparable eloquence, I would resort to copy-speech. "How *you* doin', kid?" I'd shoot back. In fact, I came to call him "Kid." And, in time, so did everyone else. It was a name that caught on in the family the way nicknames always do: first with an ironic smile, eventually without shadow of attitude. I was the firstborn grandchild and, as such, put my stamp on much of the local fauna and flora.

I felt sure that Mickey would be enchanted with my grand-father, and I could tell by the glint in his eye and his attentive silence that he was. For Kid was a man's man. He was doubtless as crafty and pitiless in certain pursuits as your latter-day Do-minican, but I knew nothing about that side of him. The Kid I knew was a page come to life from Damon Runyon: he fol-lowed the nags, loved deep-sea fishing, and—and this was the matter I was growing to—was absolutely bugs about boxing. In my earliest memory, Kid is in his den, crouched in a two-fisted posture upon the coffee table. It's the end of the work-week and the Friday night fights are beaming from one of the first idiot boxes RCA ever made, and my grandfather is match-ing slants with Kid Gavilan, holding his own against the tricky Cuban. My Kid even has an answer for the Kid's famous bolo punch.

My grandfather had a collection of pasteboard boxing cards, which were put out in the early part of the century as an ad-vertising gimmick by rival tobacco companies. The cards came in cigarette packs. Mecca, for example, featured full-length studies of bare-knuckle champions Jem Mace and John C. Heenan rigged out as if for the opera, while Mayo presented such post–Marquis of Queensbury idols as Peter Jackson, the original Joe Walcott, and Jake Kilrain, stripped to the waist and frozen for posterity in the on-guard position. Kid would sort through the cards, and sucking his teeth in a way I found fetching in the extreme, he'd suddenly pull out the likeness, say, of Joe Gans and be moved to dilate upon the immortal lightweight's theory of "straight hitting" in an era of "wide swingers." Or he would reminisce about seeing Dempsey-Carpentier at Boyle's Thirty Acres in 1921, or going up to Pompton Lakes in 1938 to watch Louis prepare for Schmeling, or, the week just past, hopping over to Greenwood Lake with Mac and Monte to see Marciano put through his paces by bowler-lidded trainer Charley Goldman.

For years, I played Desdemona to Kid's Othello, aching for the retailing of yet another adventure, however vicarious, in the garish foot-lit world of prizefighting. My grandfather and I were bound together, not just by blood, but by presumptive expertise. There was no end, for example, to the pleasure we took in 1955 when Dr. Joyce Brothers, who'd won the "$64,000 Question" in the "boxing category," picked Bobo Olson to retain his middleweight laurels against a refurbished Ray Robinson. Foolish woman! What did she really know, statistics apart, about the Manly Art? There were field trips, too. Kid took me to the Ring Museum, where I peered through the glass of the oaken cabinets at the very gloves Louis used to dispose of Billy Conn. They looked even then, as I remember, like a pair of spaniel puppies curled in sleep. . . . But, *basta*. Enough. I merely wanted to get Mickey's best engines going, and I did.

"My father dies when I am born," he said. "To me my older brother is my father, and long as I can remember I want to be just like him. The funny thing, to be like him is to be like this." No more than five feet six inches himself, Mickey held his hand at chin level.

"In them days the Puerto Rican people don't believe too much in marriage. A man walk in, he can take care of the woman with the kids, that's all they think about. So we all living, my brother and my mother and me and the three little girls, with this fellow I call my stepfather. Then this stepfather move out, and my mother goes to New York to work in some rich lady's house and send us the money. We living in Santurce in a place they call 'el Fanguito'—"

El Fanguito? I interrupted. On the Martín Peña Canal?

"Yes."

I'd seen the place, in English "the Mudhole." A population of 100,000. Squatters, mostly, holed up in shacks on stilts pounded into the putrid water. The tides came in twice a day to chase the pigs and goats indoors and redistribute the garbage and sometimes to drown the little ones asleep on the shack floors.

"This stepfather named Vasquez, he was a fancy man. My mother, although she have three children with him, only lives with him a short time. She is one of his victims. When he hear that she leaves for New York, he want the little ones back. It's a macho thing. But my brother is already trying to send us to my mother in New York."

You and your brother have the same father?

"No. My mother have Rafael with a black man, that's how come he so dark and have that beautiful black curly hair, like a midget Indian. But her family make her abandon Rafael to people named Tejada, who bring him up. At seventeen he find out the name of my mother and that's when he come to live with us and when he have the trouble with the stepfather. Because my brother come home from work, where he fix ice cream trucks, and there's the stepfather come for the *nenas,* the little girls. My brother has a fistfight with this man. He chase the stepfather out of the house. Then he put all four of us in a public car and he takes us to the airport." Mickey smiled, clearly savoring the memory. "I remember when they call out my name for the plane, 'Rosario.' And Rafael he tell me, 'Go on, that's you.' Then they ask him his name and he say, 'Tejada.' Finally, they come to the *nenas,* and they say, 'Okay, now, these little girls, they are Rosario or Tejada?' 'Neither,' say my brother. 'My sisters are Vasquez.' They look at him. They look at me. They look at the *nenas.* We all of us different colors. And they say, 'Aw, hell! Let the whole bunch on!'

"There are little things I will never forget. Like my brother, when he ask the pilot to let me see the cockpit. Or like the taxi when we reach New York. In them days the taxis got them Jeep fenders and sun roofs and they kind of like a Cadillac in front. I will never forget how cold it is when we get to New York. How my brother take each one of us and he squeeze us through the roof and show us the New York skyline and he say, 'Look, you home now.' "

"My brother get a job over here in a radio shop. He has to stop everything in Puerto Rico, college, everything, just to be with us. Only the radio job don't pay enough. He has to help my mother who is on welfare, 'home relief' they call it back then. So he get a job at a factory. That's no good either. Then, one day a friend take him to Jamaica, Aqueduct, Belmont, one of them racetracks. He take my brother to do what they call the 'pony-walk,' which is just leading the horse around the track. For some reason, I don't know why, this man named Jim Fit, Jim Fitz or something, he take a liking to my brother and start to teaching him to ride horses."

"Sunny" Jim Fitzsimmons, the famous trainer?

"I think so. My brother become a jockey in less than a year. Jackie Tejada. Maybe you heard of him? He rides against Arcaro, this fellow Woodhouse, this other fellow Pincay, and Willie Shoemaker. All the top jocks. He go to Hialeah, Santa Anita, everywhere, and he wants me to become a jockey too. But I am so possessed by the City, the City is in me already, even at this tender age, that I can't go to the suburban area. I was always so wild. I guess it's because of all them years leading the gangs—"

You were a gang leader? I interrupt.

"Yes, but we talking about my brother here. I listen about you grandfather, right?"

Yes, you did. Sorry.

"Like I say, he just a little fellow, my brother. And he got none of the gift of gab that all these people got today. But he stick to you and he command a room, like, like you grandfather.

I was always so wild, but whenever he come here, even today, for some reason I got to tremble. I don't know how to carry myself. If I got something in my hands, I going to drop it on the floor. I become speechless. He talk to me on the phone and I got to ask for his *bendicion*, his blessing.

"You see, my brother taught me everything I know in life. First of all, I think, he taught me love, although he also taught me to be a son of a bitch sometime. Whatever I do that's good, that's, you know, from him. Whatever I do for these kids, for my sons. The only reason I'm not a junkie or in jail now is I got too much respect for him." Mickey paused, then chuckled. "Plus I always know I will have to answer to him when he come home from being a jockey. And he could hit, for a little midget."

The very next day I went down to the Lower East Side. I went down to Izzy Zerling's G&S Sports Shop on Essex Street, one of the top boxing outfitters in the City. I needed to pick up some hand wraps, bag gloves, a rope, and gumshield. Mickey Rosario had agreed to let me hang around his gym, even, if I wanted, to train me.

Chapter 3

JUST NERVES,
IS ALL

To get to the Rosarios' gym from my place on the Upper West Side I would often ride my bike. This was when the weather was good and I expected to be equal on the return trip to coaxing my old Schwinn back up Morningside Heights. Mostly, I caught the bus at Broadway and 106th, which jogged up St. Nicholas and traced the lower reaches of Morningside Park to 116th, where it made a concerted push east, past the lunar landscape known as "the Valley" and into Spanish Harlem itself.

At Fifth Avenue, El Barrio reared up and announced itself with a flourish. Which is to say, with La Marqueta, a parade of awnings in autumnal colors, beneath which one might find answers to most of the body's needs and not a few of the heart's desires, as well as an unrivaled chance to haggle. Tiny girls' dresses crocheted on the premises by leather-skinned ladies from the Caribbean; the latest in designer jeans and footwear and their knock-offs; yard goods; ceramic saints and animals; herbs and spices; flowers and candles; fish glistening on beds of ice; parts of the pig unknown to polite society; guavas and avocados; yams and yucas; plantains and papayas; sun-rouged mangoes with their taste of turpentine; tamarinds to make a mouth-puckering drink called "tamarindo"; banana leaves for wrapping sweets; *cuchifrito* stands with *bacalaitos* (codfish cakes), *pastelillos* (fried turnovers with meat or cheese), and

51

rellenos de papa (mashed potato balls stuffed with meat and glazed with egg), the whole multifarious operation wrapped in a cellophane of sound, salsa music by Tito Puente or the brothers Palmieri.

At First Avenue I would step off the bus and onto the remaining commercial thoroughfare of Italian Harlem. Making my way down to the gym at 112th, I would walk past Tocco's Sea Foods, Santarpia's Wines and Liquors, the gleaming Cimbali espresso-machine store, as well as the Kanawha Political Club, starring, according to a marquee in the window above the Delightful Restaurant, Frank Acosta, with Frank Rosetti and Wilma J. Sena in supporting roles. These were the surviving artifacts of a once-vibrant Sicilian colony. These plus a trio of funeral parlors, flagships of the old neighborhood, now a mothball fleet moored along 116th between First and Second avenues. Actually, Pleasant Avenue, a ribbon of domesticity between First Avenue and the FDR Drive, was still solidly paisano. Every now and then, the old guard in their pie-shaped caps and cardigans could be seen bowling in the dirt behind the ironwork fence that defined the park.

The Rosarios' gym was in Thomas Jefferson Park. It was in the park's public pools. To be precise, it was in the girls' locker room, which is not as curious as may sound. For no one, not even the well-heeled enthusiast, sets out to build a boxing gym. It's simply not done. Custom and use forbid it. The unspoken rules collected in an unwritten book (apparently read by everyone) say that the would-be owner of a boxing establishment must discover, not create, his site. He must engage in what passes for visionary activity among the citizenry of Palookaville. Which is to say, he must read the essential form of *gym* between the murky lines of some edifice down on its luck in an area that's probably seen better days.

There is wit in this. For at some level, I take it, the game is to set up shop in the least likely spot possible. Take the Jerome Boxing Club, which operates in the South Bronx out of a Mauve Decade post office complete with wainscoting and intricate twenty-foot tin ceilings, as well as—to further confuse things plebeian with things patrician—a subway rumbling along the casements in back. Or consider the Bedford-Stuyvesant Club, which conducts its business in a failed branch bank, peach in color. Or the Atlantic B. C., which does its in a pair of disused temporary school buildings, grounded mobile homes unzipped at ends like soup cans and riveted together in the exurban wilderness of Mastic, Long Island.

Lodged in the old Italian Park by the East River, the Rosarios' gym had about it an almost pastoral air. Approximately a quarter of a mile squared, the park contained a couple of baseball diamonds, several basketball and handball courts, as well as walking paths and play areas for children. It was sprinkled, by way of grace note, with crescent-shaped benches and tables with built-in metal umbrellas. The globes that topped the ten-foot lights spaced throughout the grounds had mostly been eclipsed by the neighborhood deadeyes, and much of the architecture, including the red brick pool building itself, was festooned with ghetto steno. No matter, not really. The park was still pleasant, comfortable, especially in the summer with the breeze wafting in from the river and being fanned by the trees.

The Rosarios' little setup in the park by the river made me think of Ancient Greece. I was reminded in particular of the gymnasia of Athens. They were also erected amid fields and by the side of water. They were located just outside the walls of the city and had about them a country aspect. But they were governed by urban sensibilities, by *gymnastai,* or instructors, like Mickey who were as intent upon the development of the ephebe's mind and spirit as his body.

There were three gyms of note in Athens. There were the Academea and the Lyceum, garden spots frequented by Socrates and his ilk, which trained up the cream of Athenian youth. Then there was the Cynosarges, where Mickey himself might have found work. For the Cynosarges was reserved for outsiders—for bastards and kids whose parents were not Athenian.

* * *

I'd been coming to the gym for better than a month when I decided, rather blithely, to start training.

"Sure," said Mickey. "Bring you stuff tomorrow."

The next day I pushed open the heavy metal doors and entered Casa Rosario as if for the first time. It was an illusion in which the gym's very atmosphere seemed to conspire. By this I mean, the air was heavy that day with an odor that had nothing to do with sweat or liniment but was redolent of the antebellum South, of men and women in white engaged in slow conversation in the green shade of a veranda. Odor of verbena. It was unmistakable. For a moment, I felt as though I were passing through the portals not of a boxing gym, but of a Faulkner novel.

I looked down the perfumed hall toward the entrance to the gym proper, where Negra was on the phone, doubtless chatting up her mother or one of her several sisters, great *bochinches,* or gossips, all. She smiled in my direction. Whatever it was that had raised her hackles—a miscreant spirit sent perhaps by an envious neighbor or rival trainer, whatever—she must have felt she'd chased it by burning the verbena. (Later, I would know to look for traces of San Miguel. Recipe from the *Spiritist's Cookbook:* Fill a glass with water and a pinch of salt. Write on a slip of paper the name of the party believed responsible for the haunt and stick it in the water. Turn the works upside down on a saucer. Light a stub of white candle and place it on the overturned glass. Do this a certain number of days and invoke Saint Mike each time and, with any luck, the saint will reverse the whammy, just as the glass has been reversed.)

I peered into the office, where Mickey was seated at his desk. I waited until he glanced up, then held my nose.

"Don't ask," he said and started to laugh. He sobered quickly enough, however, as he looked past my shoulder to where a kid was standing.

"I hear you teach boxing," said the kid. He was black, medium size, probably in his late teens. He was a picture of studied nonchalance. Arms folded across his chest, he leaned against the doorjamb as if he, and not Mickey, were master of what there was to survey.

The trainer couldn't look at the kid. He got up from his chair and, keeping his eyes fastened on the floor, extended his right hand, palm up. "Give me it," he sputtered. His capacity for speech appeared to be deserting him as well.

"Huh?" The kid turned to me for help, but I was fresh out. Besides, I was interested in what came next. I noticed a strip of pink on the kid's neck, a birthmark that crept up from his shirt like a fantastic caterpillar.

"It's the earring," said Negra, materializing suddenly. "Mickey can't look at it. It make him sick."

Negra reached up and popped a tiny gold stud out of the kid's right lobe and handed it to her husband, who put it in a large manila envelope, bulging, presumably, with other such trophies that he kept in his desk. The trainer was instantly whole again.

"You want to join the gym?"

The kid indicated that he did. He was more than a shade less confident now, somewhat at a loss for words himself.

"Okay, first thing you got to know is the rules. We don't allow no cursing here. We don't allow no fighting, except in the ring. I ain't here to waste you time and you ain't here to waste mine. I don't smoke and I don't drink and I don't chase womens. Sure, I like pretty girls. But I'm just looking. I got nice furnitures up at my house. I can take my wife out and have a dinner somewhere. I work. I work in a hospital and if I can't work in a hospital, I work as a mechanic. I got license number two and three. I can drive whatever kind of truck. I can work in drugstores. You understand?"

The kid clearly did not.

"What I'm saying, I'm sacrificing my wife and my kids and myself for you, you sure as hell going to sacrifice youself for you. Rules is rules, my rules, no argument. You understand?"

"Yes," said the kid. He'd been drawn in, as if on a string, to stand in front of the trainer's desk.

"If you right you wrong, if you disagree with me. Understand?"

"Yes."

"I say six rounds of rope, I don't mean four. I say 'jump,' I want you to jump."

"Yes."

"And you don't come down till I tell you."

"Yes."

"If I tell you."

"Yes."

"Ain't but one boss here."

"Yes."

"And you looking at him."

"Yes."

"Understand?"

"Yes."

"Still want in?"

"Yes."

"Sure?"

"Yes."

"Okay, I need you birth papers. I need four pictures. I need fifteen bucks for the ABF card. I need another twenty-five dues for the year. . . ."

You could see the weather start to change in the kid's face. See the lines begin to collect in the plain of his brow and pour down along the slope of his nose, as he started to drift back toward the door, then seemed to catch himself and hover in the middle of the room between the desk and the door. Which is to say, between worlds.

The trainer didn't really expect the kid to come up with the money, I was sure of that. I knew that three-quarters of the youngsters in the gym did not. Mickey forgave their dues and paid for most of the ABF cards himself, held the odd smoker to raise funds for gloves and headgear, put the arm on the local blue shirts and fire boys for a few bills now and then. He mostly made do. Or, better, did without. It wasn't the money he was after. It was something else.

"What you doing with youself nowadays? School? Working?"

"Well, I'm kind of between things just—"

"You a bum."

The kid jerked back as if he'd been struck. He stared at the trainer in disbelief. Then quickly looked about him to see who else had heard the taunt, his eyes lighting on my eyes, using them as blocks and sprinting off. After a while he spoke.

"Yes," he said, "I'm a bum. But I don't want to be one no more."

"You going to hate me," said Mickey, finally gentling. "That come first. Later, you going to love me."

"Ha!" said Negra, smirking in the doorway.

Negra knew better. She always seemed to know better. She knew Mickey and she knew the kids and she knew the gym. She knew that eight out of every ten youngsters who entered Casa Rosario washed out within a matter of weeks, if not days. She knew that the typical kid never stayed long enough to get into the ring and see how he liked fielding punches with his face. That he never got past the rude foreplay of the initial days of training, never got past hating Mickey to see him clear, much less love him.

I was of course going to be a case apart. I mean, I'd sat at my grandfather's knee, read all these books about the Manly Art, devoured the Great Fights on film. Plus I was an athlete—admittedly, at thirty-eight, not in first flower. But I'd played varsity hockey and lacrosse, two rough-and-tumble sports, in college, even got some All-American notice in lacrosse. And I was reasonably fit, I ate right, was pretty good about drinking, smoked just one cigar a day when writing, tried to run four miles a day four days a week. . . .

I never did learn how the Pink Caterpillar ended up feeling about the trainer. By the time I thought to interview him, he had long since disappeared into the gym's collective memory. I do know that it took me some time to love Mickey, or even to regain the affection I felt for him before we started training. It's all there, alas, in my diary—a document I share here in the interest of science and against my better judgment, a chronicle so drenched in self-pity you could have wrung it and filled at least one of the two pools outside the gym.

DAY ONE. Arrive with Channel 13 tote bag containing shorts, sweats, jock, T-shirt, hand wraps, and 9 ft. jump rope (9 ft. too short, need 9½). He starts me light: stretching, loosening up with half a dozen other kids in the ring. Then he has me go four rounds on the heavy bag. I notice the Pink Caterpillar remains in the ring with Refugio [the assistant trainer]. Refugio has him moving slowly across the canvas: advancing left hand and left leg, right hand and right leg, left and left again, like he's a small train choo-chooing up a grade. Isn't that the usual way to start a kid? Teach him basic footwork? Plod before you run?

"Relax," Mickey tells me when I start in on the bag. Naturally, the countersuggestion takes hold and I tighten up. "Don't bite you lip," he says. "Close you mouth. Breathe through you nose. The reason that bag is spinning, you ain't hitting it right."

After two rounds I'm exhausted. My knuckles are grapes being ground into wine, my arms dull spikes being piled into my shoulders. Am getting light-headed. Between trysts with the bag, he has me doing push-ups and squat thrusts in sets of ten and twenty. Keep thinking of "A Town Without Pity." Who sang it? Roy Orbison? Gene Pitney?

Four rounds of rope. Don't even know how to jump rope. Keep telling the pickaninny who gather round me that where I grew up only girls skipped rope. Double Dutch, Bear in a Beehive, Shoein' Old Dobbin, that sort of thing. The little gym rats look at me with skepticism. The good part is Mickey goes off to torture another kid.

Next, this medieval device for sit-ups: a board angled over a railing at 45 degrees. The otherwise genial Refugio oversees this torment. Put your feet under the rail at the top and lie back on the slant, your legs jack-knifed. Now bring your body up a third of the way and hold it. Count to twenty. Do this four times and you wish for death. Now do it an entire round, spiced with sit-ups in sets of ten, hands behind head, elbows kissing opposing knees.

Mickey is back with the medicine ball. I know about the medicine ball. I've read about it in sports medicine magazines. The medicine ball is bad medicine. It doesn't harden the abdominals, it ruptures blood vessels. You could bust your spleen with it. It's a bill of goods, a piece of boxing hokum like training in the mountains, which doesn't teach the body to absorb more oxygen because it has to, because the air is thinner up there. Rather it causes you to lose blood plasma, punks you out when you get back to earth. Hell, the reverse is probably true: fighters should train in caves hundreds of feet below sea level; they'd be dynamos.

I want to share this expertise with Mickey. But discretion gets the better of me and I don't say a word. I just lie there on the mat and the trainer looks off, talking to someone else, as he drops the sucker on my middle, high up in the cavity just below my ribs. Then straddles me, pushes down on the ball half a dozen times. Raising his feet off the ground, the little prick. Never giving me notice. Surprising my guts, which threaten to pour out around the ball.

He expects me to run three miles. I tell him I ran already in the morning. A lie. We both know it.

"Good," he says. "But that was this morning."

I feel the tears begin to mass behind my eyes and pray the dam holds. That's all I need, Liquid-plumr. The trainer deliberates, makes me twist. Finally, he speaks. "Okay. Go shake out in the ring. But remember." He looks at me, not unkindly, perhaps, but meaningfully. "This is just a taste."

I'm so wiped, I trip stepping through the ropes and a playful ten-year-old swats me with a right hand as I lumber by. Jesus, what have I gotten myself into!

Over the next couple of weeks I tried most everything to escape him. Notably, I tried coming early. I would arrive at the gym with Negra at about 4:30, half an hour to an hour, say, before Mickey himself appeared. My thought was to get well into my workout before he showed and had his way with me. The trainer was puzzled the first couple of times I did this and, as I came to learn, with good reason. For a real fighter never begins a training session on his own. A properly groomed kid will wait all afternoon and evening for his trainer to show up. If by some chance the fellow fails to make the appointment, if his subway derails, or his wife finds out about his girl friend and he has cause to work on his own footwork at home, well, the kid simply will not train that day, even if he knows what he's meant to do. Waiting is, of course, a condition of the powerless—just one of the many perks of being poor. Yet it is also, at least where boxing is concerned, a tribute paid by shining youth to age. It is an act of optimism.

In any case, Mickey was quickly on to me. On some days, I gather, he instructed Negra to open the gym an hour late. Other days he came early himself, no doubt getting some fellow timeserver at the hospital to punch him out on the work clock at the prescribed hour. I don't know much about all this, about Mickey's part in the charade, since he was not about to dignify my behavior by discussing it with me, either during the run of my performance or after. His response was simple and direct: It was to turn the temperature of my training up a notch.

DAY SEVEN (or eight? or eighteen?). This morning I have trouble raising my left arm to brush my teeth. My butt is so sore, I have to ease myself on and off the throne. My toes are bent over like little hammers. This is hardly news. They've been that way from Day One, thanks to the stunted shoes of my childhood. The news is this: Last night the little cripples took the cure. They raised up as if clapped on the brow by Oral Roberts. They threw away their crutches and snapped to excruciating attention, shooting bullets up my legs that seemed to detonate in the base of my spine. I jerked out of sleep several times during the night, screaming.

Hands. Never thought much about them before. Never had to. (These old things? Had them for ages. So convenient, too, the way they hang at your side.) Now they won't leave me alone. Left one's maybe not so bad. At least I can push a pencil with it. Right one's a different story. Can't put it in the pocket of my jeans without forethought, without gentling it in on the bias. Lord, do me this favor: Save me from meeting someone new and having to extend it for the shaking or, almost worse, having to explain why I can't.

This is to say, my right hand is traumatized. I can neither fully open it, nor ball it into a fist; only a middling lax position is possible without some sharp reminder. There are visuals too. The skin is pouched over the outermost knuckles. In the pouch is a pool of blood, what looks like the continent of Australia etched in violet. And these are the good knuckles. The first two, as you go from thumb to pinkie, are far worse off. They're the punching knuckles. . . .

But, let me wade out here from this stream of complaints and try to give some order and substance to this discussion of the fighter's hands. To begin, there's nothing between the skin and the knuckle of the hand but a tiny bit of subcutaneous tissue and cartilage. Cartilage is a fragile, semilucent affair, minimally irrigated with blood. Now, every time a fighter takes a swing at something solid and connects, he busts up the cartilage on his knuckles. The cartilage does not take this lying down, but puts in a call for help. Think of a fire. The knuckles are on fire, only the fire is in a rural area where there are few hydrants. The blood is pumped in, but the real work is done by the smoke jumpers, which is to say, by the inflammatory cells who parachute in and start hauling away the debris, the broken shards of cartilage.

The inflammatory cells work in tandem with a second contingent called the "fibrositic cells." Indeed, you might say that the inflammatory cells are the work force, the brawn, the heroes who brave the blaze, and the fibrositic cells are the artisans, not quite the brains of the operation. Ideally, once the fire is under control, the fibrositic cells come in and start rehabing the area, knitting the cartilage back together again. The trouble is, of course, that the blaze is never actually brought under control. For the fighter, meathead that he is, is typically impervious to the drama going on beneath the skin of his knuckles. (Pain, after all, is his element.) The fighter trains every day and every day he busts up still more cartilage. Thus, the inflammatory cells are never able to keep up with the debris, to flush it as waste through the lymphatics. As a result, the teamwork with the fibrositic cells goes crazily awry. What happens is the fibrositic cells get hold of the busted cartilage and start weaving the stuff into an increasingly three-dimensional tapestry. What happens, in short, is something called "bossing"—cartilage piggybacking on cartilage, heaping up and adhering mostly on the second knuckle, often forming what looks to the eye, and feels to the touch, like a petrified grape.

Hands. Dempsey claimed he toughened his by bathing them in pickle juice. Professor Mike Donovan, a turn-of-the-century conditioner, had his charges soak their hooks in beef brine and varnish. Trainers today paint their kids' knuckles with vitamin E. Alas, there's no help for the fighter's hands. Stay in the game long enough and somewhere along the way you're probably going to have trouble with your knuckles. In fact, the harder you punch, the greater the trauma and, therefore, the more trouble you're likely to have.

The funny thing is, the skin along the knuckles is loose. There is ample slack to make a fist. What's more, the skin across the knuckles retains good blood supply when you make that fist. Compare the hand to the knee. Flex the knee and the skin pulls taut and the blood makes for the nearest exit. Clearly, man was not meant to fight with his knees. It may well be, however, that Nature in her wisdom fashioned man to fight with his hands. That, as Edwin Campbell, top fight doc in the City, likes to say, "When man put down the club, he picked up the fist." So much for the metaphysics of hands.

Yesterday Mickey worked me eight rounds on the bag. The last two he held the thing for me, a service generally reserved for palsy victims. He exhorted me to punch at the rate of three blows per second for six straight minutes, oh, yes, with a minute's breather between the segments, during which I was invited to take my ease with a dozen push-ups.

"If you notice," he said, "you stay the whole round in that one little spot. You going to wear it out, and then what we going to do? We got nothing to fill it in."

As my hands moved slower and slower, the trainer raised his embrace of the bag, telling me to hit above his arms. I was sinking to the floor, drowning in the morass of myself, even as the s.o.b. was elevating the waterline.

"There's this thing you got to know about me," he said. "For some reason I'm afraid of cuts. I'm like the fat lady who see a mouse and don't know what to do. What I'm saying, it may be I will faint at the sight of you blood when I put you in the ring. So do me this favor and protect youself."

He paused, sensing that I was either too exhausted or too angry, or too both, to get his meaning.

"Keep you hands up. Okay?"

I scanned his face for some tic of sadism, for any emotion at all. I saw none.

It's eerie upon first experience. One minute, what with the drum of leather on canvas and the slap of rope on concrete, it seems as though you're in a closet with Mongo Santamaria and his pack of mad percussionists. The next minute you're in an aerie suddenly bereft of birds. Or in a sculptor's loft down in Soho, alone in a large space but for a population of statues.

What I'm getting at is, every three minutes in any boxing gym a bell will sound and all activity will cease. Instantly, completely. Only to start up again full-tilt with a second bell a minute later. Pavlov would have counted himself a king in this nutshell. For every aspect of a fighter's training, excluding his roadwork, is governed by the round bell. To the point where some kids joke that they breakfast exclusively on three-minute eggs, dream only in three-minute trailers, etcetera. The truth is, fighters get used to the round bell much as people living next to airports get used to planes taking off. Both pause instinctively in the midst of their activity, whether it be punching or conversing, and wait, unruffled, for the signal to begin again. They pay no more mind to the noise, or its nullity, than does the ordinary citizen to the systole of his breathing or swallowing.

It was in these lulls between rounds that the kids completing their workouts sought a brief audience with Mickey. They would line up often three and four at a time. They would tell him their weight and explain, perhaps, why they'd not shown up the day or, cause for lecture, week before; and if they were Latino, they would ask for his blessing. The trainer would inquire into their lives outside Casa Rosario. He would question them about school, and if he suspected they were truant or doing failing work, he would make them produce their report cards for his perusal, threatening to close the gym doors to any kid who refused to do so. Generally, the trainer would have been in recent contact with the youngster's mother or guardian (there was seldom a father). Or he would have spoken to the kid's homeroom teacher or guidance counselor, his parish priest or probation officer, and he would already be abreast of the kid's progress in the world beyond the gym walls.

It was in these oases between rounds that I gradually came to see the obvious, what would have been clear to me had I not been perceiving the trainer for the past several weeks through a scrim of self-pity. Mickey bore me no animus. He was not grilling me, not making an example of me, not really. He was training me a little more vigorously than other new recruits (I watched enough of them come and go to get some feel for this). This, I suspect, was because the kids in the gym knew I was a friend of his, and he had to make a show of impartiality. Otherwise, the trainer was handling me like any other fighting stiff on the premises. Which is to say, he was treating me as if I were as wayward as the rest of his flock.

Above all, I think Mickey wanted me to know in my bones, even if I were to pack it all in tomorrow and go back to being purely his friend, something about the special bond between a trainer and his fighter. He would go so far, I believe, as to stage small dramas that enacted the relationship. (Again, I don't know for certain what he was up to because there were things we simply didn't speak about. There is, of course, a protocol among males, one that locks into place when men are busy being men together. It's an etiquette that says certain things must be felt and understood in the blood and must never be brought to speech, lest they lose their power and validity. Mickey and I often found ourselves in the grips of this etiquette.) *Stage* may be too strong a word, as I suspect these little dramas would have unfolded anyway, whether I was present or not. Still, I had the sense that I was the audience the trainer was playing to, since at the show's conclusion his eyes would invariably rove among the spectators until they caught and held my own, for just a second, no more, long enough to underscore meaning.

I'm thinking, in particular, about an evening some weeks after I started training. On that evening, during a sparring session, another relatively green kid pushed Mickey to do something that pained him: to articulate this relationship between trainer and fighter, which is as artificial as a flower arrangement and, in some ways, nearly as delicate.

"How you feel?" Mickey asked the kid between rounds. You could see that the kid was exhausted and probably intimidated by the more experienced fighter he was in with.

"Tired, for the first time," the youngster said.

"I don't want to hear that," snapped Mickey. "You a fool if you not tired."

"I feel all right," said the kid, realizing he'd said something wrong.

"The rules here are funny," said the trainer. "I know you tired, but that's not what I want to hear. I want you to say one thing and one thing only. But I will know you mean another. These are the rules." Mickey paused to give the kid a chance to absorb what he'd said, then began again as if the first exchange never took place. "How you feel?"

"I feel good, Mick."

"All right!" The trainer slapped the kid's gloved hands with his naked fists. The kid returned the gesture with gusto. "You had enough," said Mickey. "Come on out."

"No," said the kid. "I'm okay now."

The trainer looked at the kid with wonder shot through with annoyance. He was no fonder of bravado than he was of cowardice. The lesson for the day, which the kid had bungled, was not about machismo, not purely, anyway. Rather, it was about metaphor, saying one thing and meaning another. It was about the code language of men. About the dance of sympathies between a trainer and his fighter, a dance conducted largely in silence in which the trainer always leads and the fighter always follows, taking his cues, however creatively, from the way the older man steers him through the music.

"Okay, Mick," said the kid, hastening to vacate the ring. "I'm getting out. I'm out, see?"

If Mickey didn't see, it was because he was looking at me.

* * *

It turned out that I got to know the kids in the gym first as boxers and only later as people, which must have been the way it worked for most newcomers. For the gym operated as a family, with the older or more veteran kids looking after their smaller, less seasoned or able siblings. Skills were handed down like clothes in a large family. Each kid was but the custodian of the know-how some bigger kid had entrusted to him and was obliged, in turn, to pass it along to the next youngster in line.

Thus, Mickey's treating me like everyone else worked to my advantage. I was not merely a gym novelty, not just some honky pal of Mickey's touring the playgrounds of the Third World. I was an aspirant, one of them, someone to be helped along, introduced to the mysteries of the training floor. I was also, at six feet and 180 pounds, considerably larger, as well as years older, than most of these adoptive brothers. It was only natural, I suppose, that they called me "Cooney" for a spell, after the lily-white strong boy whose name was continually in the head-lines. (Fortunately, for me, if not for him, following the dustup with Holmes, Cooney retreated from the sports page to the gossip columns and kindly took his name with him.)

One of the few to spare me the tag was Ariel. Ariel was a gorgeous black swan with large slightly Eurasian eyes and an infectious whinny of a laugh. He was one of several black kids in the gym who lived in the Flatbush section of Brooklyn, whose voices still bore traces of the Caribbean islands and whose gestures were so graceful they were almost effeminate. Ariel would soon be going to medical school, but I didn't know this for quite some time. It was hardly the sort of ambition one would expect to find in a young fighter. Nor did I know that Mickey and Negra were ambivalent about his presence in the gym.

"Truthfully," Mickey would say to me during the Golden Gloves, "Ariel should not be a fighter. He got his whole life in front of him. He's going to be a doctor."

Then why let him fight? I was tempted to say. Why not explain to the kid that he's too finely made for the game, that, never mind his getting hit, one ill-sped blow to an opponent's head could shatter his hands and thereby his dream of being a surgeon?

This was churlish. I knew why Mickey and Negra let Ariel fight, apart from the fact that he was good at it. I knew why, even if they didn't. It was as plain as the light that stole across their faces when the kid merely entered the room. They loved him too much to bear to part with him, even for his hypothetical own good.

It was the rope that brought Ariel and me together. I knew only that the kid swung a mean one and that he saw me as a challenge, which I was, of the rudest kind. He started me, mercifully, without the rope on a small wooden platform. He had me jump in place with both feet together, knees bent slightly, hands held about six inches from my hips. The object was to land in the same spot after each jump, to flex my toes and feel a natural rhythm course up my legs to my hips. The point was to turn my body into a sort of piston; for the rope, once it is set in motion by the hands, should continue to make its way over head and under feet with no help from the arms and little encouragement from the wrists. The job of the wrists, actually, is to resist the force of the rope created by the up-and-down motion of the body and, thereby, by a logic of contraries, to make the thing scoot around all the faster.

The business of getting a rhythm was not helped by the trainer's improbable taste in music. For Mickey was not, as might be imagined, a fan of salsa. Nor did he care for the hard-driving funk or rap music that clotted the air of every other boxing spa in the City. No, Mickey was big on country-and-western music, the more maudlin the better. He was probably the only Rican this side of the Cumberland Trail who preferred George Jones to Rick James or even Rubén Blades. Invariably, when the trainer entered the gym, his first stop was the boom box in the corner near the equipment cabinet, where he put the quietus on Grand Master Flash in favor of the FM radio.

"What number's that WKIK?" he would ask Reggie, say, who'd be whirring his rope hard by.

"Dag, Mick," Reggie would complain. "Not that hillbilly crap. How you going to do ropes to that?" Then, mostly under his breath, "I should have brought my own radio."

"What you need a radio for?" Ariel would ask Reggie.

"Music, man. What you think?"

"Say what!" Ariel would whinny. "You hearing music all the time, the way you get hit." Slaps all around.

Every kid on the training floor, it seemed, had some choice bit of advice for me. Chino Number One, for instance, taught me how to catch a rhythm and do ropes even while Tammy Wynette was standing by her man. The trick, he said, was to say a rhyme to yourself.

What kind of a rhyme?

"You know," he said. "Like the one you say when you a kid about Cinderella. You know."

I didn't know.

"You mean you was always old like this?" he asked. "You was never a kid?" Chino flashed his famous harbor-light smile, nearly bleaching me with his self-delight. He then proceeded to repair the gap in my education.

> *Cinderella, dressed in yella,*
> *Go downtown to meet her fella.*
> *On the way her panties busted.*
> *How many people was disgusted?*

Johnny Luna thought I should get a haircut. "Sure, it look nice and everything to have it long," said the burr-headed young pro. "But you in a fight and you get hit and you hair fly up, and you know what? That judge he going to think it's a much better punch than it is."

For his part, Smooth talked to me about the mirrors that were tacked up on the walls. The mirror, he said, was the fighter's principal training tool. It was where you got to see yourself as your opponent saw you. It was where you worked on your form and your balance. "The mirror," he said, quoting the original and sweetest Sugar Ray, "tells if you got your guns where you can use them."

As far as boxing skills went, Smooth and Johnny Luna were the class of Casa Rosario. Smooth, I would discover, was as formidable outside the gym as he was within it. By this I mean, he was a "player." In what he called the "old" days (maybe five or six years ago), he'd been tip top at the hip hop with the Rocksteady Crew. These were the kids who used to burn up the City street corners with their "egg rolls" and "helicopter swipes" and graduated—at least, the group after Smooth did— to performing their Electrik Boogie in the movies. Nor did Smooth confine himself to breaking dance steps. He put the hurt on some hearts, too. In fact, his girl friend of the moment was so smitten she was saving to buy him the sort of ride he saw himself getting accustomed to. Something boaty and throbbingly conspicuous. Maybe an Eldorado. A stylish wisp of a Latina, the girl friend had already on secretarial wages bought him a VCR and given him a line on her Master Charge. This even though she had a couple of kids whom she paraded through the gym in Fauntleroy suits and pinafores and could not have had much spare change jingling in her purse.

The kids conducted their real clinic at the heavy bag. During my first weeks of training, pretty much every fighter in the gym took time off from his own workout to watch me belabor the sack for a round or two. Inevitably, each kid would find something in my performance that he liked and, in the next breath, would try to make me over in his image.

Take Jackson, the gym heavyweight. At six feet four inches and 240-odd pounds, he was an imposing physical specimen and an agreeable sort, to boot. When he smiled, which was often— heavyweights tend to be gentle beasts outside the ring—his cheeks came up like billiard balls and his eyes sank like raisins tossed in cookie dough. Everything about the kid was slow, ponderous, from his gait to his voice, which you found yourself waiting for, the way you might the splash from a stone heaved down a well.

Jackson, I would learn, was the oldest of twelve children reared to be upstanding citizens by a lone welfare mother in the Richmond Hill area, a stretch of Tobacco Road in Queens. He went to community college. He worked with retarded children. He wanted to be thought of as a boxer, not as a fighter. Which is to say, he regarded himself as a man of measure and nascent accomplishment, as a sensitive, reflective human being. I was impressed. Unduly, thought Mickey, who submitted that Jackson was "a animal," beginning and end of story.

How can you call him that? I'd say.

"Listen," the trainer would answer, exasperated as ever by what he took to be my unflagging innocence. "When I say the kid's a animal, it don't mean I don't love him same as the rest. It just mean I don't have to look out for him so much. Hell, I'm glad he's a animal! Wish they all was. Maybe I could sleep at night."

Jackson talked jab to me. He talked feinting and footwork. But even I, disposed as I was to take him for Ralph Bunche redux, even I could see that it was his right hand that talked to the bag during these demonstrations. And that it talked in language most any Neanderthal would have understood.

By comparison, Milton Street was utterly candid about his ongoing affair with the hook. Apart from Chino Number One, Milton might have been my favorite kid during my first days at Casa Rosario. If he was, it was because he was nearly the anomaly there that I was. Milton was cerebral, self-educated, a reader. He spotted his conversation with words like "irony" and "nostalgia," deployed them in a quenchless flow of patter to which he always stood somewhere on the slant, in some self-conscious relation. In a word, Milton was complex. He was a walking anthology of the styles of bad-assedness, each with a peculiar spin on it, available to a young black man growing up in New York City during the seventies. Which is to say, by age

WILLIAM PLUMMER

twenty-two he'd already been a small-time gangster, someone who'd marketed the favors of his girlfriend, traveled with a ring of pickpockets, and engaged in shootouts.

At present he was working in a Wall Street firm. He was trying to purge himself of his ghetto ways and blend with the Caucasian mainstream. He was only a gofer with no promise at the firm of anything more. No matter. He adopted the prevailing plumage anyway. He wore business suits, pinstripe and Glen plaid simulacrum of Brooks Brothers and Paul Stuart standards, which he purchased at Syms men's store ("At Syms, an educated consumer is our best customer") and topped with a conservative fedora, a Panama hat come summer at the raciest. Milton was a confection of quotes and allusions, a queer sum of his eclecticism and seldom purely what he seemed to be. The kids in the gym didn't get him at all. They called him "Clark Kent" and regularly put him through the ranking mill known as the Dozens:

"Yo, Clark, where you coming from looking like that?"

"Work."

"You making all that money?"

"I'm a millionaire."

"Yeah, and still taking the train." (Slaps all around.)

Milton dressed for success. But he also wore nerdy-looking open-frame glasses with a rim of serious plastic on top, which were a fair piece from the regulation tortoiseshell of the successful stock trader. The glasses were an homage to Milton's all-time hero, Malcolm X. He'd cut a picture of Malcolm's specs out of an old magazine—just the specs, because he didn't want to have to hear any static about what a "rotten weirdo" Malcolm was—and took it to an optician. "No one wears these anymore," the optician told him. "I don't care," said Milton. "You got them or not?" The fellow managed to root a pair out of two decades' dust in back.

Milton favored the hook because it was the thing itself, an "old-timey punch." "Look at the old flicks and what do you see?" Milton would say. "Guys throwing hooks. Not all of

72

them. Not the dancing masters, the Benny Leonards and the Willie Peps, not so much anyway. Just the hard rocks, the guys who were really down."

Milton studied the old fight films, sifted them for telling detail as if he were an actor trying to find his way into a part and, by turns, in and out of himself. He noticed that the old pugs wore black leather shoes. They didn't go for these tasseled red, white, and blue drum majorette deals the sugar-nipples were wearing today. So he scoured the stores and turned up the black high-laced Ethiopia-brand shoes he wore in the Gloves, wore them in the face of the derision of his numb-nuts gym mates. And Milton hooked, hooked, and hooked.

In the end, it was Refugio who taught me the poetics of punching. This was surely by design—Mickey's design—for the assistant trainer was approximately my age. Plus, just a few years earlier he had performed the same dance with Mickey that I was currently enduring. Refugio was clearly meant to be my inspiration and model, even if our backgrounds could not have been more dissimilar.

Refugio had grown up in La Perla, the community anthropologist Oscar Lewis called La Esmeralda in his book, *La Vida*. I knew the place. It was an agglutination of green-roofed shacks, a menage of squatters not so very different from those that made up Mickey's El Fanguito, only Refugio's native pesthole was still more perilously situated. It stood defenseless, even asking for it, you might say, at the base of sheer cliffs rising up out of the Atlantic and serving as pillars for scenic Old San Juan. Each year, as sure as there were tropical storms, the ocean would roar in and swat the several dozen shanties closest to the sea wall, reducing them to kindling.

Refugio came to the states in the fifties at the height of the Puerto Rican diaspora. He worked for a time picking vegetables in Jersey, then caught on as a pin-spotter out in Long Island, stayed there for three or four years, living in the back of the building until he was "Brunswicked," or phased out by automation. Lately, he'd caught on as a janitor in one of the City's junior high schools, an out-and-out sinecure. About eight years ago, however, when he first entered Mickey's orbit, Refugio was a rising barrio entrepreneur. He and his wife owned a combination stationery store and botanica. They had also purchased from a friend one of those hole-in-the-wall social clubs. They bought the club—little more than a bar, a nest of tables and chairs, and dibs on a basement rental on 130th Street—for $1,100. Eventually, they nursed the business to where they were able to squeeze $15,000 to $20,000 a year out of it, just hustling booze and soda. The living was good, but the club life-style had its down side. "I was getting into a alcohol habit," Refugio told me. "That's when I meet Mickey and ever since then I stop. I tell him I want to change my life and he train me like a fighter. He train me hard, and I am grateful for that, because I was very depressed and he wake me from this depression. Mickey make me a better man than I was. He make me see the value that life has."

According to Negra, if Mickey spruced up Refugio's internal man, he worked a sea change on his external one. Which is to say, the trainer so upgraded his fighter's palpable self—trimming forty pounds from Refugio's frame and adding definition to what remained—that women virtually accosted the recast Adonis on the street. Alas, this did not sit well with Refugio's wife, who loved him for his ready smile and cobalt blue eyes. It got to the point, apparently, where la Señora Refugio forbade her husband to do any more training, where she would allow him to return to the gym only with the express understanding that he limit his activity to assisting Mickey on the training floor. In the interim, of course, she fattened him up considerably.

"Bill," said Refugio, during our first session together. He was holding his left hand about chest-high, palm up. There was a coin in it. "I got a half-dollar in my hand, see?"

I nodded.

"I want you to reach and take that half-dollar from my hand."

I did as he said.

"You notice anything?"

I started to look at the coin, thinking it was a Kennedy head. PRs used to be crazy for Kennedy, many still were.

"No," said Refugio, laughing. "I mean the motion you just make. Here, give me the half-dollar. Now, reach again, slowly. This time I think you will see the motion is how we throw a punch."

Ah, I get it.

"Slowly, now. Start you hand from up by you shoulder. See how because you reach for the half-dollar you pinch the fingers and make like a fist? See how you turn that fist at the end of the motion? You should do this when you punch. It's called 'burning in' the punch. It make you punch short across the chest and with the knuckles. Always punch with the knuckles."

Refugio worked with me for half an hour most days. He taught me all the punches and how to throw them in purposeful sequence. Always, however, he came back to the jab. One day, as he worked with me, I noticed Mickey sidling over from an adjacent sack.

"All we going to do is jab," said Refugio, who was also keenly aware of the trainer, his mentor. "I want you to forget everything but the jab now. Just move the jab."

Refugio watched me for a few seconds, as did Mickey, silently, from our perimeter. Finally, the assistant trainer stepped in to still the bag and to offer an analogy I'd heard Mickey himself make on more than one occasion. "See," he said, "it's like a new car. You got the jab, and then you got everything else. The power window, the whitewall, the radio, all these things is what they call 'optional.' Only the jab come 'standard.' The jab will take you where you want to go."

The jab, the redoubtable Barney Ross once remarked, is a totally artificial punch. It is the one punch in the boxer's repertoire that you will not see in a street fight. The hook, the overhand right, even the uppercut are, by comparison, natural punches, available in the rough to any hothead looking to be creative with his anger. The jab is the only punch in the boxer's fight kit that is both offensive and defensive and at the same time. It jumps out—Ali called his a "snake-licker"—thereby preventing the other fellow from digging in and bringing up more powerful relations. Meanwhile, it scores points. The jab is employed at a remove; thus, it both keeps the opponent at a comfortable distance and, like an outstretched yardstick, enables you to gauge that distance and the time it takes to close it with a following right hand. The jab is the honest workman in the fighter's employ. He's not the celebrated guest, but a menial at the feast, someone who probably set the table.

Curiously, the old Greeks did not have a jab. I say "curiously" because, contrary to reputation, the Greeks were not oafish bloodletters, but cautious, methodical, even thoughtful fighters. The Greek boxer stood upright, head erect, feet apart, left foot forward, in what is rightly called "classic style." He apparently had a knowledge and appreciation of footwork. Or so one would be led to believe by Theocritus' "Dioscuri," in which the lithe and nimble Polydeuces evades the thuglike rushes of the giant Amycus, slips a massive uppercut, and rattles the big fellow's chops with a counter one-two. For the Greeks, boxing was first and foremost the art of self-defense (Dion Chrysostom speaks admiringly of a fighter who could hold his guard up for two days and thus forced his opponents to yield before any blows were struck). And yet, curiously, if the paintings on the surviving amphorae are to be believed, the Greek boxer held the left hand out, fully extended; thus the jab was obviated. The left was reserved for parrying, maybe for cuffing or pushing the other fellow off balance. The right was held back, cocked just behind the ear. It was the right hand, as Mushy might say, that carried the cure for insomnia.

The jab, as we know it, came along shortly after boxing's rebirth out of fencing in seventeenth-century England. Yet its first great champion was not a Brit, but a Yank. He was "Gentleman Jim" Corbett, who used the jab to defeat the great John L. Sullivan. James J. Braddock, the "Cinderella Man" of the thirties who leapt from the welfare roles to the heavyweight title of the world, based his fairy tale almost entirely upon the jab. Gene Tunney dismantled Jack Dempsey with his. My grandfather, who was there, said that by the end of their second get-together Dempsey's face was so slashed and swollen he couldn't see. He was not so benighted, however, that he could not admire Tunney's rapier skill. "Lead me out there," said Dempsey to his corner after ten memorable rounds. "I want to shake hands with him."

"Look here," said Mickey, no longer able to stay mum on our periphery. Mickey held his left fist six inches in front of his chin and unloaded it at the bag twice rapid-fire. "A good jab don't travel but a foot. And the snap, see how I get the snap on it."

I nodded. Vaguely, I guess.

Mickey thought a moment. "Remember them old-time movie cowboys that come on TV late at night? Remember the one that got a whip?"

"You mean Hope Gipson?" asked Refugio, who was always eager to be of help to his benefactor. But the trainer didn't answer his assistant. His eyes appeared to be focused inward, where he was no doubt screening a favorite oater.

"Now, sometimes," said Mickey, "that fellow throw that whip out there kind of lazylike, and it don't do nothing. He just playing, wrapping it around a fence pole or a heroine or something." To illustrate, the trainer lobbed an imaginary whip toward the bag. "When this fellow get serious, look out! He going to snap that thing. *Yap!*"

Mickey shot out that same whip. Only this time he canceled it in midair and had it back and coiled on his belt before you could say, "Lash LaRue."

"You got to be anywhere tomorrow?" asked Mickey.

It was a pleasant late summer afternoon several months into my stay at Casa Rosario. The windows of the gym were open and the sun was streaming in upon the training floor, which was painted a bright tourquoise with salmon-colored spots beneath each of the half-dozen heavy bags.

No, I said. I'll be here.

"Okay, but do you got to look pretty for anybody?"

Just you, I guess.

"You sure, now?"

Yeah, I'm sure. What's this all about?

"I just don't want you wife getting mad at me when you come home all busted up and everything."

It was in this manner that I learned I was to be put to box for the first time. My opponent was to be a fellow named Tiburón, or "the Shark." A strange choice, I thought, to the extent that I could think at all, the way my mind was suddenly racing.

Tiburón was a dapper on the order of Smooth. I'd seen him come in just a few minutes earlier in his brown-and-white saddles, tangerine slacks, and blue sateen shirt with a white kerchief at the throat. He was an adept, I gathered, in some exotic branch of the martial arts. He was also a professional boxer whose local fame rested on his dropping a close decision some years earlier to a kid who went on to fight for the World Welterweight title. Which is to say, Tiburón was the most experienced hand in the gym. I had thought that when Mickey did get around to boxing me that he'd throw me in with some other naif and—this was my hope and expectation—that my natural athletic ability would have a chance to wend its way to the surface, where it would effloresce in deft defense and thoughtful combinations.

For his part, Tiburón could not have been more gallant. I scarcely knew him, but he seemed to sense my nervousness and to try, as best he could, considering what we were about to do together, to get me to relax.

"Let's take it slow and easy in there," he said with what I took to be a collegial smile, as we donned the sixteen-ounce sparring gloves. "Let's just try and get some work."

As Tiburón turned and walked toward his corner, Smooth came up and said, "I seen him talking to you. He give you that jive about 'taking it easy'? He did?" Smooth thought this hilarious. "Dude does that with everybody. Why you think they call him 'Tiburón'? Know what I do when he ask me to spar?"

I couldn't imagine.

"I go up to Mickey and I say out loud, 'Can I box him? Can I? Can I?' Then I whisper real lowlike, 'Say *no,* say *no.*' Hell, I ain't sparring with nobody like Tiburón. Dude can hit me all crazy and hard. Then when I start going berserk on him, he say, 'Take it easy! You going too wild! We trying to get some work here.' "

Great, I thought. Just great.

DAY THIRTY. Boxed two rounds today with Tiburón. Each round lasted three minutes or an hour, honestly couldn't say which. This because of what happens to time in the ring, where it gives up any pretense to being absolute. It's also because somewhere along the way, I gather, Señor Tiburón managed to ring my bell, and while I didn't leave my feet, I did, apparently, briefly take leave of the premises. I visited another warp—one much like our own, except that everything in it was wrapped with gauze.

I'd seen Tiburón box other fellows and was familiar with his style. Enough to know that he was weird in the ring. I knew that he liked to fight off the ropes. Liked to screw himself up like a pretzel, to turn his back on you the way Luis Tiant did when he pitched for the Yanks and Red Sox, leaving you wondering where he'd gone and whether, when he came back, he'd be firing torpedoes from below or heaving grenades over the top.

Which is to say, I don't know what Tiburón hit me with. Must have been a grenade. How else to account for this buzz behind my eyes?

We were both tentative at the start. Nothing unusual about that. Boxing is a kind of conversation in which the principals ask increasingly more difficult questions of one another. Most fights begin as do the best conversations, even the dialogues of Plato: with small talk. I quickly discovered, however, that I was ill-equipped to chat. I had no patter, no store of breezy remarks. I had no language, not even stock response, with which to answer Tiburón's quizzing rights and lefts. The most astonishing thing, though, the thing I was not prepared for, was that I could not see his punches coming. I could not see them at all. No, check that. Some punches were the merest blurs along the curve of my vision. By the time I picked them up, it was too late, they were upon me. Other punches I saw with preternatural clarity. I am reminded of the scene in Tom Jones when Albert Finney, I think it was, turned and stretched his hand out to cover the lens of the camera that was making the movie. Finney was about to dally with a lady and wanted to do so without the moviegoer cheering him on. These punches of Tiburón came into view much as Finney's hand did. They bloomed before my eyes, as I stood there, fascinated, incapable of getting out of the way.

Soon I was finding it difficult to see for other reasons. A few taps on the nose and my eyes began filling up with sympathetic tears. A few more taps and blood started to pool inside my nostrils. Had to suck great gobs of air through my mouthguard. Was encountering difficulty breathing. I spit the hunk of rubber out, whether purposely or not I can't say. All I know is they pulled me into the corner where they washed the thing and Mickey said stuff to me I could not hear because the blood was not just in my nose but pounding in my ears.

It was at this point, I believe, that the dialogue began. Not my dialogue with Mickey. As I said, though I could see that he was talking, I couldn't hear what he was saying. No, I mean the dialogue within myself. I looked across the way at my sparring partner, who was up on his toes, looking very athletic in the opposing corner, and I remember hearing a voice say something like, "Tell me, Bill, what is it exactly that you've got against this fellow Tiburón? Nothing, right? If I'm not mistaken, Tiburón is all right in your book." This voice went on to suggest that Tiburón and I replan our afternoon, that we step out to an early supper, maybe catch a show and afterwards try our luck at some place like Xenon's. This was the voice of sanity, of culture and detente. It was upstaged a few beats later by another voice. (By this time I'd been shooed back into the center of the ring.) "Jab, jab, jab, just move the jab. Don't be ducking, now, son. Slip the straight punches and weave under them wide ones. Get you rhythm. Remember you combinations. Double jab, hook, right hand, hook again. Always finish with a hook, so you can start the new series." This was the voice of craft and ring experience. It sounded alternately like Mickey and Refugio, and may actually have been them, since they were both in the corner, carrying on what looked to be a rather vigorous dumbshow.

It was the third voice, in any case, that got me into trouble, if you could call it a voice. It was actually more of a sneer. "Know what, sucker? It's Tiburón's fault you in this fix. That's right, Tiburón. T-I-B-U-R-Ó-N. Weren't for Tiburón needin' to 'get some work,' you wouldn't be in here gettin' you map rearranged. Know what else, dickhead?" Pregnant pause here. "Dude's been talkin' 'bout you mama!"

I was suddenly so angry at Tiburón that, oddly, under the circumstances, I wanted to fight him. *Fight* him, that is, not box him. Screw the candyass Rules of the London Prize Ring, I wanted to tear Tiburón's head off and piss down his neck, whatever it took to stop this goddamn train I was on. I wanted to get off, please.

Then it happened. I don't how exactly, but the next thing I knew I was raging across the ring, swinging my arms wildly and scattering, not just my sparring partner, but those of my gym mates leaning against the ropes. I couldn't see at all now. And I was having trouble breathing again, only this time it was serious. I don't know, I must have taken a jolt, maybe that's what did it, or maybe it was the anger and the frustration and the exhaustion, the three of them ganging up on me, I don't know. All I know is I couldn't breathe, *couldn't breathe,* somebody something had grabbed hold of my lungs was squeezing them dry was not letting any more air in my lungs were screaming my throat was dredging up bile I couldn't stop it I couldn't start breathing it was like a child my own son Nicky with croup that night when I thought about cutting a hole in his throat just a little one size of a dime to let the air in thank heavens I called the doctor he said turn on the hot water in the sink hold him up to the steam Jesus I was so damn scared. . . .

Something had happened to me. Something I'd never experienced before. Something mortifying. I had lost control in there with Tiburón, gone off the deep end. I wanted to know why. I wanted Mickey to explain it to me. But he wouldn't, at least not in any way that I found useful or consoling.

"Nerves," he said.

What do you mean "nerves"?

"Just nerves, is all. It happen sometimes."

I don't understand, I said. I've played sports my whole life. My whole youth, much of my relationship with my father, was based on sports. And I don't mean bowling or golf, either. I mean real sports, the kind where you push yourself past empty and nobody gives an inch. How could it be "nerves"?

"You can't compare fighting with other sports," said Mickey, looking me directly in the eye.

The trainer started to say more, then didn't. We were in that zone again—invisible curtains had clattered down on either side of us. We were in that stark, laconic space where men were men and where the important, the troubling things could only be alluded to.

"It's just nerves," Mickey repeated. "You'll get over it."

I'm the sort who prefers to talk things through, who likes to lay seige to a problem with words and overcome it by understanding it. But we were in Mickey's building, where rules were rules, his rules, no argument. I observed the house form and stewed in silence. A couple of weeks later I boxed again.

"You in trouble again, buddy," said Mickey, smiling as he tossed me the gloves.

This time I took the news with relative calm. Perhaps it was because I was to be paired with Chino Number One. Chino might have been the toughest kid in the gym, but there was no aura of mystery about him. He was my friend, which seemed to make all the difference. Naturally, things speeded up considerably as I stepped through the ropes, and the gloves felt like those large foam rubber clubs people with marital woes use to learn to "fight fair." But, for the most part, my heart seemed content to stay inside my chest and my breathing somewhat under control. To my amazement, I discovered that I could see many of Chino's punches coming and even head off the odd slowpoke with an open glove. More amazing still, I found that I could reach the kid with my jab, actually beat an irregular tattoo on the front of his headgear, which caused him to take a share of razzing from those at ringside. Only once did I charge across the blood tub like an enraged animal. Only once did I take a good lick from my opponent, a straight left hand to the nose that caused me to leave a trail of claret across the canvas.

"My God!" said Mickey in mock-horror, as he inspected the carnage. "You nose, it's over here now!"

It was all very cozy. Mickey was right—each time I set foot into the ring, it got easier. But Mickey was wrong, too, wrong about my getting over my "nerves." I never did. I trained for four more months and stopped, just like that. This despite the trainer's visiting upon me a range of perplexed and wounded looks, despite his silent plea that we continue our dance together, his tacit protestation that there were still some cuts left on the record, any number of steps we hadn't tried. . . .

As I think about my training, two incidents stick out. Neither had to do with my dance with Mickey per se. But both, in retrospect, seem to illuminate my reasons for quitting, reasons which, at the time, were obscure even to me. One took place a couple of weeks before I boxed for the first time. Like most fighters, I was enjoying my condition. I was tired and sore much of the time, but I was also oddly exhilarated. I felt as though my senses had been scraped clean. I could smell coffee brewing in restaurants from outside on the street. I was, in fact, foolishly emboldened by my condition and the little bit of boxing technology I had managed to absorb. I would walk down the streets of the barrio, down past teen-age punks collected outside the candy stores, past groups of derelicts lolling by abandoned buildings, and I would imagine, even wish, that one in the number would step out and dare me to raise my dukes. In my fondest B-movie fantasy, I would jab the hapless fellow dizzy, then, finally, mercifully, close the show with a monster right hand, leaving the multitude dumbstruck with admiration.

One afternoon I was on the bus, traveling across 116th through the wasteland of the Valley. The bus stopped to pick up a group of women. As it did, I chanced to look out the window and see two men by a third man who was lying on the sidewalk. One of the two men appeared to be standing guard as the other kneeled over the third fellow. The pockets of the latter had been pulled inside out and looked like elephant ears in a children's book. Finished with the pockets, the kneeling man was reaching down past the supine man's belt, down through his trousers into the region of his vitals, from which he extracted a black leather purse with a gold clasp.

"That's all right. Joker ain't got no use for the money no how," said a black fellow sitting in the seat in front of me. He was peering out the window, too, and laughing.

Turning back to the scene outside the window, I noticed that the man on the ground had a long red gash on the side of his face and that his eyes were frozen wide open. I saw all this in the time it took the bus to stop, hiss to its knees, collect the women, and sweep back onto the road.

The second incident occurred some months after my interlude with Tiburón. I had started doing a number of free-lance magazine pieces, whatever I could get that would bring me into conversation with the top people in the sport. One such assignment took me to the hardscrabble country outside Sacramento, where I visited with Junior Lightweight Champ Bobby Chacon. Chacon lived with his girl friend and several young children in a sprawling aluminum house mounted on concrete blocks. He was called "Schoolboy" by his fans for his young looks and bubbly demeanor, but the face he held up to the world was misleading. Chacon was thirty years old and he had just, after ten years of fighting nobodies for nothing, become a world champion for the second time. He had persisted in this mission to attach a second title even after his wife, his childhood sweetheart, had committed suicide in her despair at not being able to convince him to try another line of work.

I liked Bobby Chacon and I was moved by his story—how could I not be? But what got me, even more than the part about his wife, were the goats, the soft, snow-white kids his children were playing with as we sat outside on the stoop. The goats were pets, but the genitals of each had been wrapped tight with twine. When the balls finally desicated and dropped off, Bobby sunnily explained, he would take each goat and slaughter it.

I knew, after spending time with Bobby Chacon, that I could never be a proper fighter. There was something missing in me. Or, better: There was *not* something missing in me. There was no lead-lined area of unfeeling in me, no cold and brutal place from which I could draw strength as a fighter. If this second vignette affirmed what I already knew, the first reminded me of something that in my euphoria I had forgotten. Which is, that I was a sojourner in Mickey and Negra's world. That my role was that of observer. And that, if I played my part well, if I was thoughtful and attentive, thereby, maybe, hung a tale.

Chapter 4

LIBERACE'S TROUSERS

It was late, past seven, when we arrived at the Felt Forum and started pounding on the corrugated steel doors to get in. It was so late that grizzled old Cerberus hardly bothered to mess with us, but contented himself with muttering something choice under his breath about "Portorickens," as we breezed by his jealously guarded checkpoint. Maybe five months had passed since I had gotten smart and said uncle to what Mickey called my "nerves" and packed in my training. More to the matter at hand, just a few days had elapsed since Reggie and the two Chinos had traveled out to Rockaway to make their collective bow into pugilistic society. Buoyed by their success, we were back for a second round of Golden Gloves preliminaries, this time with Milton, Smooth, and Jackson in tow.

We descended to the bowels of the Garden, where we found that the usual group of suspects had already been rounded up and was decorating the corridor that wound past the half-dozen dressing rooms. This is to say, the Golden Gloves coaches were out in force, taking their conversational ease prior to the entertainment. Their kids had made the weight, and there was nothing for them to do just now but put time out of its misery as painlessly as they knew how, short of heading across the street for a couple of cool ones.

It was one of my favorite moments at the Gloves, a leisurely caesura in the march of the night's activities characterized by warm fellow-feeling, a share of yarn spinning, and a good deal of plain old-fashioned talk. I felt the pull of the moment as we plunged through its field of force and, weak vessel that I am, readily succumbed to its allure. I paused to troll for local color as Mickey and Negra and the three young warriors continued on down the corridor.

"You might say it's a tale of two Willies."

A fellow named Willie Dunn was explaining how he'd come to lose a fighter he'd had since the kid was knee-high to a ring post. He was telling how he'd lost this youngster to Eddie Futch, the peripatetic trainer of Michael Spinks and Larry Holmes and other leading men. It was an old story and, therefore, to my taste at least, all the more beguiling in the telling. It would be familiar in outline form to pretty much any amateur handler in the City—that is, to anybody who'd been in the game long enough to develop a prospect and to see him, when it came for a little remuneration, go off with some mug with a sparkler on his pinky and a wad in his pocket fat enough to hire himself a name trainer. Sometimes in these situations the kid felt a sense of obligation to his Willie Dunn, this man who for close to a decade had been his confessor, advocate, and all-purpose angel. Sometimes when the kid moved on to Eddie Futch he took Willie Dunn with him. Took him to Phoenix or Vegas, where the amateur coach was put up in a run-down motor court and was reduced to donkey work. In training camp, to executing the principal architect's grand design. At the fight itself, to wielding a bucket and generally playing Tonto to Kemosabe.

Willie Dunn's eyes glittered like mica chips as he rehearsed his tale. He was stoic, philosophic, gay even, after the manner of his breed, in sharing his particular set of facts.

"Like I say," he perorated, "there these two Willies. Now, Willie Shoemaker, he get to ride the good horses. They leave that old swayback pony for Willie Dunn."

There was a murmur of assent among the listeners. In the number was an olive-skinned, pirate-featured fellow named Sinbad Rios, who got about on a wooden leg. He and his sidekick, Jay Kortwright, ran the Ringside Gym on Eighth Avenue and Thirtieth Street. Kortwright, who topped out at Sinbad's none-too-lofty shoulder, had a bum wheel himself as well as what looked like a Woody Allen fright-wig. The two men were regular attractions at the Gloves, always buzzing with news and strategems as they pogoed along the corridors.

"People ask me why I bother with the amateur," said Sinbad. "They ask me what I get out of it." Sinbad chuckled. "I tell them it give me a chance to waste money on gas and cars driving all over the place to the Golden Gloves shows. But, you know, when the kids win, I feel good. Everybody talking like crazy and the air smell so pretty you could bottle it for perfume."

A few yards away, Al Gavin of the Empire S.C., who had made the transition in a modest way from amateur coach to professional cutman, was regaling his own circle with news of his recent motorcade through New England. Gavin had been as far north, apparently, as Portland with a string of fighters that included a young heavyweight nicknamed John "the Baptist." I'd met the kid briefly. He'd been a Gloves finalist a year ago. He was also a Hell's Angel, which meant that he consorted with the usual collection of beer-bellied "outlaws" in piss-stiffened levis and anorexic "mamas" with kelplike hair and uplift bras. None of which endeared him to the Golden Gloves purists.

"Shit, a biker," said a snub-nosed white fellow in a snap-brim and green PAL sweater.

"Hey," replied big Al, who'd apparently given the matter some thought, "I didn't like Hitler either. But you got to admit, he had a helluva army."

There was assent to this too.

The Rosario dressing room was oddly quiet. Mickey was standing against one wall along with Refugio, Chino Number One, and Reggie, who had come down to support their gym mates in this their trial outing of the season. The four of them had the aspect of stiffs banking a catacomb. They were staring across at the evening's warriors, who seemed scarcely warmed-over themselves.

Smooth was hunched forward on the edge of a bench, rubbing some kind of lotion onto the backs of his mocha-colored hands, giving special attention to the knuckles, which were intractably black from use. The normally loquacious Milton had put on his trunks and robe and was hooked up to a Sony Walkman. Eyes closed, he was leaning back in a folding chair. Jackson was a matching picture of repose, his great brown legs spanning the tiny room like a pair of transatlantic cables. Yet he was clearly not at ease. His face was etched—it was difficult to tell—with either pain or concentration. Rounding out this wan ensemble was Negra, who was balled up at Jackson's side. She looked, in her striped sweater, like a pair of argyle socks fresh from the wash.

There was something in the air, and I thought I knew what it was. The three kids who were fighting this night were different sorts of people with different ambitions and ways of carrying themselves both in and out of the ring. But they were alike in this: After years of finding their sustenance in a steady diet of leather and regular attendance at the Gloves, all three had skipped last season's festivity. Each had his own reason for sitting out. Yet Jackson could have been speaking for the lot, I suspect, when we talked some days earlier about his current frame of mind. "Whenever you've been away for a period of time," he told me, "your mind plays tricks on you. You say, 'Hey, do I still have it? Can I come back and do it, or am I making a mistake? Can I get off, put my punches together without getting hit? Or am I going to make a fool of myself, maybe even get hurt?' You worry that you've lost the instinct. It's important, when you come back, to win that first fight big."

Jackson had been a perennial Gloves contender, losing in successive years to Eddie Gregg, Mitch Green, and Carl "the Truth" Williams, statuesque black men who had gone on to become main-eventers in the pros. Every year, it seemed, Jackson was a pretourney favorite, and every year some dark knight emerged from the forest to deprive him of what was rightly his. The big lug was human. He got discouraged, started to hanker after a more "normal" existence, one in which you did not work or crack the books all day and go steady with Mickey at night. So he sat out last year, only to see a willing side of beef of Italian extraction walk through the tournament. Another kid might have been terminally bummed out, or at least railed at the gods for his misfortune. Not Jackson, who could locate the silver lining in a mushroom cloud. "I said, 'Wow! if this guy can do it, I know I can do it, because I'm three times better than him.' That's really what made me come back. I also said, 'These people who lead normal lives, *snorrr!* It's boring.' You know what I mean? Going to movies, parties, enjoying your leisure, after a while you get tired of it. It may sound strange, but I wanted to get back to that world where you got curfews, you got to be in the house, you got to rest, you can't hang out or smoke or drink, you can't be fooling around with too many women."

Ah, the ladies! Ah, sex and boxing! This may be the place to talk about them. For it is an article of faith among boxing folk, dating back at least to the Sophist Philostratus (A.D. 170–245), that sex is anathema to an athlete, that the quality of a kid's performance in the ring is in inverse proportion to the quantity (and vigor) of his efforts in the sack. "If one comes from sexual indulgence," wrote Philostratus in his classic *Concerning Gymnastics,* "it is better for him not to take training. For where is the manhood of those who exchange the wreath and the herald's cry for vile sensual pleasure?"

Where indeed? Some fighters say that a night of dalliance ties anvils to your feet and turns your knees to Slinkies. Others say it puts a hole in your bellows for upwards of a week. Some argue that masturbation is worse than partnered sex, because, well, think about it: If you put twice as much into it, it's got to take twice as much out of you. Still others hold oral sex to be the most draining sex of all, because—as a fast-living young featherweight once explained to me—"We're talking Bela Lugosi here. The stuff is hoovered right out of you!"

Through the years the fighter's semen has been accorded properties comparable to those granted in biblical legend to Samson's hair. Which is to say, there is a belief among boxing folk that semen is magic, a sort of philosopher's stone or elixir of life. There is, for instance, a trainer at the Times Square Gym, a natty, well-spoken fellow named Syd Martin, who claims, rather portentously, that "it takes sixteen drops of blood to equal one drop of semen." Thus, he argues, a fighter should no more think of spilling his seed before a bout than he should consider putting a knife to his arm and opening a vein. Either, suggests Martin, is a form of vocational suicide.

Among the cognoscenti, it is widely believed that a boxer should horde his sperm for at least a month prior to getting in with a worthy opponent. In part, the drill is psychological. Abstinence is thought somehow to whet a kid's appetite for fighting—it is the sauce that makes a fighter want to tear into the other fellow and eat him alive. In other and, to my taste, more interesting part, the drill is physiological—or, better, metaphysiological. By this I mean, there is a belief in certain rarefied corners of the boxing world that the horded semen actually is spent, that it is somehow fired inward, into the bloodstream, where it is recycled in a self-contained, self-enriching, Escher-like system. Lightweight champ Ray "Boom Boom" Mancini, a disciple of this school, once told me that he knew he was at the absolute peak of physical condition, ready to stop training and go fifteen rounds, on that day that he started having nocturnal emissions. Other mystics begrudge even this midgelike loss of executive power. Indeed, said Bundini Brown, Muhammad Ali's colorful aide-de-camp, of the whole titillating, purposely frustrating ritual known as the training camp: "You got to get the hard-on, and then you got to keep it. You want to be careful not to lose the hard-on and, at the same time, cautious not to come."

As for Milton and Smooth, their problems were female in origin, but they were not, strictly speaking, sexual. By this I mean, they came, not from fooling around with too many women, but from trying to get serious over one woman in particular. Both young men were stuck in mercurial relationships with dumpling-shaped girls who had made them the ambivalent fathers of little boys. Milton's girl Tina had had him on a string for five years, yo-yoing him in and out of her affections as she lived at home with her folks and essayed to lead the life of Archie's pals, Betty and Veronica, complete with high school, slumber parties, dates with other guys. All this while letting her own mother and Milton and his mom split the job of rearing Milton, Jr.

Two years ago, Milton sought order and clarity where he had always found them before: in the gym and the monastic rituals of the training floor. He entered the Gloves as a matter of course, and *wham!* got knocked out for his troubles, five seconds of oblivion courtesy of a slick piece of goods and former Gloves champion named Luis Hernandez. It was not the sort of respite that Milton was looking for. "I don't care how good he is," said Milton of Hernandez. "He's not supposed to be a knock-out puncher. And you know what I can't understand? I felt so vicious that day. So *bad,* so *down.* I don't get it, man. I never been hit and felt my brain click like that."

Milton sat out last year to brood, to worry that he was not the man he thought he was, but a fictional character in his own life. Given my own turn around the floor with Tiburón, I understood him perfectly. More puzzling was Smooth, a gym icon in disrepair. Three years ago Smooth won the Gloves 125-pound Open Class title, a truly remarkable feat considering that he'd been stopped the previous season in his trial outing in the Novice tournament, a decidedly lesser competition. Then, two years ago, in his initial fight of the Gloves, he quit on the stool between the second and third episodes. He was winning the fight— that was the weird part. He offered no excuse for his behavior but withdrew into an envelope of silence. Later, he spoke variously about cramping up, about not being able to get his breath, about shooting pains in the region of his jewels.

Like everyone else, Mickey was perplexed by his kid's behavior and was not above scrounging for an explanation in the usual places. By this I mean the trainer recalled that Smooth had brought his woman to the fight that night. That he had actually brought this girl, unmistakably pregnant, backstage with him. Brought her back to sit with him on the runway, as, garbed in gloves and headgear, he waited to be called into the ring to fight. Or, as it turned out, as Mushy might say, to take a dip in the pool.

"Truthfully," said Mickey, telling me all this a year later and still reeling from the scandal, "I blame Smooth's woman for what happen to him. Women are a curse to fighters."

What about Negra? I asked, nodding toward the trainer's wife. She's a woman, isn't she?

"Negra don't count," Mickey replied.

"What you mean, *Negra don't count?*" said the lady in question, who had been listening to the conversation and was, per usual, drawing her own emphases. "I'm plenty of woman for you once, Mr. Rosario. I tell you this, I'm sixteen again and I see you coming, I'm going to run. And this time, you scrawny little runt, you ain't going to catch me. . . ."

Meanwhile, back in the dressing room, on what was shaping up as Comeback Night, Smooth was the only one stirring. There were five of us stiffs now holding up the wall, and we watched him with dumb fascination and no little gratitude for the shred of life he represented. We watched as he moved purposefully about, tending to his wardrobe, as he carefully folded his black turtleneck sweater and his black leather pants, after first removing the black-and-white mock-lizard belt with a gold buckle, from which there was suspended by a gold chain a three-inch replica of a Colt .45. We leaned in with unfeigned interest as Smooth, dressed now in black briefs and black-and-white high-stitch cowboy boots, pulled one of those spongelike lint brushes from the pocket of his black leather jacket and began running it around the oval of his navy velour hat. Holding it up to the light. Flicking a manicured nail at invisible grit. Finally, placing the hat atop the pile of his other things. Carefully, crown first. I could see the combs, the sort women wear as barrettes, that he'd sewn front and back into the lining, so that the hat would better hold his modest Afro and not fly off at the first intimation of a breeze. I could see, as he produced a rake and started picking his hair, that the handle of the rake was shaped like a fist, a black fist. That it was designed to give the black power salute as it peeped from the back pocket of his pants. . . . I was thinking these things, drawing deeper into the minutiae of Smooth's livery the way one sometimes goes into a photograph or a painting and actually moves about within it, when, suddenly, Mickey burst off the wall.

"By golly, jingo bells!" he whooped. "We fully equip and ready to whip! Right fellows?"

Smooth ignored the trainer. So did Jackson, who let out what might have been a moan. Milton furled an eyelid maybe halfway.

"Milton," said the trainer. "You not talking to me, son."

"I hear you."

"You hear me, but you still ain't talking to me."

"I don't want to talk. Every time I talk I lose. I was babbling two years ago. I'm trying to get mean, like Duran. This year I'm taking my *mean* pills!"

Milton flashed us a ferocious, Duran-like sneer, adding a "*Grrrr!*" for good measure. Then he sank back into his chair and shut his eyes, while turning up the volume on his Walkman to preempt further conversation.

The trainer was wired, however, and not to be denied. An elephant had entered the room and was kneeling on the chests of his fighters, squeezing all capacity for speech and perhaps the very fight out of them. This, at least, was what I felt Mickey himself was feeling and preparing to do something about. The trainer was a species of psychologist, a student of the mind without certificate whose laboratory was a boxing gym and whose couch, at the moment, was a bench and a couple of fold-up chairs in the maze beneath Madison Square Garden. He was, admittedly, an odd sort of dream sleuth *cum* anxiety hound. For in keeping with his cherished masculine code, he could bring himself neither to name nor talk about the mind's favorite chimera: about fear. (There! I've said the word myself.) But that didn't mean he didn't know the beast, didn't recognize its peculiar stink when it hunkered down before him, or that he didn't have his own way of confronting it. Which is to say, the trainer was not about to stand there, thumb buried where the sun don't shine, as his kids marinated in silence. No, he was going to get someone in this sorry-ass company to open up and talk, talk about anything at all. It didn't much matter what, so long as it got the juices flowing in the room and thawed out the rest of these candidates for a meat locker, so long as it reversed the process by which the doubts his kids brought with them this night were swelling into visions of failure, metasta-sizing as fear and paralysis. If this evening's warriors were less than garrulous, well, what the hell, any port in a storm, the past evening's would simply have to do. Perhaps catching this drift, Chino Number One and Reggie began to move toward the dressing-room door. Chino actually had his hand on the knob when the trainer started in on him.

"Now, Chino, don't let youself get carried away with this victory you have," said Mickey, referring to the fight in Rock-away a few nights earlier, the one where Chino snuffed his opponent at the opening bell. "This is only one fight, buddy."

"I know," said Chino Number One.

"The next one is what matter."

"I will train even harder."

"I want to tell you from the get-go, I am happy that you won. But, truthfully, you did not impress me."

Chino was baffled by this critique. He had, after all, eclipsed his man with a single blow. What could be more impressive than that?

"I don't know," chimed Refugio. "Chino lookeded kind of slow, didn't he, Mickey?"

"Slow?" said Chino. The two men had his attention now.

"In fact, I never seen Chino look slow like that," said Refugio.

"Well, he's a slow fighter," said the trainer to his assistant. The two men were discussing the kid as if he weren't standing there in front of them, a few feet away, hands on hips now, no longer baffled but indignant.

"He's a taker, really," Mickey continued. "That's what Chino is. He can punch. But the thing I don't like, he walk into too many right hands."

"Capoolo!" came a cry from the corridor. Gloves officials were seeking a kid for an upcoming bout.

"How can I take 'too many right hands'," Chino wanted to know, "when I sneak the guy and he don't even hit me? You know why he don't hit me?" Chino canvassed the room with his eyes but, alas, could muster little interest in his plight. "You know why?" Still no interest. "I tell you why. 'Cause he's lying there cold as a fish in a newspaper, that's why."

"Capoolo!" came the voice once more.

"Capoolo, that's a helluva name," said Mickey. "Got a friend of mine by that name. Only it ain't 'Capoolo,' it's 'Caputo' he mean."

"That's Spanish, right, Mickey?" asked Refugio.

"Eye-talian," said Mickey. "All people that ends in 'o' ain't Ricans, you know."

"So what?" asked Chino, still seeking justice in an imperfect world. "How do this guy hit me with a right hand? In his dreams?"

"Capoolo!" The voice was faint. The official was seeking the kid at the other end of the corridor now.

"Watch this," said Mickey. "Yo!"

"Capoolo!" cried the voice. It was coming back our way again.

"Yo!" shouted Mickey.

"Capoolo," laughed Refugio. "It sound like *culo*. Or *chulo*. Bill, you know what *chulo* mean?"

I shook my head.

"Pimp."

"*Chulo* can also be handsome," said Mickey. "Like a pretty boy."

I thought *majo* meant pretty boy, I said.

"*Majo?*" said Refugio. "What's *majo?* You mean *mono? Mono* is pretty, like, you know, cute. It is also monkey."

No, I said. *Majo,* like the paintings of Goya. The *Maja Desnuda* and so on.

"You mean the vegetables?" said Mickey. "They got pretty boys painted on them?"

No, no, no, I said. Not Goya food products. I'm talking about Goya the artist. Fellow from Spain. Painter. Lived a long time ago. You know, Goya.

"Yeah, you know, Goya," Chino sneered. "Remember him? Kinda slow, walk into too many right hands."

Mickey stared at Chino, wondering at the edge in his voice. He'd entirely forgotten about the youngster.

"Ignacio Free!" A second official was calling for yet another kid now.

"Yo!" shouted Mickey.

"Free!"

"Yo!"

"Capoolo!" The first voice was just outside the door now.

"Shhh! Quiet, quiet," said Mickey to the rest of us. We were starting to giggle.

"Robert Capoolo," said the voice. It was speaking into the door now, speaking calmly, deliberately, sensing it was being trifled with. "You ain't upstairs in ten minutes, you out of this tournament."

Mickey waited for footfall in the corridor. Then he sprang to the door, cracked it and gave a final "Yo!"

"Capoolo?" Silence. "That's it! You hear me, Capoolo?" More silence. "*You're out!* I ain't going crazy over you!"

Mickey threw open the door, so that it crashed against the cinder-block wall. Then shrieked in a ludicrous West Indian falsetto, "Gim'me a break, mon!"

It was more than we stiffs could bear. We cracked up, howled, crashed about the room and into each other in our boundless hilarity. Like some poor man's Orpheus using laughter as his lyre, the trainer had gone down and retrieved the lot of us from the deadly gloom within us. The lot of us, that is, but Chino, who pouted theatrically in the corner. And Jackson, who seized the moment to toss his cookies all over the place.

Smooth stood in the corner just above me. His back was flush against the turnbuckle, and Mickey and Negra were pressed fast against him from outside the ropes. They were reaching through on either side to massage him, to pull on his arms and legs and rub the hard spots out of his midsection. They were moving up and down his frame, all the while saying things I could not quite make out, soft things, honey-coated things, cooing in his ear so to keep him slack and lubricated, so to keep his body from tying up and betraying him.

The fighter himself stared across the ring at his opponent, who was a Latino—Fernandez by name, the ring announcer was saying. I tried to see the kid from Smooth's vantage, tried to read the kid as I imagined Smooth did, as a system of signs, starting with the *cola,* the tail or single plait of hair that poked out from the back of his headgear. The *cola* was surely significant. It was the badge of the Spanish bullfighter and, more to the point, of the badass Nuyorican. Given this sort of advertisement, the chances were that the kid had come to fight. His buddies seemed to think so. Their heads tied off with multicolored scarves like so many dime-store Cochises, they were camped at the bicycle rail just behind us, from whence they spent a quiverful of wit on Mickey's fighter.

"Hey, Chorty. I hope jew got a gun wit jew. Jew gonna need it." Yuk, yuk, yuk.

There was something else about the kid that struck me. He

was wearing black and white, the colors of the Bed-Stuy Boxing Club, whose presiding genius was a fellow named George Washington. George was a New York Gloves landmark, a 260-pound monument to affability and good eating, a onetime sparring partner of Joe Louis and sometime poetaster who tutored his kids in a punching sequence he called the "Cherry Tree Special."

> *The Cherry Tree Special,*
> *A punch guaranteed to tell no lies.*
> *A jab, followed by a hook, then a right hand,*
> *And down he flies.*

You could forget the hook. Most of George's kids did. They had what Mushy liked to call the "Panamanian disease," which is to say, they were right-hand crazy. This was less in defiance of the trainer, I suspect, than in deference to his top pupil, a six-foot-three-inch, 147-pound fighter named Mark Breland. Breland was a prodigy of nature, "an animated licorice stick" (as they called "Panama" Al Brown), "a bundle of loosely joined fishing poles" (A. J. Liebling on Sandy Saddler), who had been endowed with certain grotesque advantages, among them a predator's wing span of nearly 78 inches. A mere welterweight, Breland had greater reach than two-thirds of the men who had held the world heavyweight title, including Louis (76 inches) and Dempsey (77½ inches). But reach was scarcely the half of it. For three years running, the kid had stopped every opponent Gloves officials had the temerity to place in front of him. Most of them in the first or second episode. All of them with a straight right teed up by the jab, hold the hook. Breland was the amateur World Welterweight Champion. He was the mold of fashion in his gym. I figured Fernandez would be looking to drop the right hand early and call it a night. Mickey thought otherwise and better. He used his eyes.

"Look how he got them legs spread so wide," said Mickey,

addressing Smooth from behind the turnbuckle. "You can go in and out on him. He can't catch you. See how deep and even his feet in the canvas. He can't change direction like that. He's made for you, son. Look how tight them muscles in his legs. He got to be set to punch. Pressure, that's you game. You back him up, he can't do nothing, I promise you. See the way he carry them hands. This fellow got one way to win, a big left hook. But you ain't going to let him get off."

As it turned out, Smooth did let him get off. Fernandez came out hooking with impunity, lofting high, wide, and arcing pieces of business that failed to land but still managed to cheer the little tribe behind us. Especially as Smooth chose not to counter. Especially as Fernandez took time out to stand in the center of the ring and pose as if for a ceremonial coin, to gesture toward Mickey's kid to come and fight.

"Jew got that gun we talk about, Chorty? Jew betta jews it, bro." Yuk, yuk, yuk.

Smooth's answer, when it finally came, maybe a minute into the round, was typically thoughtful and elegant in its near-tautological simplicity. Which is to say, Mickey's kid, who stood but five-foot-three or -four, got short, or "chort," on his opponent. He bent at the knees. Lowered his hind end so that it nearly brushed his calves. Swayed like a snake in a basket. Then, suddenly, he was exploding up. He was screwing a right hand into the place where the ribs leave off and the stomach begins, even as the kid started to wave another gaudy hook across the top of his head.

Fernandez's reaction, most of it involuntary, was something to see. He crumpled from the waist down, bringing to mind the old skyscrapers in the Movietone newsreels, those musty brick-and-mortar Atlantic City boardwalk hotels brought down with dynamite in the interest of a Glass-and-Steel Age, the ones where for a few delicious slo-mo fractions of a second the top floors keep their integrity, even as everything else goes to pieces beneath them. Fernandez did not lose consciousness, which must have been the worst part of the ordeal. Rather, he sat there on the canvas, his legs arranged inconveniently on either side of him, a look of mortal anguish chipped into his face.

The kid had been hit in the pit of the stomach. Which is to say, in one of boxing's erogenous zones. He'd suffered a blow that was at least as venerable as the bareknuckle era, when the punch was called "hitting to the mark." It was a blow perfected at the turn of the century by "Ruby" Robert Fitzsimmons, who gave it its lasting name: the "solar-plexus punch." A ring physician from the Pacific Northwest named Jack Battalia once explained to me how it works. "Having the wind knocked out of you is the least of it," he said. "The solar-plexus punch does a lot of things. It stimulates the autonomic nerves near the stomach, it changes the blood pressure, it changes the heart rate. Above all, it causes a mysterious shunt in the spinal cord, an electrical reaction that cuts the fighter's legs right out from under him."

So much for the objective view. Mushy filled me in one day on the subjective particulars when I foolishly chanced to question the phenomenon.

"What?" he said. "You tellin' me you don't believe the solar-plexus punch exists?"

Oh, I expect it exists, I started to say. I just find it hard to believe that it's as devastating as—

Before I could complete the heresy, Mushy shot out his left hand and dug his fingers, just the stiffened tips, into the area of our difference.

"Now, where was I?" he said, looking on with amusement, as, doubled over, I strove to keep my feet. "Oh, yeah, the solar-plexus punch is a honey of a punch. It leaves you wondering which end you wanna soil yerself with."

Perched there on the canvas, Fernandez seemed to be fairly secure in his continence. He appeared, in fact, to have moved on to the next level of self-inquiry: whether to rest on remembered glory or to get up. Finally, as is usual in these cases, public sentiment tipped the balance. Refugio and Reggie and, especially, Chino Number One were leading the crowd in out-right horse laughter at Fernandez's expense. Yet the contingent from Casa Rosario was kind, if anything, in comparison to the fighter's own band of admirers. The latter had broken camp and were powwowing anew within yards of the neutral corner where their hero had fallen. *Mariposa* (butterfly, or roughly, faggot) and *"pendejo"* (prick, or coward) were just some of the blandishments they used to entice him to his feet.

Fine. He was up. But that didn't mean he was going to fight. Each time Mickey's kid came in to shoeshine his middle, Fernandez lunged and grabbed the shorter fighter, draped himself across his back. Within a matter of seconds he had regained the use of his legs. He was, in any case, no longer wobbling about the ring like a top in need of further impetus. But, again, that didn't mean he was going to stand and deliver his hook and thereby expose himself to ruin. Uh-uh, he started running—what else were legs for?—flicking shoo-fly jabs in transit.

Mickey's kid emerged from his crouch. It was time for Chorty to get tall, time to set a new trap. Which is to say, Smooth took a few of Fernandez's jabs, just a few, so to imbue his opponent with the beginnings of confidence, so to still the flying hamster wheel of his brain long enough to do a little thinking, long enough for him to entertain the notion that maybe, just maybe, the compact little fellow from across the way had caught him with a lucky punch, what Mush would call a "Hail Mary."

As Fernandez grew in confidence, his jab became more committed and predictable. Smooth timed it. He came back over the top with a right hand, clipping the kid in the temple and shaking him. The referee was tolling a standing eight as the gong sounded to end the round and offer the kid a reprieve.

That was it, all she wrote. Smooth knew it. Within seconds Mickey knew it too.

"How you feel?" the trainer asked his kid. It was a routine enough question, only Smooth failed to come up with the expected answer.

"Not so good," he said. "I can taste the blood in my throat."

The Latino from Bed-Stuy had not hit Mickey's kid, not meaningfully anyway. It was an inside job. Which is to say, it was Smooth's own perplexing malady that was wringing his innards and misting the blood up into his throat. Fortunately, Fernandez did not see that Smooth was hurt, or would not believe it, which amounted to the same thing. The Latino from Bed-Stuy would not go after Mickey's kid, even though Smooth was slow getting off the stool. Even though Smooth did little more than sleepwalk through the last two rounds. Even though the little band of renegades drew back its bow and darkened the ring lights with its flights of abuse.

Fernandez was clearly convinced that Chorty was baiting one last hook, chumming him toward some final catastrophe.

It was his undoing.

Milton also fought a Latino, a kid from some PAL in Jersey with huge purple welts on his shoulders that looked like epaulettes. Milton came out fast, shooting the jab. But he allowed Epaulettes to catch him and mug him on the ropes. Milton sat on the lower strand, as the referee started his eight count. Mickey and Negra bellowed for his attention, as did Chino and Reggie, who angered the referee by running up and down the aisle at ringside. But Milton was too busy riddling his opponent with mean looks to cast an eye in their direction. Seconds later, Milton dropped the kid and stood menacingly over him the way his beloved oldtime fighters used to.

"Are you looking at me?" asked Mickey, slapping his fighter between episodes to the delight of the crowd. "You notice this fellow is a southpaw?"

Milton nodded.

"How you fight a southpaw?"

"Right hand."

"Right. I know you like that hook, but you can't be hooking this turkey. Do me a favor: Let's slip that right hand over and go home. Okay?"

Milton dropped the kid again in the second round, this time

with a double jab mopped up by a right. But he took another eight count himself, as Epaulettes walked through his left and mugged him once more. One minute Milton was a pair of beat-up old brogans, the next he was what? Liberace's trousers. One minute he was dazzling, the next barely serviceable. Whereas Smooth emptied his gun in the first round, Milton seemed to be rationing his ammunition. It was as if each kid, in this his initial comeback venture, was aware that he had a finite amount of fight in him, as if each had a different notion of thrift. This time Negra weighed in between chapters.

"Man, you going to lose this damn fight!" *Wap!* up the side of the head. "You hear me!"

"Hey, Conchita," came a voice from the crowd. "Why doncha hit 'em witcha ponytail!"

No need, Milton won the last round big.

On our return to the dressing room, Mickey and I found Smooth and Jackson, who had mercifully been given a bye, still in their fighting togs and deep in conversation. They were discussing what all Jackson had had to eat that day, a portion of which still hung like bunting on one of the walls.

"He say he get up at six," said Smooth, seeing us come in, "like he's going to do his roadwork. Only what's he do instead? Eat. All day. Man, you ain't going to believe what this dude put away."

This is a list, according to Jackson's recollection, of what passed through his gullet mere hours before the entertainment:

6 poached eggs
3 bananas
½ gallon orange juice
2 pounds macaroni and cheese
2 packages frozen green beans and peas
3 2-pound chuck steaks
½ loaf Wonder Bread
1 gallon milk

My God! I said. No wonder you barfed. You must have put on ten pounds!

"Fourteen," said the heavyweight, smiling sheepishly. "I couldn't stop eating. I guess I was a little more nervous than I thought."

Did you take a good dump?

"No, I was going to save it until just before I went in the ring." Jackson chuckled. "I wanted to be jet-propelled. I guess I'll go for it now."

As Jackson lumbered toward the john, Mickey walked over and kicked at his equipment bag, which was liberally sprinkled with the heavyweight's lava. The trainer turned and cocked a knowing eye at me.

"And you don't think he's a animal."

A few beats later, Milton came swaggering into the room. "Stamina!" he exulted, visiting a flurry of punches upon the air. "I don't got it now, but wait till I get my stamina. *Whooeeee!* I got to talk, talk, talk! I think I'm going to stay up all night and talk. See, look here. Here's why I won."

Milton untied his black high-lace Ethiopia-brand shoes, pulled back the elastic on one of his socks, and extracted a photograph. It showed Milton, Jr. in diapers and a He-Man shirt. Plastic sword in hand, he was fit to do battle with the infamous villain of Snake Mountain, Skeletor himself.

Chapter 5

CHILDREN OF
THE NIGHT

Fathers and sons. In a real and sometimes, I thought, almost pathological sense, Mickey acted the father to us all. It hardly mattered whether you were eight or thirty-eight, or if you were yourself, as I was, the progenitor of a male child. If you were in his gym, the trainer considered you to be flesh of his flesh, his son by proxy, and therefore proper meat for his concern. "Where you been?" he would ask whenever he saw you. This was no ordinary greeting. The trainer truly wanted to know where you'd been, and clearly suspected the worst. You could hear the worry standing just outside the question, straining to get in and strip it of its formal banality, and you knew the others that were sure to follow would be similar pieces of urgency in polite disguise, minor inquisitions. "How long you were there at this place you go to?" "What kind of place is this?" And so on.

At first it was flattering, this extravagant concern with your daily itinerary. It was touching when he wanted to know if you knew where to stand in the train during nonpeak hours (wherever the bulge of humanity was the greatest), or what stop to get off at when traveling to the gym at night (any stop but 110th, because "sometimes the only exit they got is the one with the teeth, and the junkies could be waiting in the dark"). It got old fast, however, for me at least, when Mickey and I and another gringo buddy of his named Al went out one evening to a fashionable groggery on East Eighty-sixth Street. Shortly after eleven, the trainer got up to leave, which was fine, except that he wanted Al and me to point for home as well. I thought he was kidding and laughed. Mickey laughed too. But there was that worry again, leaning hard against his voice. And in case I missed it, the trainer was standing there holding my coat.

A couple of days after Smooth and Milton survived their comeback adventure at the Gloves, we were sitting, Mickey and I, in his apartment eleven stories high in the Wagner Houses overlooking the Triborough Bridge. We were lounging in the living *cum* dining area, which was done, you might say, in Contemporary Ring Museum. By this I mean, the room was hemmed in by boxing trophies, most of them topped off with the same little man looking very pugilistic in gold or silver. The walls were littered with memorabilia, with snaps of Mickey and kids from the gym and prominent personalities from the Cauliflower Trade, as well as with sets of gloves that hung by their laces and were covered with signatures and must have commemorated famous victories. The gloves told of the presence of a lady in the house: They were set off with bows confected from the bright-colored sashes of boxing robes and looked, I thought, like giant, doofy corsages. As Mickey and I chatted, Negra passed continually through the room, pausing to freshen our cups of chocolate and mop at the dark linoleum floor, which was so clean already it winked in the midday sun.

The conversation turned toward the trainer's own kids, his biological ones. Mike Jr. was in his early twenties. He was married, had two small children, and was working just now in the lab of one of those seven-hour photo parlors. I didn't know Mike particularly well, as he trained late at night. But it was apparent even to me that, his three Golden Gloves titles notwithstanding, the kid was going nowhere as a professional boxer. Mike's problem as a money fighter could best be viewed through the little glass window of the bathroom scale, where it told that he weighed but 112 pounds. Which is to say, the kid's problem was that he was a flyweight; and watching flyweights get it on, in the opinion of most New York fight bugs, is nearly as entertaining as watching a pair of sissies squabble over a tube of eye-liner.

Mike was a victim of his metabolism, of his draw from the gene pool. But there was more to it, I felt, than that. He had a thin, El Greco-esque countenance (I thought of Saint Sebastian, all those arrows perforating his side, the martyr as pin cushion) and a shy, vulnerable, ingratiating manner, which made him pleasant company but maybe not a ravening carnivore in the ring. Ralphie, Mickey's younger son, was something else again. Where Mike seemed beaten down, hair-shirted by life, Ralphie was that curious entity in the ghetto, a youngster with a strong, even exalted sense of his own worth. Where Mike's conversation was diffident, amiable, you were lucky to get Ralphie into conversation at all. If Mickey's younger son were walking down the street with his mother and you chanced to approach from the opposite direction and he didn't care for—for what? . . . the lotion in your motion—well, he might just amble off a few yards and give you his back, stare haughtily into the distance, until you'd had your quota of disdain and moved on about your business. Twice, to my knowledge, Ralphie had been thrown out of shows for dropping his opponent in the dressing room prior to the fight, which, from the other fellow's perspective, had to be something of a blessing. For when it came to fighting, Ralphie left his airs outside the building; he turned into a thoroughgoing hoodlum with few compunctions about raking his elbow across your face or stepping on your feet or making thoughtful use of the outside as well as the inside of his head.

"This one is like his mother," said Mickey, pitching his voice so that Negra couldn't fail to hear him from the next room. "He will tell you how you were born and how you will die. And if that don't do it, he will use force and slickness."

The remark did its appointed work. "Bill," said Negra, emerging, spatula in hand, from the kitchen, "let me tell you about Ralphie. When I am pregnant with him I have a hard time. Just getting pregnant I have a hard time. We have just lost two kids by miscarriage, and after Ralphie we lose five more. Mickey think I have abortions because I don't want a child. Mens think dirty things like that." Negra paused and gave her husband a withering look. "Ralphie is special. You know why?"

I didn't.

"Because he's born with one ovary."

"One ovary?"

"Yes, because after Mike is born I have woman problems. There's a cyst and they got to take the ovary and they say I can't have no more kids. Then I have a operation, and after that I would walk and I always see this little kid behind me. Sometime it would slip out my mouth, 'Grab the baby.' And Mickey would look at me. 'What baby?' You see, in my religion, when there's a child to be born, his spirit will wander the mother around. So I know Ralphie is coming. Later, when I'm pregnant, I'm so sick I'm in bed all the time and nobody ever see me and they all think he's adopted. That's why I tell Mickey before Ralphie comes, 'As hard as I been getting this child into the world, that's how mean he going to be!' I also tell him, 'Man, you in trouble. You going to pay for every bad thing you ever done with that child!' " Negra laughed delightedly. She loved Ralphie's naughtiness, his bell-to-bell arrogance.

"You know how evil Ralphie is? One day his father and I are just kidding around with him, right here in the living room. He's only a couple of months, but he's a devil. He make out like he wants a kiss from Mickey and a kiss from me. He put his little cheeks out to us, and soon as we go to kiss him, he take our heads and smash them together. Mean. Ralphie used to get these angers when he's one or two years old. He would get them when I won't give him the toy he wants. He would take his head and *bang! bang! bang!* he would hit it right on the wall or floor. His father would be spanking him on the rear end and telling him, 'Don't do that because it's hurting your brains!' I remember one time when he just four years old. It's raining and Mickey used to take Mike to school and take Ralphie too. But because it's raining I don't let Mickey take him. I don't want him to get wet and catch his death. Oh, Ralphie, he is furious at me, and he say to me, 'Now, you see, you don't let Poppy take me. Now I know he's going to his girl friend's house. I know his girl friend.' *Eee-vil.* Ralphie was so evil. When he was five or six he was playing with this Mexican kid. The kid was twelve and Ralphie bit him on the stomach and stood there on the stomach until he made a hole. We had to pry his mouth off."

"Ralphie is so different from Mike," said Mickey. The trainer had been listening closely to what his wife was saying and taking it somberly to heart. "Mike was my firstborn, and I guess he have to pay for my mistakes. I had Mike in a glass case. I shield him, keep every drunkard and addict from him. I shield him so much it make him timid. I put him in a Catholic school to keep him away from the sons of bitches, and it turn out they got more sons of bitches there than anywhere. You know how bad I was with Mike? When he took the elevator, I ran down the stairs to make sure nobody would hurt him. He was my prize. I kept him in a cage." Mickey shook his head. "I wanted to be such a good father, but I guess I blew it."

"You still blowing it," said Negra.

"What you mean?" said Mickey.

"I mean you trying to keep Ralphie in a cage too. Tell Bill about Ralphie and them special schools. Go on, tell him."

Mickey shrugged. "There was these two schools Ralphie wants to go to, and I guess I took my time thinking about whether he should go to them. Soon it was too late for one of them, the one in West Harlem. The other one was in the Bronx, and I definitely was not going to let Ralphie go to the Bronx."

Wait a moment, I said. You're not talking about the Bronx High School of Science?

"Yeah," said Negra. "That's the one."

They took him?

"They took him there and they took him at the one where they draw or something," said Negra.

The High School of Music and Art.

"Right," said Negra. "Ralphie's very good at art. He could do all these beautiful drawings. You never seen them?"

Now, let me get this straight, I said, not quite believing what I was hearing. Ralphie got accepted at the Bronx High School of Science and at Music and Art and you wouldn't let him go to either of them?

"Well, he picked the High School of Printing," said Mickey, "because it's on the West Side and it's about two steps away from where I work."

"You mean *you* pick it him for him," said Negra.

Do you know about Bronx Science? I asked. It's probably the most famous high school in the country. Nobel prize winners go there. Do you know that people kill to get their kids in there?

"All I know," said Mickey, speaking very slowly, the way one does to foreigners, "it's in the Bronx and I'm here in the City, and if Ralphie get in trouble I can't help him in the Bronx."

It was one of those laden moments in our relationship. One of those indelible spots in time where the two of us just sat and stared at each other, silently, incredulously, across the cultural divide, wondering if we were even of the same species. Finally, the trainer spoke.

"You think I overprotect Ralphie too much, right?"

He's your son, I said.

"But you think so, right? You think I overprotect all these kids too much?"

It doesn't matter what I think, I said. Like you're always telling me, I'm not from here. I'm from—

"That's right, you not from here!" Mickey said sharply. Then, a few seconds later, "Look, maybe you right. Maybe I do over-protect Ralphie and the others too much. But you know why

I'm always on these youngsters, asking them where they been, what they been doing?"

No, not really.

"I'll tell you this, it ain't because I don't know. I know exactly where they been and what they been doing. Because whatever they do, I done it already myself. See, the world revolve around, and it always come back to the starting point. I been through hell in my life, and I'm going through hell all over again in the minds of these youngsters. Remember, you ask me once about the gangs?"

Yes.

"Well, maybe we ought to talk about that. Maybe you could understand me better." Mickey laughed. "I may look the same as any other Rican, but I'm not. I think different and I act different, and I think maybe it's because of all them years leading the gangs. Anyway, first thing you got to know is I was always like a little ruffian. I was always good with my fists, which is lucky, really, because, at that time, just after the world war, there ain't too many Puerto Ricans in the City. It's all Italians over here, all Irish, and their favorite word is 'spik,' 'greaseball,' whatever. School and me, we don't get along too good. At first they have me at a grammar school on One hundred and third between Park and Lexington. Then, for some reason, they move me to a school named Patrick Henry at One hundred and first and Third. I never really graduate from one grade to the other. They push me up because of my age. I never learn to read and write until I'm twenty, when I start to work in drugstores. Also then I learn to do my sums.

"My anger starts in school. My trouble is I can't speak English and I develop the habit, which I still got today, of speaking so fast the words all come together. I don't know, I must be thinking if I speak real fast, nobody will notice I don't know what I'm saying. But they notice all right. The white kids spend all their time laughing at me. Anyway, I'm so frustrated I'm fighting all around the clock. I'm fighting in school and I'm fighting out on the street. I'm getting very street-wise too. It's funny. I have a good home, not too broken like all these kids I got in the gym today. My mother and brother, they give me everything I need. I never go to bed without eating. I always have clothes on my back and two–three dollars in my pocket. But there's something in me, I need a challenge, and I don't find it in school. I need a 'high,' but I ain't interested in drugs. I like to fight, one on one. Roll up you sleeve, let's see what you got.

"I became more or less a gang leader. You know, 'action clubs.' This was the early fifties, and by this time there is more and more Hispanics and we feeling closed in by the Germans and the Italians. We used to try to go to swim over to the park on One hundred and twelfth, where we got the gym now, and the Italians, they would run us out of there. We used to roam over to Yorkville, underneath the El. We used to steal the fruit from the vendors, but not because we hungry. We used to steal the fruit so they could chase us. It was like them old-time cops the way they come after us, like the Keystones. They used to have gangs up in that area too. There was the Redwings, which was Italian, and the Yorkville Dukes, which was German. Then they had a group called the Enchanters, which was mostly blacks. And then there was this Hispanic gang that claim the turf from One hundred and twelfth to One hundred and tenth. They used to call themselves the Dragons.

"I want to tell you, my friends and me, we thought we was in hell. We couldn't move here, we couldn't move there. Whenever we went out we was in trouble with somebody. Maybe they was black, maybe they was German or Hispanic. So one day a bunch of us from the One hundred Street area, we get together in my house and we create our own group. We get about ten fellows and we start to fighting. Nothing fancy, fist fighting is all. We start with the blacks, the Enchanters, until finally we control them. We say, 'At last, we can roam over to Park Avenue.' I say, 'We got to move into Yorkville now. That's where they got the movies. That's where they got all them fruit vendors.' We call ourselves the Comanches. The Hispanics used to have groups called the Viceroys, the Latin Aces, the Scorpions. The Dragons was the most feared Hispanic gang of all because they started importing weapons. But the meanest of all was the Redwings because they got the Mafia behind them. They got cars to transfer them around from the fights. Big limousines! With chauffeurs!

"So we move the Enchanters out of the way and they become one with us. They elect me president of the organization. Then we start with Yorkville, which goes from Ninety-ninth down to the Seventies from Fifth over. We fight with them and start breaking ground for Hispanics to go through. We was like the pioneers, John Wayne and all them wagon trains. Even the older people who was afraid to go over there was now going over and shopping and things like that. Even the blacks, who always been afraid to go over there. But the Redwings, that's the turf we want because they got the swimming pool in Jefferson Park and, you know, during the summer, it's so hot, you could cook an egg on the pavement. I remember one day we have collected some weapons from Yorkville—zip guns, you could make them with a toy airplane launch, so they could throw a bullet maybe fifty feet. And we got knives, switchblades, machetes. We never have weapons before—and I hope my sons never hear this—but I figure we need some protection against the Redwings. Anyway, the Redwings are having a club meeting up in a vacant building on One hundred and sixteenth. We learn this and we go up there and just walk right in. One fellow in my gang has a forty-five. I don't know where he got it. I almost push the panicky button when I see him flashing it around, it's so damn big! But I force myself to talk to the Redwings. I tell them, 'Blah, blah, blah. We don't want no problems with you. From now on we going to come over here any time we want. Blah, blah, this and that. If you start any problems, we going to burn up the whole place and run all of you out.' Well, God must have been smiling, because nobody got hurt that afternoon, and pretty soon all the youngsters from our neighborhood start migrating with us to the swimming pool.

They go under our colors, Comanche colors. 'Now,' I say, 'it's time to go for the Dragons.'

"Now, it happen that I know the head of the Dragons visits this girl on One hundredth Street, which is our street. One day this fellow come in a cab, so we wait until he goes in the house and we seal off the whole of One hundredth Street between Park and Lex. We got Comanches on the roof, Comanches behind garbage cans and stoops. We got this fellow covered because we afraid he has a piece. So this fellow walk into the hallway and I'm in there. I'm only fifteen or sixteen, but he's a mature man of twenty-four or -five. So I stop him and I say, 'Yo, what you doing here?' He looks at me down this long dark hallway and I speak to him again. 'This here's Comanche territory. This is Little Mickey talking to you.' Because that's how I was known then. I say, 'You want to go one on one?' Now I know I could never take him, because he's bigger than me. But I ain't no dummy either. I got my henchman behind me, this kid named Cesar who's a weight-lifter. Cesar is my strong arm. So I snap my fingers like this, and I say, 'Cesar, come on over here.' Then I say to the fellow, 'What you going to do? Fight me one on one? Or are you going to stop this bullshit and call it a truce right here between our peoples?' He say, 'We never have no troubles with you fellows.' So I say, 'Well, you going to have troubles with us, if you don't let my people go back and forth between One hundred and twelfth and Park and all this here.' He says, 'It's not me that decide these things.' We start haggling back and forth, until finally I say, 'What you going to do? You going to call the shit on here? Or not?' I step back and Cesar starts to grab him. Then I say, 'Hold on, Cesar. Let the turkey slide. Get you ass out of here.' The fellow go away angry, but he come back with three or four others and we make a truce. We become friendly. Before you know it, him and me we start going back and forth together. We lay down the law between us: We say we don't go in for mugging, drugs, alcohol. We just like to fight. By this time I got about thirty in my gang. I got Cesar, Lefty, Wildcat, Panther, Manuel,

Negro, Saoul, Apache, Jubul, Jose. Finally the Dragons come in with us, and we go out together and push over the Trojans. The Latin Aces fade out. The Viceroys, they were the ones that came and got me after we got control of everything east and west. We was called the Comanche-Dragons at that point."

What about Negra? I asked. How did she figure into all this?

"The way I got Negra is one day something happen in the Bronx, and my people came and told me about it. We went to the Bronx to a dance, one of them canteens they always having for the youth. We walk over from here across the bridge at One hundred and thirty-eighth Street. Once we get over there for some reason the people start getting nervous, because my name is already known. 'Little Mickey this, Little Mickey that. He's this crazy little fellow,' and all that. I have about thirty youngsters with me. We ain't going to fight. We going just to let them know how strong we are and let them know what's going down."

What was going down? I asked.

"Well, a friend of mine got shot on One hundred and third Street by a gang member in the Bronx. We had gone to the hospital and gave blood for him. He was crippled but he lived, so I was angry and I told one of my people, 'Do what you have to to the fellow that did this.' At that time my word was final, no questions. Anyway, I never hear about that fellow again. Also some other fellow had pulled a knife on me up there. So they was having a dance, and Negra had come with some girl friends to the dance. Right?"

"No, Mickey, we meet over here in Harlem," said Negra, who had rematerialized from somewhere in the apartment. "I was living in the Bronx then, but they was tearing down the houses where I live and I am going to move down here, so me and my girl friends Baby and Sugar we come to check the neighborhood out. My girl friends say, 'Let's start at the church.' So I go with them on Easter Sunday to a dance, which is at the church on One hundred and third Street. We met this guy Bobby Fish and make friends with him and another boy. Then I meet Mickey's sister, whose name is Millie. Somebody tells Millie something about her brother, something bad. Millie don't say nothing. She just laugh and walk away. But one of the boys hear it and he goes out. All of a sudden, Mickey walks in, the small little shrimp. So I say to Bobby, 'Who's that boy?' And he say, 'He's the *law,* he's the *law!* Whatever he say go.' I say, 'Hmph! I don't like him. He's a bully. Get him away from me.' So Mickey walk over and Bobby introduce him to Baby and Sugar. Mickey looks at me and he say to Bobby, 'Introduce me to you friend.' But Bobby say, 'She don't want to meet you. She don't like you.' So Mickey think I'm Bobby's *novia* and he gets mad and he say, 'Bobby, I'm going to take her away from you.'

"A couple of days later, we go to the candy store, which is owned by an old guy called Juju. They introduce me to him and he say, 'Ah, you the girl the Cowboy likes.' They used to call Mickey that. Juju says, 'You better watch it. The Cowboy catch you with Bobby, he going to shoot you!' The old man used to try to scare me, but I say to him, 'Baaa!' And I walk away. The old man used to tell everybody if they argue with me or anything, 'Don't mess with her. She belong to the Cowboy.' It was terrible because I couldn't go nowhere without somebody saying I was Mickey's girl. I would go to a dance and nobody would dance with me because they say I belong to Little Mickey. Nobody would want to walk me home. I had to walk home all by myself."

"Anyway," said Mickey, "there was this fellow over at the candy store that I want to bang up. For some reason I don't like him. I guess it's because I know he's my competition. I'm afraid he is going to take control, and I guess they have told him about Negra and if he bother with her he will have me to answer to. So I go over there to the candy store and we have words. Well, the old lady she put a horseshoe on the newspapers to keep them quiet. This fellow, I remember, he go to grab that horseshoe. *Wham!* I hit him a shot and he falls over like in a western movie. I don't give him a break. He gets up again and I kick him, I punch him—"

"Oh, he lookeded pitiful," laughed Negra. "Then I hated Mickey for it."

"I know it's either him or me," said Mickey. "In them days they used to have railings in the stairways, which they don't got anymore. There's enough room for a head to go through. I just kick his head in and out of that small space. Then I walk away."

"After that I was poison ivy," said Negra. "No boy would even look at me. Finally the girls say to me, 'Why don't you go out with him? You ain't going to go out with nobody else.' But I wouldn't. This go on for a year. One day, my girl friends Baby and Sugar tell me they have this blind date for me. His name is Mikie, they say. I say, 'I hope this ain't that Mikie from One hundredth Street.' They say, 'No, Negra. This boy is nice.' Guess who it is?"

"These girls used to get me anything I wanted," said Mickey, preening. "I was likable."

"Ha!" said Negra, "You know what it was? He always used to work. Whenever he got paid, after he paid his mother's rent, gas, he used to buy the girls presents. He would buy them manicure sets. They would have to do what he want."

I take it you two finally got together, I said.

"What else I'm going to do?" said Negra. She looked genuinely pained. "He even got my best girl friends working against me!"

What about the gangs? I asked.

"I was getting back to that," said Mickey. "I'm seventeen and I'm washing dishes at the Hotel Commodore, making forty dollars a week, which is good money for them days, but I'm still leading the Comanches. One evening I decide to go to the movies. I cross over to One hundredth and Lexington, and these two fellows step out of the dark. They are Viceroys. They know we have beaten them, but they don't want to give in. Anyway, one of these fellows scream out my name and starts to shooting. He pump two bullets into my chest. It's like dynamite hit me, throws me back on my behind. I see he's still aiming. I'm holding onto a sidewalk railing. I'm sort of zigzagging while he's firing the gun at me, missing me. I get up and run. I'm going haywire. I run up to a taxi and there's these two nuns in it. I tell them, 'I been shot! Let me in, I got to go to the hospital!' They say no and they lock the door on me, which maybe is why I don't like the church too much. So finally this other cab come along and take me to the Metropolitan Hospital, straight the wrong way down a one-way. They operate on me. They take one bullet out and leave the other. The same day I check out of the hospital. I'm angry as hornets. I want to go look for the fellow who did this. But I go home and start to thinking. You know who I'm thinking about?"

Negra? I said.

"No. Well, yes, Negra. But, no, the one I'm really thinking about is this youth counselor, Eugene. I ever mention him before?"

Never.

"For some reason—you know this about me—I don't like to be told what to do."

I've noticed.

"But Eugene, he was different. He was the one person, beside my brother, who really got to me. He was a black fellow, what they call a 'high yellow,' maybe forty, give or take. In them days the blacks live all on the West Side, but Eugene used to come over and mix with us rice 'n beans. I don't know how that creep walked into my life. Must have been God sent him. He said I was a leader and if he could straighten me out, maybe the other kids will take notice and straighten themselves out. It's funny, but he didn't say much. Just a constant pain in the neck. Always there, waiting for me to talk to him. I couldn't do nothing. I wake up in the morning and there he is. My mother let him into the house. He used to be sitting in the parlor, reading the papers. I try to sneak out. But whenever I come back, he's there."

"Everywhere Mickey went, Gene went," said Negra. "When we got married, Gene said, 'Well, now I'll leave him alone.'

But he still used to come around. The habit was too deep. He would wake me up on Saturday mornings."

"To make a long story short," said Mickey, "the day I get out of the hospital Eugene take me down to enlist in the army, and I break with the gangs forever. I join the Eighty-second Airborne and get into boxing. At first I do it to avoid K.P. and guard duty. Then, I am able to win the First Army championship at one hundred and twelve pounds, and the sport, it kind of gets into my blood. But, Eugene, it's not until years later that I realize the importance of this fellow. By this time my pro career is finished and Mike is about eight years old and I'm starting to work with him and the rest of these youngsters and, truthfully, I'm thinking about how I want to be with them. I start to thinking about my brother, Rafael, and about Eugene. I start thinking about these two men and how they were with me and what I can apply to these kids. See, my brother was like a little dictator, 'Do this, do that.' Which is the way you got to be sometimes with youngsters, because there's so much temptation out there and they such hardheads. But Eugene, he was different. He was, how do I say this? Just watching me. I could talk to him and he would listen. But mostly it was like he was sitting there on my shoulder, like what's that cricket they got in the movies? Jimmy?"

You mean he was like a conscience? I asked.

"Yes, that's it. I want to be like a conscience to these youngsters, somebody they got to answer to. Because there's always somebody you got to answer to in this life, and most of these kids don't know this until it's too late. Then, all of a sudden, the one they got to answer to is the law. Or a gun. You see, we playing for keeps in this neighborhood. But here, let me tell you one more story. Short and sweet, because we got to get over to the gym. Anyway, you know how I love walking along the streets. I love it when the kids that's hanging around the candy stores and the tenements, when they see me go by and they say, 'Hey, Mick, how you doin'?' Now, I know these youngsters are smoking reefer. But I like it when they throw the cigarette away when they see me coming and they act like they on the up-and-up. Negra will say to me, 'Mickey, you got to go talk to these kids. You got to tell them what trouble they getting into with that reefer.' But I tell her, 'No, Negra. I can't do that, because these kids don't want me to see that reefer. They throwing it away because they ashamed of this weakness they got, and they don't want me to know about it.'

"See, these youngsters, these ruffians on the street, they respect me. And once you get a young man, I don't care how mean or nasty he is, once you get him to respect someone or something, there is good in him. Now if I see this in a youngster, believe me, I'm going to maneuver myself into his life. Before you know it, I'm going to be like a conscience for him. Sure, I'm going to yell at him, but I'm going to listen to him too. It may be that sometimes I will be all over this kid, wearing him like a glove the way this fellow Eugene was all the time wearing me. It may be that sometimes, I don't know, I'm even going to, to . . ."

The trainer pulled up and went silent, tilted his head ever so slightly to one side, as if listening to distant music. I couldn't resist. I volunteered a finish to his thought.

It may be, I said, that sometimes you're even going to overprotect him too much.

The trainer looked at me, blinked twice, then laughed.

"Aw, hell," he said. "Ain't no use talking to you. Let's go to the gym."

Mickey Rosario was an east Harlem institution, a stay against the confusion of growing up black or Latino in the ghetto. Which is to say, of being twelve or fourteen and under daily hormonal assault, or of being eighteen or twenty-two and all dressed up with no place to go in the Land of Opportunity but down. Boxing was the instrument Mickey knew how to play. Fortunately, he was a virtuoso, and the music he made was the kind the kids, the best, the more salvageable among them, would listen to. Boxing is clearly not for everyone. Nor should it be. Yet it occurred to me, as I watched Mickey operate, that even the diehard opponent of the sport, the person who was utterly indifferent to its sculpted and liquid beauties, would have to concede that it was at the very least a sick way of getting healthy.

A case could be made that the primary disease of the ghetto is violence. In keeping with this conceit, Casa Rosario could be seen as a sort of field hospital and Mickey as the croaker perpetually on call, dispensing a brand of medicine that was closer to the "homeopathic" than to the "allopathic" ideal. Which is to say, the trainer did not try to cure his kids' disease in the conventional way, by attacking their symptoms. Rather, following the principle that "like cures like," he sought to bring his patients to health by inducing in them symptoms that looked a good deal like the symptoms of their disease. Much as the homeopath might, for example, remedy hay fever with grass cuttings or diarrhea with a laxative, Mickey taught these youngsters who were schooled in the cycle of ghetto violence, who were forever fighting, how to fight.

It is a truism that violence breeds violence. Yet on Mickey's ward, when administered in controlled doses and under close supervision, when refined by art and defined by rules—in short, when tricked out as boxing—violence did not act to perpetuate, but rather to neuter itself. For the truth is, while boxing may seem to be an emblem of ghetto living, the very stigmata of violence, it is actually an antidote to the disease. More: It is a remedy not just for the violence kids brought up in poverty commit against society, but for the terrible tattooing they give themselves as well.

Take a moment and think about it. Boxing is premised on conditioning (thus, it is anti-drug and -booze). It teaches patience and discipline and stick-to-itiveness, what we gringos call the "work ethic" (thus, it is anti-immediate gratification). It instills respect for legitimate authority (the trainer, the officials). Most paradoxical of all, it sows pacifism and reaps a harvest of tolerance and civility. (Such monsters of the midway as "Two-Ton" Tony Galento and Roberto Duran notwithstanding, boxers are a gentle species—and why shouldn't they be? Who else gets to go toe-to-toe with his demons on a daily basis?)

The old Greeks were apparently onto all of this. Or, at least, so suggests the German classicist and powder keg, Friedrich Nietzsche. Before Homer, asks Nietzsche, what kind of life was there? "A life ruled only by the Children of the Night: strife, lust, deceit, old age, and death." A life marked by savage hatred and the wish to annihilate, one typified in theogonic myth by the terrible dark doings of the Titans, beside whom the Olympian gods seem like mischievous Yuppies. Confronted with the legacy of undifferentiated violence, the Greeks found it necessary to establish the idea of the agon, or "the contest"; it was imperative to set up games for serious stakes in order that the citizenry might play out its patrimony of hatred and envy—in order, in Nietzsche's phrase, that they might "preserve the health of the state." Thus, in the post-Homeric or Olympian scheme of things, the patron of boxing is not, say, Ares, the war god, or Dionysus, the divinity of let-it-all-hang-out. Rather, it is Phoebus Apollo (the Delphians sacrificed to "Apollo the Boxe"). For the Greeks aligned the sport of boxing, not with the Forces of Darkness and Irrationality, but with the "Shining One," with the god of order and perception and proportion, the god of music and sculpture and healing, the god whose bywords were "know thyself" and "nothing in excess." In short, they associated boxing with the god who made life, not merely possible, but worth living.

It struck me that if there were any juice left in the old myths, then Mickey Rosario must have operated beneath the protection of Apollo. For the trainer was also in the business of imposing order on chaos, of turning his own "Children of the Night" into boxers and, thereby, with a little luck, into serviceable human beings. . . . I was thinking these things, in fact, or something very much like them, later that afternoon down at the gym, following my conversation with Mickey about the gangs. Several of us were standing by Negra's desk in the bottleneck between the outside doors and the gym proper. Negra herself was on the phone, trying to console a cousin whose son, an irregular at Casa Rosario, had just OD'd on heroin at an upper West Side disco and was now recuperating in a hospital. Mickey was talking to Luke about his upcoming Golden Gloves bout—he and Ariel were slated for the next night—when a kid I'd never seen before burst through the gym doors and gestured to the trainer to join him in private conversation.

The two of them huddled by the doors, and you could see that the trainer was surprised by the kid's news. As the youngster began to speak, Mickey actually took a step back, as if the kid's tidings had knocked him off-balance. Thereafter, the trainer stood his ground and listened, nodding his head, slowly, listlessly, as if the matter, whatever it was, were beyond remedy. The news, we learned after the messenger receded, was that Cuba was dead.

"They put four slugs into him," said Mickey.

Who did? I asked.

"The kid didn't know," said Mickey. "It could be almost anybody. He was always asking for trouble."

"He told me he was fooling around with gay guys," said Jackson.

"Could be," said Mickey. "He was fooling around with a lot of things."

Jackson didn't really know Cuba. Nobody did. Nobody did, that is, but Mickey and Negra. To me, the kid was an enigma, an unsettling one, a dark thought with jaundiced eyes and preternaturally white teeth knifing through the Rosarios' gym and apartment. To Mickey, he was obviously something more. To start with, he was a human being.

"He believe in all that stuff about the saints too," said the trainer, who was becoming abstracted. He was not talking to us so much, it seemed, as aloud to himself. "He is a refugee from Cuba. You know, from that *flotilla* that floats."

He was a Marielito? I asked.

"He's a little cracked. Like a little child, really. He write his name all over on everything."

You mean graffiti?

"I call his attention to it. He say he don't do it. But I think he just want the people to know about him, to know that he's a somebody."

"Yeah, graffiti," said Jackson, answering my question. "That stuff done played out. That was the seventies, man."

"He's quick tempered too. But he must have been high, because he don't have the heart to do this on his own."

Do what on his own?

Mickey put down briefly from his reverie and looked me full in the eye. "They say he broke the window of a restaurant on One hundred and nineteenth Street, and they shoot him for this." The trainer shook his head in amazement. "*Quatro tiros,* the kid say. Four bullets. Neck, chest, stomach, head."

"Dag!" said Jackson. "These guys weren't taking no chances!"

"I have him in my house for months. Then he disappear, and when he come back I put him over here to sleep in the gym with Johnny Luna. I guess I should have put him back in my house. Maybe I could have kept him safe."

Everyone was silent.

"I don't know," said the trainer, who was still abstracted, still wondering at it all. "You see, he came to this country to look for better things."

"Yeah," said Negra. "Look what better thing he find."

Chapter 6

LIONS LYING DOWN WITH LIONS

Refugio was a vision in white. On what was, as far as Casa Rosario was concerned, the final night of Golden Gloves preliminaries, and one of the coldest nights of the year to boot, the assistant trainer wafted into the gym as if on a spring breeze, wearing white duck pants and a thick white cable-stitch V-neck sweater over a white dress shirt embossed with a pattern of tiny curved swords. This daring new look for boxing seconds was founded upon white leather sneakers and attained new heights with a cream-colored fez. It did not go unnoticed.

"Yooooow!" screeched Ariel, who, along with Luke, was scheduled to tread the boards this night at the Jerome Avenue Gym in the South Bronx. Ariel put a hand up to his face to cover his eyes, staggered about as if momentarily blinded. "Somebody throw a blanket over it! Quick, I can't see!"

"Wait, wait!" shouted Chino Number One. "Let's see what flavors he got. Because he got to be selling Good Humor."

"Man, that ain't no Good Humor man," rumbled Jackson. "Because I didn't hear no bell, and Good Humor always be ringing a bell."

"So who is it?" Chino wanted to know. "Tom Carmel?"

"No, no," said Jackson. "That's got to be Casper. You know, The Friendly Ghost."

Things went on this way, with most of the gym entering into

the merriment, including Mickey and the always quiet Luke and even the indomitably good-natured Refugio himself. In fact, the only one who failed to find Refugio's costume a source of great amusement was Negra. But, then, Negra was probably the only one present, apart from the assistant trainer himself, who knew what his getup was all about. (Actually, I knew too, but, unlike Negra, had nothing at stake.)

Refugio was in the grips of santería, a sort of voodoo that more and more New Yorkers do, thanks, I gather, to the latest wave of credulity sweeping up from the Carribbean. Negra didn't care for santería, in part because it struck her as faddish, as arriviste, as—what with its embrace of the saints and demonic possession and its horning in on the candle, rag doll, and potion trade—pretty much her own Puerto Rican spiritism gaudied up for popular consumption. Negra had a point. Yet my reading and nosing about suggested that she was wrong to dismiss santería as a Juan-come-lately.

"The Religion," as it is called by its adherents, is several centuries old. It dates back to the arrival in the New World of Yoruba tribespeople, who were stolen from their villages along the Niger River and pressed into slavery. Naturally, the Yoruba had their own gods, and just as naturally they brought these gods, or *orishas,* with them from Africa—divinities with names like "Obatala" and "Oggun," a decidedly human lot, reminiscent in their capricious and lusty behavior, as well as in their inordinate demand for sacrifice, of the old Greek pantheon. The trouble for the Yoruba was that they were set down in places like Cuba and Haiti, which is to say, in a nominally Roman Catholic corner of the New World. And zealotry being what it is, they were not permitted to openly worship their gods.

Yet the Yoruba were a people of wit and ingenuity, and they found a way to smuggle their rites into the daily round. The slave owner may have ruled the Yoruba's body, but he did not control his mind. By this I mean, there was no way for Massah to know that when his chattel seated himself before a statue of Saint Anthony of Padua, it was not really Saint Anthony the man prayed to, but "Ifa," a similarly disposed Yoruba "god of impossible things." Massah must have been given pause, however, when he saw his man place before a statue of Saint Barbara a glass of rum and a lit cigar. What Massah would not have known was that when the slave gazed at Saint Barbara he did not see the delicate likeness of the fourth-century maiden who was decapitated by her father when she declined to lay down with the man of his choosing. Rather the Yoruba saw "Chango," a giant black god with an ear-to-ear grin and the nonstop appetites to go with it. How did the Yoruba come to this curious bit of syncretism? Easy. According to Catholic hagiography, Barbara's dad was struck with lightning the instant he lopped off her head. As for Chango, well, he was the Yoruba fire and thunder god, who sidelined in lightning as well.

If santería was born of the forced coupling of African gods with Christian iconography, it had of late lost its quality of desperation. It had, in fact, fallen upon commercial times. Nowadays, the business of becoming a santero—of learning, that is, how to manipulate the saints into helping you cure illness, win lovers, crush enemies, and so on—was major bucks. It could cost as much as $5,000. Assorted *babalawos* (priests) and *padrinos* (godfathers) were said to be doing rather well for themselves, some, allegedly, commuting into the barrio from Westchester.

Refugio was merely a santero-in-the-works. He was a novice going through a period of "purification," a stint of sacramental hazing (ergo the white costume, which struck me as an Arabian fantasy of Bill Tilden). It scarcely mattered to Negra, however, that Refugio was not yet the full-fledged item. The mere sight of her husband's assistant was enough to make her stomach churn, which meant that she was doubly afflicted this night, since she was of course already deep in the throes of her usual prefight cramps. Negra did manage to raise up from her desk to glower at Refugio and to share her qualms with me.

"He come here a couple of weeks ago and he say to me, 'Negra, they tell me I got to spend five hundred dollars for my powers, and that's only the beginning.' 'What!' I say to him. 'You got to be born with powers! You can't buy them. You know what's the only thing you could get for five hundred dollars? The bad luck of the person who sell them to you!' "

Negra was hot when Refugio first told her about this *santería* business. And, her cramps notwithstanding, she was hot now, just thinking about it. Little threads of smoke were spiraling from her eyes.

"Bill, let me tell you something. I believe in spiritual, but the spiritual I believe in is different from cutting off the heads of chickens and drinking the blood!"

This said, the trainer's wife clutched her runic middle and sank down into her chair. When Mickey, always looking for that elusive leg up on the competition, came by to inquire after her pains, she smiled and seemed to suggest that Ariel would win. The jury was still out, apparently, on Luke.

"So how'd you like the riot the other night?"

What riot? I said. I was just a few yards inside the door of the Jerome Avenue Gym, the old dinosaur of a post office that had been resuscitated by pugilism. Mickey and Negra and Refugio were upstairs with Ariel and Luke weighing in, gearing up, etcetera, and I had remained behind to chat with the cognoscenti. I was talking to Phil Monahan and Tommy Hanrahan, members of the mostly Irish mafia that ran the Gloves for the *Daily News*.

"You mean you weren't there?" said Tommy. Tommy was a news hound on the city desk who covered the Gloves as well. He was a big, auburn-haired fellow in his late twenties with a push-broom moustache, a Princeton degree, and a lovely taste for the ludicrous.

Where? I said.

"Bleeding Heart in Queens. Everybody was fighting but the fighters. They couldn't because there were about thirty people in the ring. It was amazing. Wasn't it Phil?"

"Yeah, it was really something," said Phil. A hard-boiled,

chain-smoking splinter of a man, Phil had been one of the tournament's principal organizers for going on thirty years. "I mean I'm not going to say I've seen everything. But I've seen most of what's going to happen at the Gloves. I seen a guy get so scared he run across the ring dropping turds out his pants. They had to stop the fight right there. Another time a guy got bit on the shoulder. As I recall, all they did was give him an eight-count. I don't know, maybe he got a tetanus afterwards. But that was nothing. I saw another guy one year crawl out the ring. He'd had it. He crawled right out on his hands and knees and the other guy was after him, *wop! wop! wop!* on the back of the head as he went for the apron. The guy must have hit him a dozen times before the referee could step in. Then there was this other time at the old Sunnyside Garden they had a big brawl. Things were so bad a cop shot three times in the air just to get everyone to quiet down. And, then, what do you think happens? We look up and all this rain is coming through the roof and landing in the ring. That night was a pip. But this other night was pretty good, too."

What started it? I asked.

"I heard it was a racial thing," said Phil. "Tommy was closer. I was in back making the fights. All I know is the priest got decked."

"He did?" said Tommy, surprised. "I didn't know that."

"Yeah, Father Mike."

"The little fat guy?"

"Yeah, they put ice on his head and took him to the hospital."

"Great," said Tommy, laughing. "That was the only element missing."

"You know what else?" said Phil. "He knew the guy that did it. It was one of his own parishioners."

"No!" said Tommy and I at the same time.

"Yeah, I figure the guy was probably going to throw a punch," said Phil, "and, you know, Father Mike ain't exactly built for speed. He probably walked into it. He was trying to be a peacemaker between this parishioner and a black guy and, well, good ol' Father, he must have bought a piece. I mean they were putting ice on him."

"God!" said Tommy. "That's too much."

"You know what he said?" asked Phil.

What who said?

"Father Mike. He said, 'I know who that guy is, and he's going to catch hell tomorrow.' "

Jesus, he probably meant it, didn't he?

"When a priest tells you to go to hell," said Tommy, "you got to take it seriously."

"Yeah and don't forget," said Phil, "this all happened on a Saturday night. The next day was Sunday, which was a workday for Father Mike."

By the time I got upstairs, half the fights had already been made. They had been typed up in order of battle and posted just outside the room taken over by the Gloves field command. As usual, there was an interested group of bystanders idling by the door, awaiting the publication of each new batch of pairings.

The kids who would be boxing this night were almost all open-class fighters. A handful of contests between novice heavyweights was scheduled for the tag end of the card; but, for the most part, the evening was to be given over to junior middleweights with some mileage on them, 156-pounders who had fought at least ten times in ABF-sanctioned shows. Many of these kids already knew each other. They'd faced off in smokers staged at various spas around the City. Or, more legitimately, they'd been matched in last year's Gloves or maybe, years earlier, they'd cut a rug together in the Junior Olympics or even in the Kid Gloves, boxing's big-city equivalent to Little League baseball. In some cases, the youngsters had never been introduced but knew each other by sight or legend.

There was, I'd noticed, a certain etiquette for taking in and appraising the posted match-ups. This is to say, ideally, one should not rush but more or less sidle up to the sheet. Preferably, one should comment first on the other fights before getting, as leisurely as possible, to one's own, at which point one should look interested in whom one is paired with, but not too interested. Certainly, one should betray neither elation nor concern, which was the nadir of form. The trainer and kid standing before the match-up sheet as I walked by seemed to have the etiquette down pat.

"We got the toughest nut," said the handler, a short black fellow in a red gim'me hat with CAT written on it. "That's all right. We take him now or later, don't make no nevermind to us."

The fighter wrinkled his brow in thought. "It's fate," he said. Then, as if he had only the public's entertainment in mind: "Would have been a good fight for the finals."

I continued on into the Gloves command post, a charmless room with chipped ochre-colored walls. Sheets of black plastic were taped across the windows. Overhead, half the tubing for the fluorescent lighting was on the blink. The other half bathed Phil Monahan, Matt Cusack, *et al.,* who were sitting at the table, in a weird purple glow. To the left of the officials, several dozen strips of tape hung from the wall, as did the room's only decorator item: a photo torn from *Kayo* magazine of Tony "the Baby Bull" Ayala, a once-promising kid from a family of Texas fighters who had recently been socked away for rape.

I half-expected to find Mickey in the room, trying to talk the officials into giving him another fifteen minutes to bring Luke in at the desired poundage. Luke had problems with his weight. Luke seemed to have problems, period. But he must have been okay this night, because Mickey was nowhere to be seen.

Instead, Gloves officials were going round with a different trainer. He was an old-timer, looked to be of Mushy's vintage. He had one of those short, stiff haircuts that brush up and back like the prow of a battleship and skin that would make a good saddle. He was saying that the officials had no business objecting to his kid's fighting, not now, not at this late date. Hell, it wasn't as if his kid had never been in an ABF show before. He'd been in plenty of them, that's why he was fighting

Open Class. Besides, the kid had passed the physical back in December. . . .

I remembered the kid—remembered that he was named for a sporting goods company. I'd seen him at the physical, one of several held around Christmas in the basement of the *Daily News* building. Early on a Sunday morning I had stood behind the battery of doctors and watched and listened as they examined the youngsters who passed in a file before them. The Gloves medical exam was a model of comprehensiveness, but it hadn't always been. We are, of course, a nation of counterpunchers; thus it had taken a tragedy to make the Gloves' medical state-of-the-art. In 1979 a Puerto Rican heavyweight from the Fort Apache B. C., a kid with a body Miron or Michelangelo might have admired, had gone to throw a right hand and collapsed. After he died, it was discovered that he'd suffered from cardiomegaly, or an enlarged heart, which could have been picked up by X ray. Alas, at the time, the chest X ray was not on the examination menu. It was now, along with an electrocardiogram. Indeed, Mickey was so impressed with the Gloves physical that he got everybody he could in the gym to sign up for the tournament, whether they expected to fight or not, merely so they could enjoy the benefit of the close medical scrutiny.

At the physical, I remember standing beside a young, preppyish orthopedist when the kid in question, Spaulding something—something Spanish—manifested in the line. The orthopedist had just finished examining a would-be Golden Glover who was several inches under six feet and well over 300 pounds. The flab hung in sheets over the kid's waist. The doctor had had to lift one of the flaps of meat merely to get a stethoscope near his heart. He asked the kid if he'd started training.

"Yeah," said the kid, wheezing audibly. "I started walking."

"No running?"

"I got to get my wind up first."

"You know, I wouldn't sell you insurance. I bet you fall asleep sitting down sometimes. Am I right?"

The kid blushed and looked at the floor. No one asked him how he thought he could compete in the Gloves. He was simply rejected when his blood pressure was found to be an incorrigible 180/120.

I expected the preppy doctor to deal with Spaulding in much the same way. Spaulding was dark, fuzzy of face, Indian-looking. He had stubby little legs and an extremely large chest. His head sat right on his shoulders. Which is to say—and I mean this literally—he had no neck.

The doctor tried Spaulding's reflexes with a rubber hammer, measured his chest on the inhale and exhale, directed him to touch his chin to his shoulder, even while asking him questions designed to put him at ease. "How long have you been boxing?" Three years. "Enjoy it?" Yeah. "How old are you again?" Nineteen. "What's your best punch?" The hook to the liver. "Okay young man. Take your papers and good luck."

The orthopedist explained that Spaulding was a "Klippel-feil." He was missing vertebrae and had a fusion. There were certain cases where the ribs didn't expand, others where there was arthritis. But this kid was all right. He could fight.

Another doctor, a pediatrician with a mop of hair and eyebrows like Groucho, was attending the conversation. "Takes a specialist to identify a syndrome," he said. "You know what a pediatrician would call this kid?"

I didn't.

"An FLK."

What's that? I bit.

"A funny-looking kid."

The dressing parlor at the Jerome Avenue Gym was one huge room, partitioned off somewhat by rows of lattice-front lockers. A couple of hundred people were crammed into the space, with each gym or boxing club staking out, as best it could, its own bit of turf. I picked my way through the multitude, stepped over equipment bags and sets of legs poking out from the benches, skirted clusters of trainers locked in last-minute confabs with their youngsters, as well as a sprinkling of kids working over their shadows, trying to get up a sweat before going down to fight.

I spotted Negra first, picked her out by the yellow ribbon in her hair. She was sitting on a bench haunch-to-haunch with Luke and whispering in his ear. Next to Jackson, Luke was probably the biggest puncher in the gym, which was no wonder, one might think, given his build. The kid's upper arms looked like the hind parts of a horse or a bull. Luke was dedicated too. He worked long days as a carpenter, often carrying heavy doors up five and six flights of stairs in the small apartment buildings his outfit was rehabilitating. He still managed to do his roadwork every morning, and he seldom failed to drag his carcass, his midnight-blue skin speckled with the white dust of sheetrock, into the gym five and six nights of the week.

Yet there was something wrong with Luke, some mutiny of emotions or imp of the perverse within him that undid all those hours of hard work and sacrifice and made him a less formidable opponent than he should have been. I'd heard there were problems at home, something about his parents' being religious, their not liking his fighting, et cetera. My own theory, based on very little evidence, was that, as bulls went, Luke was more Ferdinand than Minotaur, someone who might have been happier sniffing the bougainvillea in his native Trinidad than girding up for some latter-day Theseus in the maze beneath Madison Square Garden or up here in the loft of a retread post office in the South Bronx.

On a given night one never knew which Luke would answer the bell. Would it be the cool, clear-eyed predator who went about his business with the necessary, calculated malice? Or would it be the jumped-up, reluctant pacifist who stormed across the canvas and into the destructive element, his eyes soaked with blood and both guns blazing?

On this night Luke appeared to be all right. He was quiet, per usual, but he was soft around the mouth and eyes. Negra, who was absently fingering the zipper on his warm-up, appeared to have him in harness.

Mickey and Refugio were a few yards away, klatched with a handful of other trainers, all of them Latino. They were discussing their plan, Mickey's plan, really, to take over the metropolitan ABF, which controlled amateur boxing in the City. The discussion was animated and largely in Spanish. It revolved around Mickey's belief that the kingpins of the local setup, most of them gringos, were acting as *celestinas,* or panders, between professional managers and the top kids in the Gloves. These *sin verguenzas,* or "men without shame," were using their position to gain the kids' trust and to sell them to the highest bidder. They were no better than the chicken hawks who perched in the rafters of the professional gyms.

I noticed that Refugio was paying only partial attention to Mickey's spiel, which he had to know by heart. Rather, he kept casting anxious glances over at Negra, even while fidgeting with the *collares*—or five beaded necklaces, each consecrated to a different Yoruba god—that he wore beneath his shirt as a protection against evil. I stepped in and intercepted one of these glances and asked him about Ariel. Where was he? Refugio didn't know. We decided to go after the kid, together.

Ariel had been an important cog in my training—he had, quite literally, shown me the ropes—but I was only just getting to know him. He was a blur at the gym, coming all the way out on the train each afternoon after a day of classes at Brooklyn College, alighting just long enough to work out, then getting back on the train and making for King's County Hospital, where he was using a work-study program to learn what it was to be a doctor. I had caught up with Ariel one day a couple of weeks ago, waylaid him, actually, in the dressing cage and burdened him with a new discovery about Mickey. I had been talking to one of Mickey's fighters from the early days who had been making noises about starting to train again. This was nothing new. The warriors of yesteryear were forever returning to Casa

Rosario, suiting up, banging the bags, pushing their postgraduate bellies around the battle box for old time's sake, especially during the Golden Gloves season, when the wistfulness became almost epidemic.

What interested me about this kid was his story about how he chanced to catch on with Mickey and the gym. The story seemed to add further dimension to the composite I'd been making of the trainer's "pathology," his extraordinary need to be the barrio's very own Catcher in the Rye. It suggested to me that, when it came to saving kids, Mickey was not merely an Apollonian and a protégé of Jiminy Cricket, but a dedicated ambulance-chaser as well.

The kid told his story somewhat reluctantly, I thought, but he told it all the same. He told me that he was just six or seven years old on the day that he met the trainer and already as bad as could be. It was the middle of the afternoon, going on fifteen years ago, and the kid was in a parking lot, crouched down by a car, attempting to boost a tire. Suddenly, he felt pressure at his rear quarter and he reached back and swiped at what turned out to be a foot gently jacking him up. "What you doing there, buddy?" asked the fellow on the other end of the foot, who was, of course, Mickey. "What's it look like?" the kid said, defiantly keeping his back to the trainer. "Why you doing that?" "To sell it, man, what you think? Need money for food." "How much you going to get for that tire?" "Five bucks." "Here, I got a better idea." The kid slowly turned around and saw the trainer for the first time. He saw that Mickey had a five spot in his hand and he was holding it out to him, even as he was telling him about this boxing gym he had over on First Avenue. "It's a nice place. Clean. Quiet. I like you to come see it sometime. Whenever you want is soon enough."

Ariel shared my delight with the story and told me that the kid's name was Clemente. Ariel had known him for years. He told me that Mickey had taken Clemente and made him into a first-rate amateur boxer, good enough, on at least one memorable occasion, to fight future Junior Middleweight Champ

Davey Moore to an exhilarating standstill. These days Clemente did all right. He made a nice living as a process server in the Bronx. He had a little girl he was crazy about, if no longer a wife. Ariel guessed that the young man was reluctant to talk about the trainer because he was a creature of strong emotions, and he probably dated his life from the day Mickey caught him boosting that tire.

"That Mickey, he's something," said Ariel. "He got all these kids coming in here off the street, because he's famous in the ghetto, and he's still out there prowling for more. You know how he got me, right?"

I said I didn't.

"I can't believe that, because Mickey always likes to tell people he picked me up at a gang fight. Oh, man, that was funnn-nee! But it wasn't really a gang fight."

Ariel's story went back about ten years and turned on an excursion the trainer took one weekend from Harlem to Brooklyn, out to scenic Lafayette Gardens, the Bed-Stuy project where Ariel lived with his parents. Stephen and Dennis Price, two stalwarts from Casa Rosario, had recently moved to the projects and promptly waded in over their heads. Dennis, the younger and more tempestuous brother, had beaten somebody up, which meant the locals were taking numbers for the privilege of taking him apart. To make matters worse, Stephen had been suckered by another kid named Booby and deposited on the hood of a car.

It was arranged that Stephen and Booby would meet and settle their differences in the familiar way. Mickey and several others from the gym had come out to Brooklyn to see that Stephen got a fair shake. Booby was a big fellow, light-heavy size, and Stephen was a featherweight, but he was not just any featherweight. In the interim between the throwing of the gauntlet and the actual tossing down, Booby learned that Stephen was twice a Golden Gloves champion. Thus, when the group from Casa Rosario arrived at Lafayette Gardens they were greeted by Booby and fifty or sixty of his closest friends.

Mickey was talking to Booby about this apparent inequity when one of the latter's minions, a fellow named Poochie, noticed that a member of Mickey's quadrille, a kid named Victor, had brought his own equalizer. Poochie saw Victor reach into his knapsack and heard him charge the chamber of a Saturday night special. "He got a pistol! He got a pistol!" Poochie reportedly screamed. "I know that sound anywhere."

It was at this point, according to Ariel, that things got extremely festive. "The brothers heard Poochie scream out and they saw Victor going into that knapsack and they started to fly into the buildings. And once they got into the buildings anything could happen, because they were up there in the windows and you were down there in the courtyard. You had to watch all the windows and you had to know who lived where and who had a piece. This was when Mickey stepped in and called them all back, because Booby and Poochie and the others they were getting ready to flap their wings too. Everybody started talking again and everything was cool. Then Mickey, you know how he used to run with the gangs and how, deep down inside, he hates to pass up a good fight, well, he said something that just about started it all up again. Something like, 'You all better be cool, because, if I wanted to, I could bring a whole lot of young 'uns from my gym, just like these here, to fight with you.' Well, when Mickey said that, Booby and them they didn't want to hear nothing else." Ariel recreated Booby and Co.'s furious displeasure with the trainer, which apparently involved a certain amount of jumping into the air and a lot of signifying. " 'What you *mean* you could bring a whole lot of guys down here to fight with us! Sheee-*it*, man, we ain't afraid of you. So bring 'em! Go on, *bring 'em!*' "

"Damn that Mickey!" said Ariel, laughing, his laugh a sort of ethereal horse's whinny, the kind of thing Pegasus must have had, so high-pitched it seemed to evanesce into another register. "This was like after fifteen minutes of negotiation, after he had got the brothers all quieted down and they were starting to listen and it looked like Booby and Stephen were maybe going to kiss and make up. And then Mickey says just that one thing. They said, 'What! motherfucker. You in our neighborhood, and you talkin' *that* shit.' Oh, man, that was funnn-nee!"

Fortunately, Mickey was his usual dauntless self. He simply kept talking and managed to coax everyone down from the buildings once more and to reintroduce the notion of lions lying down with lions. It turned out the trainer was such a hit with the brothers that, come the following week, several of the harder cases among them started making the long underground journey from Bed-Stuy to Casa Rosario to train on a daily basis. It didn't last, however. In the end, Ariel was the only spoils of the aborted rumble at Lafayette Gardens.

Refugio and I found Ariel on the other side of the dressing room, where he appeared to be scripting a little mayhem of his own. He was talking to Willie Dunn and George Washington. The two trainers were squiring novice heavyweights who had apparently been assigned a waltz this evening. The heavyweights were paragons of the species. Which is to say, each looked to be in excess of 250 pounds and in dire need of a brassiere. Amid such ponderous company—remember, George Washington was a big fellow too—Mickey's lithe, swan-necked fighter more than ever recalled his namesake from Shakespeare's *Tempest,* that lissome spirit of the air, "dainty Ariel." Mickey's kid was full of his antecedent's mischief too. For he was not so much talking to George and Willie, as he was darting verbally between them, drawing them into argument over who was going to win the competition that lay before them and, of all things, which trainer's "dancing bear" was lighter on his feet.

"Now I'll tell you something," said George to Willie. "My boy move faster than your boy."

"Yeah?" said Willie, misunderstanding. "Why your boy don't move so fast?"

"Huh?" said George.

"Uh-uh, Willie," Ariel interposed. "He say *his* boy move faster than you all's."

"What?" said Willie, outraged. "Your boy going to move faster than mine!"

"What's the matter, Willie?" said Ariel. "You don't understand? He ain't speaking Puerto Rican, you know."

George was tickled by this riposte. "Hoo-haw, haw, haw," he roared. "That's it, Ariel! Tell him. Haw, haw, haw."

"Wait a minute! Wait a minute!" said Willie.

"Haw, haw, haw," George continued. Ariel winked at Refugio and me.

"Wait a minute, now. Wait just a cotton-pickin' minute," said Willie. "Maybe your boy *have* to move that goddamn fast, or else"—Willie paused for effect—"or else he going to get knocked on his ass!"

Willie turned toward Ariel with his hands waist high and palms up. Ariel gave him skin.

George forced out a couple more "haw, haws." Then, abruptly wanted to know, "Where the money at?"

"Yeah, shit," said Willie again, extremely pleased with himself. He was grinning at us now. "Maybe his boy *have* to move that fast."

"Where the money at?" George repeated, suddenly all business.

"Willie," said Ariel, tapping the trainer on the shoulder. "George say it's time to put your money where your mouth at."

"He do?" asked Willie.

"Yes, he do," said Ariel. "Less, of course, you ain't got no money."

This, for Willie, was the final aspersion. The trainer reached into his pocket and fetched a thick wad of bills, as well as a handful of coins, which squeezed precariously out from between his clenched fingers. He'd obviously just been paid. "That's just where I'm starting at."

"You sure?" asked George.

"Talk to me," said Willie.

"You going to knock my boy out?" said George, incredulous.

"Talk to me," said Willie again.

"You sure, now?" said George. "You going to knock him out?"

"We ain't going to knock you out," said Willie, waving the fistful of money. "We going to beat you silly."

All of a sudden, bills and coins were flying all over the place. And Willie and his fighter—whose chest, the way it moved beneath his shirt, made me think of water sloshing in a bucket—were frantically attempting to pick the paper money out of the air, even while zigzagging down the narrow path between the lockers in pursuit of the disappearing silver.

"Hey, Willie," George yelled after them. "You paid the rent and insurance this week? Haw, haw, haw."

"That's it, George!" said Ariel, who slipped the trainer another ration of skin before heading back with us.

It was knockout night at the Golden Gloves. Kids were falling left and right, often, it seemed, with only the slightest provocation. When I remarked upon this phenomenon to Refugio, he intimated that he might have had something to do with it. It was, he earnestly pointed out, his first time in public as a "man of knowledge" (a euphemism, I take it, for santero). It was possible that the saints had set off this string of mortal fireworks as a way of saluting him.

I informed Negra of Refugio's notion, thinking that she would at last be amused. I was wrong. She was not. First of all, she said, there was a full moon out tonight and didn't I know there were always knockouts during a full moon? Second, and somewhat contradictorily, I thought, she said that I should tell my "friend" that if either of her kids happened to get flattened this eve she now knew who to blame. And the responsible party wouldn't be hard to find, either, because he was wearing "a ice cream suit."

I didn't convey Negra's message to the assistant trainer. The poor fellow was already worried about her. And, besides, I thought, why bother? Ariel was paired with an unattached fighter, a kid who hadn't aligned himself with a club and was therefore likely to be something less than a future main-eventer. I figured Ariel to be on the pitching end of the evening's statistics, as did Mickey and Ariel himself, neither of whom made any effort to locate the opposition and size him up before getting in the ring.

Ariel's foe turned out to have been worth the bother. He was truly extraordinary. In fact, it occurred to me, as I looked across the canvas at him, that I had not seen anything quite like him at the Gloves. He was white, not tall, but shortish and thick and square. His hair was long and scraggly. Hair, you might say, was his motif. He was thatched with it, apparently, all over his body. Indeed, it was not at all clear to me that he had the opposable thumb. And then there was his battle attire: high red sneakers with purple laces, green gym shorts from some upstate high school, and—*pièce de résistance*—a grungy white T-shirt with GRIZZLY written on it, handwritten in that jagged sort of calligraphy favored by Aegean restaurants. What is more, he appeared to be talking to himself, whacking himself in the head every now and then for emphasis.

With the bell, Ariel walked out from the corner and threw a straight left hand. No jab, no feint, no dancing or feeling out. Just unadorned power. The kid went down, *kerplunk!*, right on his duff, and sat there as the referee began to count.

Ariel, meanwhile, the consummate performer, whipped off a flurry in the neutral corner. He had the crowd's admiration and was basking in it. Thus he failed to see what I saw, and what Mickey and Negra saw, which was that the kid was smiling.

"Ariel," Mickey shouted, "use you jab! Don't go after him!"

"Ariel, he ain't hurt!" screamed Negra.

Hurt? The kid may have called himself "Grizzly" and hailed from the north, but it was about to become painfully obvious that he was, by temperment at least, a fighter from more southerly latitudes. By this I mean, the kid came off the floor as if he'd been born and bred in the slums that ring Mexico City. They say the worst thing you can do to a Mexican fighter is knock him down. All it does is get him interested. Señor Grizzly was very interested indeed.

Ariel, however, was a southpaw, and fighting a southpaw is not like fighting a regular person. In Mushy's time they used to turn the lefties around, basically because nobody wanted any part of them. Southpaws make bad fights. With a southpaw, an orthodox fighter is that much farther away and really can't use his jab. It's a case of mirror vision: The two jabs touch and the right hand has to be started from another county. The trick is to close the distance with a southpaw, but without leaving yourself open to his left. To do this, the book says you've got to keep your left foot outside his right foot, which brings you within range and allows you to throw lead rights to the heart and chin and to hook to the body beneath the right jab; at the same time, it acts to deprive the southpaw of his key feature, the straight left. Naturally, Grizzly paid the book no mind whatsoever, but improvised his own text, which said, Muscle your way in and whack whatever you can.

Ignorant of all this, Ariel was loaded for bear. He sped from the neutral corner toward his opponent with thoughts of finishing him. Grizzly met him in the middle of the ring, and before Ariel could get off, threw a monster hook at him, which, fortunately, did not land anywhere critical, but rather wrapped around Mickey's fighter, drawing him into a massive embrace. As the pair grappled in the center of the canvas, you could hear Grizzly talking to Ariel through his gumshield, asking, "Is that your best shot, nigger?"

A few seconds later, Grizzly ended the embrace by taking Mickey's kid and throwing him into the ropes. The ropes absorbed Ariel's momentum and, much as a slingshot, hurled him back again. As he flew back into his opponent's ken, Ariel, who was not standing behind a tree when the gray matter was ladled out, had the sense to duck, even as Grizzly hooked mightily over him and nearly wound himself into the floor in the process.

During the second round, Ariel started taking advantage of his height and Grizzly's apparent desire to put his head in, if not through, his chest. Which is to say, on Mickey's instructions Ariel started using the uppercut, smacking his opponent several times from below each time the kid sought to plow him into the ropes. The strategy was highly effective, especially as, following each sequence of uppercuts, Ariel would grab the kid and hold on as if his life were in the balance, which it probably was. Unable to find the necessary punching room, Grizzly would reach up and scrape Ariel off him. Then, briefly unencumbered, he would seize Mickey's fighter with one mitt and attempt to anesthetize him with the other. Each time he essayed this maneuver, however, the referee felt compelled to step in and remind him that there were rules to boxing and holding and hitting was against them.

While Grizzly's tactics did not please the referee, they positively enchanted the fans. When he first came out, there was a good deal of hooting and here and there a Tarzan yell. "Hey, look, it's Fred Flintstone," said one fan. "I seen better heads on lettuce," opined another.

The Tarzan yells continued, even after the Griz showed his mettle, but they seemed to modulate into affection. Now Ariel was the target of scorn. "A white man can beat you, chucker!" came a voice from behind me. Amazed, I turned and looked at the speaker. He was white himself, a speck of salt in a pepper mill. I wondered if he knew where he was.

Between the second and third stanzas, Negra was the first to greet Ariel. As Mickey brought the stool through the ropes and Refugio reached up from below with the towel and condiments, Negra ripped Ariel's gumshield out of his mouth and, in one fluid motion, slapped him resoundingly on the backswing.

"Ariel, you better not wait for him or you know what's going to happen!"

"*Cálmate*. Take it easy," said Mickey to his wife. The trainer turned to his kid, who was gasping for breath. He got down on one knee in front of him and dabbed his quivering lips with the sponge. "Listen, son, you won that one and you won the first one too. But see him over there, smiling. Believe me when I say he going to come at you with everything he got. He going to come with the kitchen sink and the bathroom sink too."

"Well, I got my own sink over here," Ariel managed to utter between heaves.

"No, no, no," said Mickey. "We want to win this fight. I want you to do everything that's sweet and cute. Understand?"

At the start of the final act, Ariel seemed to run upon the wind. He was in and out, cuffing his opponent and disappearing, before Grizzly had a chance to even think about retaliating. It was a case of Earth against Air, lowly Understanding versus lofty Imagination. Toward the middle of the stanza Ariel began dancing in place. Mesmerized, Grizzly began to dance as well, a few yards away, in inadvertent parody. The fans were delighted. "Ah-lee! Ah-lee!" they chanted and laughed uproariously. Yet the fan's laughter must have caused Grizzly to snap to, for he went after Ariel with a fury, saying for all the world to hear, "Damn you, nigger, *fight*."

Ariel, alas, had little of the stuff of champions left in him. Visibly wilting, he was thrown back upon his mother wit. He started "walking" the referee. By this I mean, the referee would move in to dissolve a clinch, then would step back to allow the free-for-all to resume, and each time he did this, each time he started walking away from the action, he found Ariel on his arm, escorting him toward the perimeter. Ariel was using the fellow as a buffer between himself and his opponent, as a levee to stem the flood of Grizzly's attack for five or six seconds at a clip. The tactic drove Grizzly mad. It also infuriated the third-man-in who gave Ariel a stern talking-to, as well as an official reprimand. But neither Grizzly nor the referee managed to discern the ruse until Ariel had plied it three or four times. What is more, the reprimand itself ate up still more precious seconds on the clock. Thereafter, Mickey's kid confined himself to grabbing his opponent, tying him up as best he could, until the bell finally delivered him.

"That was a good fight," said Grizzly after Ariel's hand was held high in triumph. Ariel was so wasted he could barely stand unaided. But the Griz appeared to be in fine fettle. He was still smiling and his teeth, visible now without the mouthguard, were as jagged as the lettering on his shirt. "When can I get you again?" he asked. "Where you train, man?"

"You want to fight me again?" said Ariel, staring at the kid in disbelief. "Yeah, sure. I train at, um, Bed-Stuy. You know, with George Washington, Mark Breland's trainer. Yeah, you can find me there almost any time."

Luke's fight was in better line with the theme of the evening. True, his opponent, a Latino from the South Queens Boys Club, hit Luke early in the first chapter and spun him almost completely around. But Luke came back and put the kid down three times. If a boxer is dropped three times in a round, the contest is automatically stopped and it goes into the record book as a TKO. But there was nothing "technical" about this knockout. The third trip to the canvas was a keeper. As Mushy might say, the kid was put out like an empty milk bottle.

The only ones in the arena who somehow failed to see this were his corner. Where most corners would have kept the kid prone and placid after the last knockdown, they let him up, with the result that he weaved like a drunk for a few steps then fell headlong into the ropes. The referee was disgusted and bawled the corner out. "The kid had no eyes," he said afterwards. "They were gone. I was over talking to the judges and next thing I knew the kid was standing up. His people didn't even restrain him. He opened up a nice gash with that fall and went into a shaking state. You know how it is with these kids, fifteen seconds later they're all right and mad as hell at you for stopping it. The corner should've known better."

The drama was not quite over. For once the kid was finally made to lie down, a young woman with an infant in her arms came rushing up to the apron, screaming, "Fredo! Fredo!" She must have been the kid's wife and was understandably terrified.

Fredo, however, wasn't having any. Still shaking, he pulled himself up on his elbow and shouted, "I ain't hurt! Get her out of here!"

Then he did a strange thing. He looked out at us in the audience, as if to determine whether we had witnessed the sorry sequence of events that had just befallen him: the kayo, the plunge into the ropes, the screaming wife. Or whether, perhaps, it had all somehow been a dream.

I found myself, to my surprise, looking away when the kid's eyes touched briefly on my own. It was as if I'd seen something I shouldn't have. As if there'd been a tear in a garment and I'd caught a glimpse of someone's private-most parts.

The knockout of the kid from the South Queens Boys Club stayed with me for a few days. As kayos go, it was more sensational, more disturbing, certainly, than most, due to the intrusion of the wife et cetera, the mix of extracurricular elements. But as I examined my reaction, I realized that I was always surprised when someone got knocked out at the Gloves (I mean truly knocked out, as in separated from the senses for five or ten seconds). And with good reason: The authentic kayo is a rarity in boxing.

This may seem an extraordinary thing to say. For everyone knows that the knockout lives at the core of the boxing mystery. Well, everyone is wrong—at least, he is statistically. According to the American Medical Association's Panel on Brain Injury in Boxing, in 1982 a total of 12,500 kids nationwide took part in Golden Gloves competitions (spin-offs of the original New York tournament). Of these, fewer than 5 percent had or would experience a true knockout during the course of their three-to-five-year careers as amateur boxers. Interestingly, again according to the AMA, which is no friend to the dulcet pastime and therefore unlikely to get creative with the numbers, the carnage among professionals proved to be pretty much the same. In the state of New York, 856 boxers were granted professional licenses between 1976 and 1981. These men fought an average of 677 bouts per anum. Of these, just 43 fights a year, or 6½ percent, ended in a true knockout.

The fact that the kayo is a statistical rarity has little to do with its allure, with its hold on the average fight bug. For the knockout is a compelling, one might say "controlling," image. It is a nexus of fear and desire with a taproot into the subconscious whose power is not a function of incidence. Consider, by way of analogy, Mark Twain's novel about Huckleberry Finn. What image comes instantly to mind? Huck and Jim on the raft, of course. Yet in the actual book the pair spends the great bulk of their time ashore; what is more, even on the raft Huck and Jim pass very few of their actual moments on untroubled waters, floating, as we forever remember them, idyllically down the Mississippi. Or consider sex and love. Sex lasts, what? five, ten minutes, twenty if you're insensate or a master craftsman. It's a mere blink in the space of even the most wide-eyed relationship. Yet sex jumps immediately to the fore when one thinks of love. So too with the knockout and boxing. The knockout is the margin of possibility in any fight. It is the frame we know a swatch of canvas by, the extreme that makes boxing a sport in extremis and gives it its special poignancy. Like sex, it is the "little death" that makes the greater enterprise, even life itself, perhaps, that much more vivid. The fact that it comes so sparingly serves to augment its power.

My own hands-on experience with Tiburón—which brought me to the threshold of the knockout, if not into the actual edifice—encouraged my interest in the subject in its multiple facets. During and after my training I conducted a minor study of the phenomenon, tracked down a number of experts, medical and pugilistic, and spoke with them both in person and over the phone. One day I traveled out to Brooklyn to talk to Dr. Harry Kaplan, who, according to the AMA's boxing people, had done the best work on the physiology of the kayo.

Kaplan was an elderly gentleman, a prominent neurosurgeon attached to the New Jersey College of Medicine, who had worked during the fifties as a ringside physician at the old Eastern Parkway Arena. Over a three-year period he administered encephalograms to scores of boxers just ten minutes after they fought; he made sixteen-millimeter movies of the fights and took notes in the dressing room on, among other things, the fighters' alertness, memory, speech, and pupillary reaction. The knockout, he told me, is a cerebral concussion. "When you receive a solid blow to the head," he said, "something happens to the reticular mechanism. The cells in the midbrain, the area that is concerned with attention, are overstimulated, causing a loss of consciousness." The shot to the jaw induces a more complex variation on the theme. "When you get hit on the chin, there aren't enough impulses to overstimulate the midbrain. But your head is wrenched on its axis and, as a result, you get neck-righting impulses, ear-righting impulses, and impulses from the skin, all of them shooting into the brain at one time. And the brain says, 'I can't handle this!' In effect, it short-circuits." Later, I talked over the phone to Dr. Jack Battalia, chairman of the AMA's brain injury panel, who agreed with Kaplan and elaborated his metaphor. He suggested I envision a house: "Suddenly, you put everything on. The toaster, the television, the air-conditioner, everything. What you've got is an overload. You turn everything on at once and all the lights go out."

For a pugilistic perspective on the knockout, I turned to such well-known fight-game savants as Ray Arcel, Cus D'Amato, and Angelo Dundee. These gentlemen gave me to understand that, if the knockout is rare in terms of incidence, it is rarer still to the man who experiences it. Arcel told me the story of a Filipino fighter in the 1930s who journeyed by car to a rain-threatened match in an outdoor arena in Long Branch, New Jersey. The kid was knocked out in the first round and regained full use of his faculties on the way home while riding through a downpour. "That's tough," muttered the kid, "the fight rained out and me needing the money so bad." Everyone in the car had to chuckle, but complications developed the next day when the kid showed up at the gym. He'd seen the afternoon paper and was irate to discover that somebody had fought under his name in Jersey and been kayoed.

The Filipino fighter was suffering from what doctors call "retrograde amnesia"—which is to say, he couldn't recall gloving up and getting into the ring. Yet even if all things had been equal, and he hadn't sipped his cup of lethe, he still would not have remembered the blow that knocked him out. The fact of the matter is, he didn't actually witness it. It is a fistic commonplace, to quote Angelo Dundee, that "the shot you don't see is that which gets you out of there." Or, to cite Professor D'Amato, who comes at the same point from the opposite direction: "Any fighter who has a competitive spirit and is hit a blow, which he sees coming, will not be knocked out. He may be knocked down. His performance will be diminished. But he will not be knocked out."

In the manly art what succeeds is not raw, but preemptive power. The knockout blow is not so much a Sunday as it is a sneak punch. This is a subtlety that has been lost on most fight enthusiasts. Take Marciano's dismantling of Walcott in 1952, probably, thanks to some lurid photography, the most famous kayo of the modern era. After the fight, the United States Testing Company contrived an apparatus to measure the clout in Rocky's right hand, which they somehow determined to be "925 foot-pounds, as against 690 foot-pounds claimed for the most powerful handgun bullets." Alas, the men of science were almost as deceived as Walcott himself. Before the fight, Jersey Joe had said he wasn't worried about the Brockton Strong Boy, because "you can always see a right hand coming." What Joe hadn't counted on was Rocky's flair for sleight of hand. "You ever seen a shell game?" asked D'Amato, who was ringside that night. "Well, Marciano beat Walcott with a Three-Card Monte trick. He feinted a left hook, which distracted his attention. Then he threw a right that hit Walcott on the button just as he was starting his own right hand." Admitted a wiser Walcott afterwards, "I never saw it."

Active fighters are reluctant to admit they have ever been

hurt in the ring, much less discuss the kayos they've sustained. "What are you crazy?" Gerry Cooney said when I brought up the subject during his training for Larry Holmes. "Don't you think Holmes would love to know if I been hurt?" Retired pugs are more candid; and judging from the things they say, the knockout, when you have to go there, is not such a terrible place to visit. Most agree with Jack Sharkey, who was put out by both Dempsey and Louis, that there is no pain in those moments, just a feeling of turmoil, like a dream. Gene Fullmer, who was dropped by Ray Robinson in 1957, woke during the count to see Sugar Ray bouncing up and down in the neutral corner. "I thought he was in great condition, doing exercises between rounds," said Fullmer. Lew Jenkins, who was floored by Bob Montgomery in a lightweight encounter in 1940, remembered gathering his wits at the tolling of eight and seeing the crowd getting up to go home. Lew got up with them. It was this gregarious instinct that saved him, for he went on to win a decision. Floyd Patterson reacted in similar fashion after being clobbered by Sonny Liston. "I felt, for about four or five seconds, that everybody in the arena was in the ring with me, circled around me like family. Somebody told me that I actually blew a kiss to the crowd."

The problems tend to come later, after the brain has regrouped and the limp body is vigorous again. That's when the pain and shame begin. The same Jack Sharkey, known as the "Garrulous Gob," wept when he came to and realized he'd been put under by Primo Carnera. Floyd Patterson adopted false whiskers and a moustache to exit unseen after his knockout by Ingemar Johansson. Jose Torres, who was knocked out once earlier in his career, came as close as he ever wanted to again during a comeback attempt in 1969. "I was on the floor when Charlie Green hit me and when I hit the floor I told myself, 'I will not let all these people see me again on the fucking floor,' and I made my decision to quit boxing right there."

It was probably the right decision. For the knockout is a controlling image, not just for the fight fan, but often for the fighter as well. "For someone who has never been knocked out," ex-heavyweight contender Duane Bobick told me, "there's always the fear of it, the fear of the unknown. And after they've been knocked out, some fighters are never the same." Most of these are kids you never hear about because they encounter their personal twilight in the amateurs, or early on in their professional careers, and they never make it out of the agate type and onto the arena marquee.

"You can heal a broken hand," Ray Arcel explained. "But you can't heal a broken spirit."

After Luke's kayo that night, I stayed ringside for the next bout and watched Spaulding mount a game but futile battle against a much taller and more skilled opponent. I was thinking about the kid Luke had put on dream street, wondering if he would ever fight again, and was not aware that Refugio was standing beside me. That is, until I heard Mickey joking a few yards away with Willie Dunn. The trainer was talking about Refugio and me as if we were a matched set.

"Yeah, ain't no way I could lose tonight," he was saying. "Tonight, I got *two* white men in my corner."

Chapter 7

STRICTLY FROM GORGONZOLA

For the most part, Casa Rosario served the more corrigible kids in the ghetto, youngsters who were able to shoulder the discipline of training, who could set goals and work toward them and would not fold at the first sign of pressure. Several of the kids in the gym, including Ariel and Milton and Jackson, had so internalized the necessary discipline they were able to do college. Everybody who trained with Mickey had to be doing something with his life. The trainer insisted upon it.

Yet I came to see that there was another constituency in the gym, one that was not required to meet the trainer's higher expectations. Which is to say, Casa Rosario had its own share of kids with broken spirits. Only they weren't casualties of the ring, but of the dice-throw at birth and the peculiar mix of their neural chemicals.

"Oh, no, I got him again today!" Mickey said one afternoon, alerting me thereby to the existence of this gym subspecies.

What do you mean? I said.

"You got eyes, right? Over there."

The kid looked like something you'd put out in the field to make the crows think twice about the corn. To start with, he was laminated with dirt. He was wearing blue sneakers that were green with mold and several layers of clothing, which he shed item by item right there on the training floor, until he was down to soiled boxer shorts and, though the heaters were hitting all nines, a scratched leather jacket with a slimy fur collar that looked, at any moment, like it might crawl off his shoulders. He was hammering one of the heavy bags with his naked fists, even while chewing furiously on his gumshield and roaring imprecations. We watched him for half a minute or so, until he lungered on the floor, at which point Mickey called him over.

"You lose you razor?" the trainer asked the kid.

"Got no money for razors," the kid replied.

"You got money for cigarettes," said Negra, suddenly manifest. "I seen you smoking."

"Over there in the cabinet you will find a cloth," said Mickey, looking steadily at the kid.

"Cloth?" said the kid.

"For that saliva you leave on the floor."

"Sorry."

"Don't be sorry. Just clean it up."

The kid did as he was told, but before long he was raving, something about somebody stealing his rings. He had three of them; one of them, apparently, was a diamond. The kid was moving along the training floor, interrogating and cajoling and threatening the other fighters. Chino Number One ("Get out my face, man!") was on the verge of popping him when the Rosarios interceded.

"Here's you rings," said Negra, kindly, pulling the kid away. "Don't you remember? You give them to me to hold while you hit the bag." There were three rings, but none was a diamond. Made of colored glass and plastic, they were the sort of thing you find in Cracker Jacks.

Mickey started to lecture the kid, telling him he had to go easy on the other fighters in the gym. "Now these that are here, they are you friends. You should not be picking on them."

"I wasn't picking on them."

"Yes, you was. You was accusing them. What happen if they say you are a loco?"

"I am a loco." The kid crossed his eyes and laughed hysterically. Then got stone-cold serious. "I been at the Belle-vue, man."

"Listen," said the trainer, "I'm crazier than you. I'm much crazier than you."

"Oh, no, no. I wish."

"And if you come into my house, you must respect my house."

"Okay, I'm sorry, man. I'm *sorry*," he shrieked.

"Easy now. I know you sorry, but I don't want you to go on in life doing these behaviors. Because you go somewhere else, you can't do this. You can't have you tantrum, because everybody get to feeling guilty. Then right away you get a punch of guilt from somebody for no reason at all. You hear what I'm saying?"

"Okay, I make a mistake."

"Yes, but I don't want you to make this mistake again. They keep on mounting and mounting. If you was crazy, I would say you was. But you not crazy. You got you common sense with you. But you can't go cursing and hollering, because, remember, wherever you go there's always one fellow that's crazier than you and he could hurt you. Believe me, if there's one rich man, there's always one richer. I never met one fellow happier than another fellow, but there's always one that's worse than the other one. Hear what I'm saying."

The kid did hear what the trainer was saying and was oddly soothed by it. I say "oddly," but the youngster's reaction was not at all strange in context. Rather, from what I'd seen, it was the norm for the subspecies. I must have witnessed this sort of exchange between Mickey and a schizophrenic youngster a dozen or more times during my stay at Casa Rosario. Schizophrenia is of course the classic disease of madness. It is marked by delusions, hallucinations, a wild disordering of the thought processes, and, alternately, by no emotion at all, by muteness, the face bereft of expression, the leaden gaze turned inward. Schizophrenia may well be the preeminent mental disease of the ghetto. Its emblem is the street person, the woman who drags her house about in paper bags, the man who stands on the corner and keeps time with the voices that rip through his brain like radio waves.

Males seem to contract the illness in their late teens, when they are required to make the stretch from adolescence to adulthood and find they can't and something snaps within them. The gyms around the City were frequently confronted with these desperate young men and almost always threw them out. But Casa Rosario was different. Mickey and Negra worked with these kids in tandem, as a sort of Mr. Outside and Mrs. Inside, a Blanchard and Davis of the mentally infirm. Mickey's portion of the labor was to hold the maddened youth to a minimum standard of behavior, to make him understand that he was welcome in the gym and that the tariff was respect for others. Negra's portion was more difficult to describe. It had to do with her religious beliefs—notably, with her belief that illnesses of the mind and body are rooted in spiritual causes. That certain people are put here to "work something out," to go through a series of *pruebas* or tests. And that such tortured souls should not be thought of as insane, but as "in development."

I am reminded of Pelota, a blond-haired Latino youth with a honey complexion and a beatific look in his eyes who simply turned up one day like a foundling on the gym doorstep. The youngster told Negra, who discovered him, that he'd gone first to the Boys Club on 114th Street, but they'd driven him off the premises. As he was leaving the building, a "blessing hand" came out of the sky and guided him to Casa Rosario.

Negra said that Pelota claimed to be able to see into the future. When I asked her what it was he saw there, she suggested I talk to him myself and promptly called him over. The kid spoke only Spanish and answered all my questions in the same clear, affectless voice, gazing in my direction but several feet over my head. He said he was sent here from the stars. He said his father had killed his mother. He said he used to go into the bathroom and look in the mirror and see his father there. He also said that he was his mother. He said that in eight years' time he would be *campeon del mundo,* boxing champion of the world, and he would have disciples, and there would be a hammer and a judge and a jury, and the judge would be his father, who was as well, apparently, el Diablo, Old Scratch himself. . . .

Nobody knew the kid's name. Each time he came into the gym and signed the daybook he used a different one, most of them lifted from the Bible. Negra called him Pelota, or "the ball," because that was the nickname of the oldest child of Mickey's dead sister-in-law. Negra had not seen Pelota for years, but she felt sure that he and this kid were one. "I don't know why I think it's him," she said. "I just meet this boy the other day. I go home and I go to bed and I keep thinking about this boy. I never have that other boy in my mind before, but now here he is in my mind. I say to myself, 'That's Pelota.' And I keep thinking about what his mother say to me before she leave this world. 'Negra, if ever I die, Pelota won't have nobody.' "

Negra was obsessed with the kid and she managed to infect Mickey as well. For if she were right, the kid was the son of Rafael, Mickey's older brother, the man who reared him. From what I could gather, Rafael had three children with Pelota's mother. After she died, Pelota was left behind in Puerto Rico to be brought up by the maternal grandmother, while Rafael carried the other two off to Miami. Mickey had not seen Pelota since he was a tot, but he had been trying for years to get Rafael to give him the other two kids, so that he might raise them himself in tribute to the brother who had been his virtual father.

It would be wrong to say that Mickey was as convinced as Negra that the Pelota at hand was the authentic article. Rather, he placed a more or less Pascalian wager on the kid. If he was his nephew, great. If not, what did it hurt to play along? As a rule, the trainer did not permit such youngsters to fight, anyway, but merely put them through the floor exercises. The main thing was to make human contact with them, which, in this case, was not easily done. Even simple matters presented a challenge. I remember one day Mickey's asking the kid, prior to a light workout, whether he'd weighed himself.

"The rooster does not want to fight," the kid answered.

"You got a rooster?" said Mickey. Like most Latinos the trainer had an interest in the cockfights.

"Yes."

"You got a fighting rooster?"

"I am the rooster. When I am born, the rooster cry three times. Then my father betray me."

Negra seemed to have better luck. But she reached the kid at palpable cost. One night at a bootleg fight out in Queens, Pelota worried that an associate of Refugio's, a public housing cop named Lester, had been sent by Pelota's father to arrest him. "No, Lester is a friend," said Negra, who, in truth, had her own separate set of doubts about Refugio and the cop.

Despite Negra's insistence, the kid would not believe her and seemed to sink into despondency. Negra did everything to divert him. She pulled his nose and pinched his cheeks, made eyes at him and generally acted the coquette. She rubbed him all over his torso as we sat there in the bleachers, the fights raging on in front of us.

At one point, Negra turned away from the kid. She was shivering, turning purple. Her teeth were banging together.

"I got a chill," she said. "I just feel a cold knife go through my body."

The upshot was, Negra got sick and didn't show up at the gym for several days. By the time she returned, Pelota had vanished. We never saw him again.

It was the last night of Gloves Quarterfinals, and although none of Mickey's kids were fighting, I'd come down to the Garden anyway. Ordinarily, there would be a bunch of us in attendance, knocking back the sights and maybe a frostie or two. But the previous night's entertainment had been expensive for Casa

Rosario—to be precise, it had cost the club Milton and Ariel and Chino Number Two. And such was the mood at the gym that nobody felt much like joining me on a busman's holiday.

From where I was standing, on the ramp leading to the back-stage area of the Felt Forum, I could see the ring. Two kids were getting it on. One was an unattached fighter, a rare sighting this late in the tournament. He was a white kid, which was the part that was not so rare. Unattached fighters seem to come almost exclusively in that one hue. Mostly, they were Irish or Italian or Slovak kids who lived with their own kind in working-class neighborhoods. They were youngsters with reputations forged in the street who didn't know the first thing about boxing. Come showtime, they would swagger into view, their jaws as blue as Bluto's, their hair awash in a sea of Vitalis, the requisite tattoo on chest or shoulder. Typically, they would load up and with the opening bell they'd sprint across the canvas, carrying their fists as if they were balancing trays laden with hot food— Watch your back!—which they would pitch into the air when they reached the other corner, never mind whether anyone was home. Invariably, they disdained the stool between episodes, that is, in those rare instances that they lasted more than one.

I was in awe of these kids, in awe of their thundering inno-cence, which I took to be edged with some kind of nutty de-fiance. Anyone, after all, with even a passing interest in the game knew that boxing was different from squaring off over some grievance, real or imagined, in a bar or out on the pave-ment. Anyone knew this, it turned out, but your tribe of the unattached palooka. I would follow them down to the dressing room, catch them before the almost certain debacle, and con-front them with the only question really worth asking: Why? Why were they doing this, putting their John Barrymores on the line?

It became obvious to me, after a few such interviews, that they did not know why. More, it was clear from the way they stammered out their answers that they had not even given the matter thought. They'd simply followed the example of their buddies and, more important, I felt, the promptings of their blood. I envied them their impulsiveness.

I was taken with the unattached kid in the ring in front of me just now for precisely the opposite reason. I knew the kid. He'd been in many of the same shows as Mickey's youngsters and I'd had several opportunities to chat with him. Ross, that was his name, taught English at a middle school out on the Island. Unlike most of his unattached brethren, he knew exactly why he was in the tournament, flip as he might be about it.

"I'm here on a lark," he told me just before his inaugural adventure. "It's sort of an experiment in masochism. I always wondered what it would be like to experience pain."

"Aw, don't listen to him," said his tousled-hair younger brother, who was prepared to work the corner. Every unattached fighter seems to have just such a recruit doing his Gunga Din–ing. "He tells me one day he's going in the Golden Gloves. Doesn't surprise me one bit. He does stuff like this all the time. If it's not boxing, it's sky-diving and rock climbing. Someday they'll shoot him out of a cannon!"

"Actually, I was teaching Thoreau," said Ross, rising up from tying his shoes and getting serious for a moment. He'd seen that I was taking notes and was doubtless as interested as the next fellow in cutting a figure for posterity. "Thoreau talks about chasing life into a corner, about getting down to essentials and taking a risk. I'm sitting in the teacher's room at school one day and, suddenly, there's this coupon for the Golden Gloves staring up at me from the *Daily News,* a paper I don't even normally read. I took it as an omen. There's nothing riskier or more essential than boxing, right?"

When Ross fought I was careful to stay below stairs. I'm not certain why. Maybe I'd overdosed on unattached fighters, which isn't that hard to do. Or maybe it was that he seemed so much a younger version of myself and I had no interest in seeing either of us turned horizontal. There was no difficulty, in any case, in keeping up with the kid's progress. The local TV stations, sensing he was not the usual Golden Gloves fare, glommed onto him early and featured him on the evening news. Judging from the clip I saw, Ross was in excellent shape, the possessor of a wooden, thrust-and-parry style that might have stood him well in a nineteenth-century drawing room paired off, say, with the game but clubfooted Lord Byron. After the first encounter, I couldn't imagine Ross winning another, but he did, and another as well. And here he was tonight with three in the creel, angling for a fourth. He also had a dandy black eye. I asked him about it earlier when we were both downstairs.

"Some of the kids in my class take credit for it," he'd said with a smile. "I got hurt in that last fight out of stupidity. I'm watching this guy throw punches at somebody, and guess what? It's me. I have to think about everything I do in there. I'm not exactly Malamud's natural.

"Actually," he continued, "the kids were kind of subdued today, which was a little weird. On Fridays, you know, you usually have to scrape them off the walls. I figured I'd have my lark and lose in obscurity. But TV blew my cover." He forced a chuckle. "I'm here on borrowed time. But I don't have to tell you that."

I watched Ross get counted out in the first minute and a half of what old Mush would call the "hello frame," which is to say, the first round. He had finally run into somebody who could fight, not a lot, but enough. As I looked on, a couple of hardened Gloves veterans posted themselves at my elbow. One of them interrupted my reverie to explain that you could always pick out an unattached kid, even when he somehow managed to get by the first few tutorials. "Look how he's holding his hands up all during the eight-count," the fellow said, pointing at Ross, who was upright but swaying like a willow in the arms of a private breeze. "A kid that's proper trained, he knows to keep the hands down. Down to his side. Know why?" I did, but I was too preoccupied to say so. "To let the blood flow back and refresh him. See, you always try, when you run a tourney like this, to match the club kids with the unattached kids right at the start. That way you get rid of the garbage and you maintain the purity of your competition. Now this kid, his being a teacher and getting on TV and all, he's what you call a 'human interest.' I figure they matched him light. Strung him along a little ways, just for the publicity. Know what I mean?"

The fellow on the other side of me, a Gloves official who had the aspect of a druggist in his white guayabera, was nodding in emphatic agreement. "These unattached kids always amaze me," he said. "I mean, what goes through their mind that they think they can get in with kids from Harlem and the South Bronx who been doing this for years, who come up through the Kid Gloves and the Junior Olympics? Some of these so-called Novices you see here tonight got better than a hundred fights. They fought overseas, for Christ's sake, and they just sixteen! I mean, you never see nobody filling in a blank for the Millrose, if they never been in a race before. And, hell, they ain't getting their brains scrambled in the Millrose. All they're doing is running."

The people in the Gloves inner circle were notably immune to the romance of the true, or amateur, amateur. They did not view the unattached fighter through the same rosy filter as I did (or, at least, as I did when I first came to the Gloves). They did not see him as a latter-day Herman Melville fending off the blahs by putting to sea in a whaling ship, as Jack London responding in kind to the call of the wild. Rather, they saw him pretty much as the old Greek saw the barbarian. Which is to say, as an unlettered putz who brought additional danger to an enterprise already knee-deep in the stuff. As a thoroughgoing clown whose mere presence served to burlesque the rites they celebrated. "You are no better than a barbarian learning to box," Demosthenes once mocked his fellow Athenians, after a lamentable performance on the fields of battle against Philip of Macedon. "Hit him in one spot, and his hands fly there. Hit him somewhere else, and his hands go there."

The unattached kid might have been saying "bar-bar-bar" when he spoke, so little did the Golden Gloves veterans understand him and his motive for invading their sacred grove. For the inner circle, the Golden Gloves was serious, if not overly solemn, business. Serious in a good way, I came to think.

Boxing, as Mickey seldom tired of telling me and as my own tour of the premises painfully confirmed, is not like other sports. Indeed, there is some question as to whether it is a sport at all. For, as Joyce Carol Oates has lately observed, "there is nothing fundamentally playful about it." There is nothing that takes place between the opening handshake and the final embrace that recalls the sunnier aspects of childhood or that even "seems to belong to daylight." This is to say: As personable and attractive as I found Ross to be, I was nonetheless repelled by his going into the Gloves as "a lark." It was, to my mind—that of a lapsed, but hopelessly tainted Roman Catholic—a little like wearing shorts to church. It lacked a sense of gravity.

My feelings on this score were no doubt intensified by the fact that the kids from Casa Rosario were beginning to tumble out of the tournament, by the fact that I'd been going home with them and getting to know them and was becoming less philosophical about what happened to them. Hemingway says somewhere that one should take care never to become friends with a bullfighter. Papa might have extended this caveat to intimacy with boxers. I was, admittedly, not especially moved by the defeat of Chino Number Two, who was too much the whiner to engage my sympathy. But Milton's loss in the previous night's Quarterfinal was another matter altogether. And Ariel's, well, it was unspeakable.

I want to say a few words about Ariel before he departs this chronicle. He was a great kid. He had the obsidian good looks and the flawless carriage of a prince of Africa, although his station in life was somewhat lower. He was, in fact, the best justification I knew for the sorry setup in this country we call "welfare." Ariel and his mother had been getting $145 a month from the government for the past year, that is, ever since the kid's father died. This modest stipend, combined with what the mother banged out going door to door for some cosmetic firm and what the kid himself picked up through his work-study program and hawking parachute bags on the street, enabled Ariel to continue his studies at Brooklyn College and fanned the dream of medical school.

Ariel's father had died of a heart attack, maybe prematurely. In any case, a year had passed and the kid was still angry about it. He told me that his father had gone to the hospital in terrible pain and was treated, not for a heart ailment, but for an ulcer. The doctors simply laced him with Maalox and sent him home, where he suffered his coronary two weeks later. "The only time we knew what was wrong with him was after he died," said Ariel. "That really pissed me off." Ariel said his father had labored for years on construction sites, and the irony was he had just found himself a sweet deal: pushing a broom at Carnegie Hall. "It was the first time in his life he could come home looking decent. My mother said, 'See, he got an easy job. It killed him.' "

Ariel and I had our conversation about his father a week or so before he took his licking from the Italian kid from the South Queens Boys Club and was excused from the remainder of the tournament. It was a beautiful late winter day. We were sitting in the park outside the gym with our jackets unbuttoned and I thought to deflect his bitterness. I asked Ariel what his father was like and, bingo, got a warm smile for my inquiry. He said that through the years he and his father had not been close. They were altogether different creatures: Where Ariel was a talker, extremely gregarious, his father was "a listener and a loner." Yet, some months before he died, "Da," as Ariel called him, started opening up to his youngest of eight sons.

Ariel recalled one night in particular as a sort of turning point. He had gone out and bought himself a carton of Chinese food. "Something happened that we weren't all eating together. My brother had made dinner for himself and didn't give me any, or something, I don't remember exactly. My father was in the kitchen when I came back, and I ate the Chinese food in front of him. I didn't think anything about it. I didn't deliberately not give him any. At the same time I didn't ask him if he wanted any, out of sheer courtesy. I didn't do either one. Then my mother came home and she noticed the container in the garbage and she said, 'Who had the Chinese food?' I said that I had some. She said, 'You couldn't leave me any?' And my father said to her, 'Couldn't leave *you* any? I was in the house with him and he didn't offer me none.' And that's when I realized the truth about my father—that he was so introverted he didn't have the ability to ask for something he wanted, but that didn't mean he didn't have wants and feelings like anyone else. That's when I realized I didn't know my father at all. When he told my mother I didn't offer him the Chinese food, I said, 'That's true. He was in the house and I acted like he wasn't there.'

"After that everything changed between us. It used to be we could be in the house for hours, just the two of us, without ever speaking a word. Now he started telling me stuff. Like he took some money out of the bank and loaned it to this friend of his. He didn't tell Ma, but he told me. I mean, to me, that was something big when he said, 'Don't tell Ma, because she'll have a fit if she knows about this.' It was something big because it was like a secret we had against my mother. This had never happened before, I mean *never*.

"Another thing he did—you know how they send you the registration to the car and there's two sides to it, part one and part two? He gave me part two. He said, 'Here, Ariel. Keep this in your wallet.' To me, that was significant, because we never shared anything before. And then, you know, we started to argue about things. After he gave me the registration, I'd be driving the car and burning up the gas without putting any back in it. So Da would start having to go to the gas station maybe twice a week, when he wasn't used to going more than once. You know what he did? He started putting in just enough gas to get where he was going." Ariel whinnied with delight at the memory. "That was significant to me, too."

You mean you never used to argue with him? I asked.

"Uh-uh. We never talked, so we had nothing to argue about.

Another thing I remember, he was a wrestling fan. I'd tell him that wrestling was a fake, and he'd get mad and say I didn't know what I was talking about. Oh, that was funnn-ee!" Ariel whinnied once more.

Did he like boxing?

"He did, to a certain extent. Matter of fact, I remember the first time he came to see one of my fights. It was in the Felt Forum, and after I won I went out into the audience. He kissed me. He hadn't kissed me since I was, well"—Ariel held his hand out at waist level—"about that tall. He was so happy, and I was happy too, because I had beaten a tough guy and he was there to see it.

"You know, a month or so before my father passed on I tried to send him and Ma to the Bahamas. The fares were cheap then and I'd saved a little money. I said, 'Da, listen, I want to buy a ticket for you and Ma to go away.' And he started smiling. Then he said, 'No, Ariel. Don't spend your money.' I said, 'I want to.' He said, 'Well, I won't be able to get the time off.' I said, 'You deserve a vacation. You could get it. Just tell them you have to go away.' He said, 'No, next year.'

"So he convinced me to wait and I didn't buy the ticket. Afterwards, a lot of things ran through my mind. I thought, Maybe if I had bought the ticket, then they would have been away for Christmas and it wouldn't have been so cold and maybe Da's heart wouldn't have had to work so hard. . . ."

Ariel fell silent, and I felt as though I should say something. I felt I should tell him that it was natural for him to feel the way he did, that children often feel regret, even guilt, for no legitimate reason, when a parent dies. That the important thing was that he and Da had found each other.

In the end, I didn't say anything. The kid's grief was so real and pure I didn't want to patronize it with my two-bit Ann Lander-ings. We just sat there, Ariel and I, and stared out across the park to one of the playing fields, where a man and a small boy were tossing a ball, getting a jump on spring.

*   *   *

I could see that Negra was taking the losses hard too, although clearly in a different way from me. Negra loved the kids, of course, and was sad to see them go down in flames. But she'd been through all this dozens of times before. Besides, she knew that most of the kids, after taking a week or two to put Humpty together again, would be back in the gym once more.

No, there was something else at work with her, gnawing on her innards. The fact is, for Negra, the losses were not simply losses, but something a good deal more sinister. They were dark installments in some vile master plot hatched by that tyro necromancer and nefarious author of evil, Refugio himself.

This was weird, even for Negra, who's probably not anybody's girl next door (unless, maybe, you live in Port-au-Prince). But let me go back a couple of weeks and sketch in the darkening backdrop for the lady's spiraling suspicions. For even if few among us believed that Refugio had brought the hard rain down upon us, most of us agreed that it was falling—indeed, that we were getting pelted on a regular basis.

First the cops called about a kid named Rory, saying he'd been sucking tokens out of the turnstiles (a neat trick which requires that you come up quietly behind your mark and—just as he's committed the fare, but before he's windmilled through—surround the slot with your lips and mightily inhale. Careful not to swallow.) The offense was laughable. But Rory had made some remarks that apparently were not. Thus the constables returned him a couple of days later with one of his eyebrows turned into macrame.

That same afternoon Chino Number One got jumped by three members of an eleven-brother contingent known locally as Los Muchos, or The Many. Chino was at the Taino Towers on Second Avenue, plying his security gig, when one of Los Muchos asked if he might leave his brand-new ride in a no-parking zone. The request was reasonable and Chino said fine, so long as someone stayed behind to move it. "Okay, Poppy," said the kid with a mocking smile.

Now, "Poppy," as I understand it, is one of those affectionate locutions that can be turned inside out and worn with different colors on its nether side. By this I mean, when the "Ps" in Poppy are made especially plosive and the whole business is wrapped in an insinuating grin, then the word implies that the referent likes boys instead of girls. It's a fighting word, if ever there was one, to a Latino, and Chino was a Latino squared.

On a Monday Ralphie caught on fire. He was in his room making a model airplane and he went to open the glue and the glue, which had been heating up in the drawer for months, burst into flames. Instinctively, Ralphie sought to rub the burning liquid off his fingers and onto his pants, but all he succeeded in doing was giving the blaze a new field on which to disport. The flames roared up his pant leg and were licking at his shirt, as he ran screaming into the living room, where Mickey had the presence of mind to throw his younger son to the floor and roll him over and over until the fire finally called it quits.

Two days later, on a Wednesday, Ralphie was outside on the street at a pay phone, using his blistered digits to touch-dial his girl friend. Mike, Jr. came along and, suddenly, words were being exchanged between Mike and the three or four lowlifes who were standing by the phone and one of these charmers apparently spit on the ground a little too close to Mike's Adidas. During the pleasantry that ensued, several other gallants came over and one produced a handgun and proceeded to massage the back of Ralphie's head with it.

Negra called Mickey at work and the trainer took a cab home. He found the fellow who had pistol-whipped his son still out on the street, still brandishing his iron, thinking it perhaps a badge of impunity. He didn't know Mickey, who walked through it as if it dealt in water ("I don't know why, but guns don't scare me—maybe because of all them years with the gangs") and stretched the fellow on the pavement. The trainer was sitting on the fellow's chest, using the fellow's head to probe the tensile strength of the concrete, when the housing cops arrived and wrestled him, still spitting venom, away.

Some days later Mickey was telling me about the incident.

He was telling me how the next afternoon he went out looking for the other punks who had assaulted his sons, how he scoured the bookie joints along First Avenue, made the books bring out their runners so he could look them over one by one, when, abruptly, in the middle of this telling, a curious thing happened. The trainer was no longer there. Oh, he was there, physically. But he gave this little shiver. His eyelids fluttered, and then the eyes themselves seemed to lose candlepower for five or six seconds.

Jesus, Mickey! I said. What was that?

"Nothing, really. The heejie-beejies. Every once in a while I get them, I guess when I let my problems get to me." The trainer laughed. "You know I got more problems than Reagan and Dick Tracy put together."

Negra knew better, naturally. She said that somebody some- where had a hank of her husband's hair or a shred from one of his coats and was doing something hellish to it. Negra's candidate for the nastiness? Refugio, of course.

Negra blamed the poor schlub for everything. She said that every time Refugio talked to one of the kids in the Gloves and told him he was destined to become champ, that kid took an immediate header into disaster. She said that the assistant trainer had changed since he first came to the gym, and the culprit wasn't that hard to figure. By which, of course, she meant santería. She said that ever since Refugio started swirling his mitts in chicken blood and his brain in the mumbo jumbo he had become swollen with pride and larded with self-interest and that it was his current, overweening ambition to prove himself a better handler than Mickey. Hadn't I noticed that Refugio and this housing cop, Lester, had entered their own dark horse in the Gloves stakes, a kid named Nelson, and that this Nelson, who was barely out of the barn, had somehow managed to lap the competition in the 156-pound class—indeed, to prance un- scathed through the Quarterfinals? "Now, Bill, you tell me," said Negra, her eyes brilliant with conviction, "how do this kid get so far, if it ain't for Refugio messing with *brujería?*"

Some days earlier, apparently, the assistant trainer had actually had the nerve to bring his *padrino* around to the gym, without saying who the fellow was of course. "I am sitting at the desk when he come in with this man," said Negra, who described the *padrino* as being thickset and endowed with the long black mane of an Indian. "Now, if another person have my religion, and I don't want him to see what I got, I could be just like a ordinary person. This godfather he take a long look at me and then, as he go out, he curse Refugio. 'You scared of that?' I hear him say. 'She ain't nothing.'

"After the man leave, Refugio come back and say, 'It's a joke. It's a friend.' I tell him, 'Oh, no, Refugio. That ain't you friend. That you godfather.' He say, 'How you know?' He's all shaking and nervous and everything, and I think maybe he going to do something in his pants. I say, 'Listen, Refugio. You tell you godfather he better watch out. I know more about him than he know about me.' "

Maybe once a week or so, I'd meet Mickey at Roosevelt Hospital and we'd go to lunch. The trainer was one of the moles who ran medical supplies up from the basement of the hospital and whose favorite question was, "What's it like out?" Yet it didn't take me long to see that Mickey was an underling in job description only—that he had, in fact, the run of the building and, as might be imagined, everyone else buzzing around for him. Not that the trainer was unfairly burdened with work, far from it. Tom Sawyer would have understood: It simply gave him pleasure to see other people doing his chores for him.

"Hey, Mick, what do you think of Boom Boom?" asked a white-jacketed resident, the staff of Asclepius gleaming on his breast. It was getting to be noon. The resident was set to board the elevator, and we were pointing for the front door.

"He's on the comeback trail," said Mickey. "I like him against this Irisher. You could bet on him."

"I could?" This got the fellow's attention.

"Sure. Listen, doc"—the trainer put his hand on the elevator to keep it from closing—"you going up to the fifth? Great." With his other hand he produced what looked to be a box of needles. "Take these?"

During these luncheons, conducted at any one of several, interchangeable greasy spoons in the badlands below Lincoln Center, we would hash over Mickey's current schemes and pipe dreams. The trainer was full of them, some grand and improbable, others wonderfully byzantine but mostly doable. They ranged from his continuing effort to topple the leadership of the local ABF, and his attempting to get up his own version of the Golden Gloves (and have the *New York Post* back it), to his driving a van twice a week, portaging about some senior citizen organization's volleyball team, so that when August rolled around and he and Negra wanted to take the kids to compete at the Ohio State Fair they could bring a little emotional blackmail and get the Golden Agers to cough up that same set of wheels for their transportation.

Mostly, however, during these hamburger-platter repasts, we talked about what we always talked about: the kids in the gym. Naturally, on this last day of Quarterfinals, we mused on the ones still alive in the Gloves.

"I got two forty-seven-pounders that still in it," said Mickey. "And, really, both should make it upstairs to the Garden. But this ain't 'Bowling for Dollars.' Anything could happen. I don't know about Reggie. He got the ability, but he fall asleep a lot and, I hate to say this, but he's lacking right here." The trainer indicated his heart. "If he know he got you, he will play you for a cat and mouse. But if it get too rough for him, he will find a back door. Truthfully, I'm glad Reggie's this way. It's this other one that give me bad dreams."

Who? Chino Number One?

"Yes."

But why? He's got a ticker that won't quit.

"That's why. See, these kids that got a Rolex instead of a Seiko, the thing about them, they know they don't got the ability. So they feel they must perform a little harder. They might hurt you, but they get hurt more themselves."

What about Smooth?

"Smooth is smart, probably the smartest I got. And he's getting over that lay-off too. He's improving his stamina, which really is in the mind. He fought one good round in that first fight, until he tasted the blood in his throat. He fought two good rounds in the second fight and all three in the last one. Smooth get a little bounce when he's going good. The problem he got, he's a little too attractive to the ladies."

How about Jackson?

"When Jackson want something, he's like a Lynch."

A what?

"A Lynch."

You mean "a cinch"?

"What, you never heard of Wall Street? A Lynch, you know, like they got in the stock market. Where they keep the bulls and the bears."

Merrill, Lynch?

"Yes."

It's good to be "like a Lynch"?

"They the best, ain't they?" The trainer smiled and shook his head. He was sorry for me again. "I don't know, buddy. I was you, I get the money back from that college you go to. Anyway, Jackson's twenty-four, twenty-five, something like that. I'm giving him his last rite. Truthfully, the only thing going to stop Jackson, there these two brothers at Bed-Stuy that want him bad. I hear they draw his picture on one of the bags and they sing out his name when they hit it. You heard about Cuchillo, right?"

No, what?

"I'm turning him pro."

You're turning Cuchillo pro?

Cuchillo, or "the Knife," was named for the scar that cross-hatched his cheek. Cuchillo was a *jíbaro*, which is to say, a rube, a hayseed, an unmitigated turd-booter from the hardscrabble interior of Puerto Rico who spoke not a word of English, except, of course, the jingles contracted from American TV. He was also an unmitigated treat. After one of the Gloves physicals held around New Year's, a group of us had stopped to eat at the Horn & Hardart's on Forty-second Street. Cuchillo had never been in a big city restaurant before, much less an automat. Thus he saw Horn & Hardart's through his own peculiar clodhopper's kaleidoscope as . . . as what? As one of those participatory theme parks maybe that are forever beckoning from the tube. Or maybe as a culinary change on the local pinball emporium or video arcade. Who knows? In any case, the kid quickly grasped the trick of the place and insisted on putting the coins into the vending wall for everyone and pulling the sandwiches and soups and pies out himself, all the while peering through the food windows and trying to catch a glimpse of the help scurrying around in back, and squealing with delight whenever a new dish cracked into view. So intent was Cuchillo on this newfound amusement he forgot to eat. Indeed, so engrossed was he in feeding quarters into the serial tea and coffee slots, he managed to overlook what, to him, must have seemed a minor detail. Putting cups beneath the spigots. The result was a dark brown flood (*con leche*) on the automat floor. No big deal, not to Cuchillo anyway, who proceeded to skate in the slop, hands clasped behind his back, after the manner of the fancy Dans on racing blades he'd seen earlier in the day on the rink at Rockefeller Center. Cuchillo had never seen ice-skating before either, but he turned out to be an inspired mimic. He plastered his puss with the fancy Dan's dreamy, self-absorbed expression. He launched on long, sleek glissades and threw his head back with such convincing élan, you could almost see the wind tousling his hair. Naturally, we fell all over ourselves laughing, as did most of the other bozos in the restaurant. The kid's impromptu didn't do a thing, however, for the automat manager who arrived to see the lot of us to the door.

At the time, I thought Cuchillo was just taking the Gloves physical. I hadn't realized he was supposed to figure in the entertainment until a few weeks ago, when he failed to materialize for his first performance. Some days after the no-show, the youngster and I were jumping rope side by side in the gym and I asked him, *Qué te pasó?* What happened? Cuchillo simply shrugged, then grinned, as a puckish thought stole through his mind. He proceeded to throw down his rope and jump under mine with me, hugging my waist and dancing on my toes like my three-year-old. I fell for the little yokel right then and there. Still, it was hard to believe Mickey was going to turn him pro.

"What I'm going to do?" said the trainer. "I know he ain't ready. But he's bored with the amateurs. I don't turn him, he walks."

I thought about a generation of men who'd gotten the little woman pregnant to save the marriage, and only ended up complicating the eventual divorce. The analogy to Cuchillo was glancing at best, and probably gringo in the extreme, but I was unduly fond of it and would have shared it with Mickey anyway, except that I'd been getting some encouragement of late to keep my mouth shut and it seemed like a good time to practice. I asked about Luke instead.

"Luke? That's one situation we got under control."

The hard rain continued to do its stuff through the next week, mostly, I thought, without help from Refugio. But, then, what do I know? What I do know is it fell the hardest on Smooth and Reggie and Luke, who dropped Semifinal encounters. But like one of those deals where you're in your yard getting drenched and the fellow next door is sitting out on his deck soaking in the beneficial rays of the sun, the downpour didn't hit Jackson and Chino Number One and—surprise to everyone but Negra and, of course, the assistant trainer himself—Refugio's kid, Nelson, at all. Which is to say, this unlikely trio made it to the finals.

Smooth lost to a good kid, which somehow made the defeat more bearable. Reggie also lost to a good kid, a kid the Casa Rosario crew called "Rat Lips" (about whom more anon). But it didn't much matter how good this Rat Lips was, as Reggie was beaten before he even went upstairs to the ring. I know because I was down standing next to him in the Gloves field command when they announced the name of his opponent. The name, as it was pronounced by Matt Cusack, had a sudden and drastic effect on Reggie's countenance. For a brief moment every particle of his fear was registered there.

And then there was Luke. It turned out that the Rosarios did not have the handle they thought they did on the kid's "situation," which, I later discovered, was fairly complicated and probably no-win no matter what they did.

Luke's troubles were brought on by his parents, who didn't want him to box, although not for the usual, unassailable reason, that boxing is dangerous. The kid's folks were Jehovah's Witnesses and as such they opposed the pastime for much the same reason they opposed saluting the flag or marking time in the army. Because it is "of the world." Because it turns one's head away from proper things (that is, from studying the Bible and featuring on Armageddon, where the "sheep"—an honorific, believe it or not—would be saved and the rest of us "goats" would make a beeline for the toilet). Because it is obsessive, idolatrous, prideful. Prideful above all, in that it is the fighter's aim to excel, to see his name blinking in neon from the heights of the foremost swatatoriums in the land. And nobody, say the J.W.s, may have a name but the Big J Himself (and, oh yes, the mincing crooner, Michael Jackson).

Luke had arms like slabs of salami hanging in a deli window. He had a dark, brooding, saturnine visage that gave his opponents palpitations, and he had the ergs in his fists to back up such an announcement. Yet in the ring he was what Mushy would call a "game-quitter." Which is to say, he went at his opponent with apparent willingness, but his willingness was just that, a wooden nickel. There was something in the kid, some deep-seated bewilderment that caused him to hold back, some infrastructural inhibitor that prevented him from discharging his punches with what old Mush liked to call "bad intentions."

As a fighter, Luke was as fickle as the rutting Jove. One afternoon at the past year's Ohio State Fair, to the astonishment of everyone, he took apart the number two ranked amateur middleweight in the country. The next day he was himself made statistical by a youngster who couldn't carry his bucket.

By Negra's lights, which were largely the lunar reflection of Mickey's, a kid's performance in and out of the square circle was of a piece. To her mind, boxing peeled back the layers of a man. It worked on him the way the sea worked on driftwood, reduced him through the friction of training and competition to irreducible character. But boxing was not merely reductive. It was creative and restorative too. It was, the Rosarios believed, a kind of smithy, a place where new character could be forged. (Forged, I sometimes thought, in both senses of the word.)

Luke, you might say, was Negra's fighter—one of her Hephaestian projects. She made up her mind to put some starch into the kid, which meant, in effect, taking it out of the Jehovahs. A few days before the Semifinals we'd found Luke in the dressing cage at the gym. He was stretched out on the bench, seemingly insensate but with his eyes darting all over. Mickey tried to get the kid to talk, to say what was ailing him. But only with Negra's arrival did he find his tongue.

"Is my father," he said in his sweet Trinidadian singsong. "He sayin', I fight it go kill him."

Negra took the youngster by the hand and led him to Mickey's office, where she proceeded to fashion a garland of Jehovah horror stories. One, which she later shared with me, involved a friend of hers named Corazón who was married to a Jehovah who did a burgeoning business selling prayer books. The friend contracted leukemia and the husband, a faithful Witness, would not allow her to receive blood transfusions. Negra said she knew Corazón was dying when she, Negra, was in her bedroom crying one night—crying about what she could no longer remember, probably one of Mickey's enormities—and she suddenly felt a hand pass slowly and familiarly through her hair. It was a gesture of sympathy and consolation, a caress really, that her friend used to make. The next day Negra found out that Corazón had expired during the night. Some weeks after the death, Negra told Luke—her eyes doubtless two-gunning significance at the youngster, as if to suggest that he was a fool if he could not draw the appropriate, sordid conclusion from the facts she was so diligently setting out—she learned that the husband had remarried and that the new wife was one of Corazón's alleged best friends.

Negra was not through, not by half. She spent close to an hour with Luke (the last few minutes of which I sidled into the office and caught), trashing his parents' belief system with a bridled fury. She knew, for example, that the kid's girl friend was Roman Catholic, and she knew that the church was regarded by the sect as the Scarlet Whore of Babylon, which made the girl friend what? A Jezebel herself.

"Luke," said Negra, "you going to leave a woman you love because you parents don't like how she bend her knee?"

"No," said Luke, iterating that his three brothers respected him because he was the only one who'd broken with the Jehovahs and moved out of the family home and lived alone.

"If they respect you for that, Luke," said Negra, "they going to respect you for doing all the things you want to do."

The kid looked at the trainer's wife and smiled.

"So, you see," said Negra, "Jehovah Witness is a boo."

Luke was fine after Negra got through with him. The kid was better than fine. He was spoiling for a fight.

But it was obvious three days later, when he slipped through the ropes for his Semifinal, that something had happened to him, something had gone wrong in the meantime. What we didn't know—and didn't find out until several days later—was that Luke had had a devastating go-round with his parents.

What had happened, I gather, was this: After his session with Negra, Luke had written his folks a letter and given it to his cousin to deliver. In the letter the youngster had told his people, apparently somewhat cryptically, that, although he loved them, he was sorry to say they were never going to see him again. Anyway, the short of it is, the parents construed the missive to be a suicide note, and they rushed over to his apartment in the middle of the night and started beating on the door and windows, pleading with their son to let them in, begging him amid tears not to take his life. Luke's landlord appeared up above and told the parents the kid was not home. But they would not believe the man and kept up the racket for hours, during which time Luke lay absolutely still and sweating a river on his mattress. . . . But, as I said, on the night of Luke's Semifinal, we knew nothing of this. All we knew was that there was something wrong with the kid, that there was a wild, harrowed quality in his eye.

With the gong, Luke thundered across the ring like an unattached fighter and surprised his opponent with a huge right hand. The kid, a mahogany-skinned Latino named Arias from the Crown Heights club, went down like a handful of pick-up sticks. Yet, to look at Luke, as he stood staring across at what he'd wreaked, one might well have thought that he was the injured party.

In a word, alas, Luke was angry—vials of wrath were bleeding out his eyes. He was obviously determined to make this kid pay for everything that had gone wrong with his life. I say "alas" because, the conventional wisdom notwithstanding, there is nothing less to a boxer's purpose than anger. Take the foolish notion of the "grudge match," which is trotted out as part of the ballyhoo for almost every major fight. "Spinks and Braxton plain don't like each other," we are told, the implication being that each kid is tied down like Gulliver before the contest, lest he charge into the other fellow's dressing closet and rip out his liver.

The truth is, anger is impolitic in the ring, the movie *Raging Bull* and other such lovely bull notwithstanding. Anger puts the boxer at risk. It causes him to go taut all over, especially in the neck and shoulders where he can least afford it, as it reduces his ability to take a punch. While, in the short run, anger may give the boxer a burst of intensity, in the long run it saps his strength and endurance. It also diminishes his ability to perceive his opponent's more subtle intentions—which is to say, it causes tunnel vision. And these are merely the defensive drawbacks. As for offense, well, England's Tom Cribb, one of the idols of early fistiana, catches the matter in a cautionary quatrain.

A hasty temper never show,
Nor strike your little friend a blow;
Far better wait till you are cool
And then half kill the little fool.

There is little mystery as to why the public persists in believing that the boxer is motivated, even enabled by anger—clearly, people need a place to put their own violent emotions and somebody to champion them. Yet there is irony in this sort of thinking, for it flies against the boxer's very uniqueness. It fails to recognize the paradox that informs his being. Which is, that in his role as civilization's designated savage, the boxer alone among men does not raise his fist in anger but only in art.

There was nothing artful, however, about the way Luke went after his wounded opponent. It was all the referee could do to restrain him. The official twice stopped counting over the crumpled Latino to herd Luke back to the neutral corner and a third time to shoo Mickey back to where he belonged.

This is to say, the kid from Crown Heights had extra time to put his house in order, to rectify the overturned tables and chairs of his cranial attic. This is to explain why, when Luke was finally released from limbo, he found his opponent almost completely lucid and more than capable of defending himself. Arias was apparently decently trained. He had the sense, in any case, to put some distance between himself and Mickey's kid, who went after him, I thought, rather like a revolving door off its stanchion.

Seeing this, the Latino took a nifty step to the side and hit

Luke a short crisp blow to the temple, dumping him right in front of me. "Whirl is king," said Aristophanes. And, for a brief moment, Luke must have understood the great comedian. His eyes spun like fruit in a slot machine, then disappeared altogether.

The main story at Casa Rosario was of course the Golden Gloves. But there were other tales, ancillary epics, playing out in the penumbra. Even as the Gloves was pushing through its Darwinian paces, the saga of Johnny Luna was winding toward its own inexorable finish.

Johnny Luna was the young pro who lived in the gym, who slept on the floor of the trainer's office and kept his worldly effects in a couple of brown paper sacks. Johnny's story was touched, I felt, with the poignancy of myth.

The kid was alone in the world and had nothing—nothing, that is, but a flaw that might yet prove fatal in the classical way and blood that was nearly royal blue. This is to say, Johnny Luna's father was Julio Luna Leon, one of Panama's greatest fighters. In the beginning (circa 1930) there was Alfonso Teofilo Brown who won the Bantamweight laurels and thus became the first Latino to ever hold a world title. Al Brown was the toast of Panama City, where he'd learned to box a decade earlier with the gringo Boy Scouts; yet he was honored in absentia. For the outlandishly tall 118-pounder who bandaged his ankles like a thoroughbred was claimed by the world. He lost his heart to Europe, specifically to Paris, where he became fantastic friends with Jean Cocteau, a boulevardier who trained on Champagne and a dozen cigarettes a day, even while defending his crown twenty-odd times without setback.

Julio Leon was supposed to be "Panama" Al Brown all over again. He was meant to usher in a Golden Age of isthmus boxing. Alas, they had to stow the dream along with the stretch limo and the confetti, when Julio lost on points to Featherweight King Davey Moore in their epochal early sixties showdown.

"Johnny's father was called *el Leoncito,* 'the little lion,' "

Mickey told me, "because of his name and the way he fights. I grew up hearing all about him. He was something out of sight. But I think, after he lose to Moore, him and Johnny's mother, they start to get into the fast lane. I think he dies in this abandoned building that catch on fire. But, truthfully, the life is gone from him long before this. He's a bum. He wear a ragged coat and shoes with holes. He been in jail and he's a addict and his liver is ruined from the alcohol."

Eventually, I would learn that Johnny Luna was taking his own route to his father's end, that where Julio Leon got there through booze and heroin, his son's preferred conveyance was PCP, an anesthetic smoked on mint leaves or marijuana cigarettes. I would learn as well that Johnny had his own young lovely partnering him toward perdition. But, as I say, I didn't know this for some time. My first impression of the kid, to employ a Mushy-ism, was that he was "dyed in the tan." Which is to say, that he was a throwback to a more rugged era.

It used to be, according to old Mush, that you could find a prizefight any night of the week in New York. There were literally dozens of small boxing clubs active within the City limits. Every neighborhood had to have its own lodge of leather-pushers, as sure as it had to have a Catholic church and a candy store, merely to be able to call itself a neighborhood. Then, after the war, television came along and the clubs started to go belly up. The neighborhood people were no longer willing to support the local fights. The thinking was: Why pay a buck or two to sit in fold-up chairs and watch a pair of nobodies crash around, when you could stay at home, notch back the La-Z-Boy, and look on for "free" as the top names in the game put on a real show?

The club fights were crucial to professional boxing. They were where the young money fighter took his lumps and learned his craft and got a little something for his pains to put toward the rent. With no club shows (and with the ordinary joe, thanks to the postwar euphoria, becoming less interested in fighting for his supper), the number of good young kids diminished and the pastime entered a period of stagnation. Technology, according to philosopher Hannah Arendt, is always violent, but TV was doubly so. It not only killed the clubs, it gobbled up what prospects there were. By this I mean, young pros were rushed onto the small screen, and therefore into major altercations, well before they were ready. It used to be that a kid would have thirty or forty professional encounters before he tried himself against contenders. But now TV was calling the shots, and it had an insatiable appetite for new faces.

Experience—in the old days, it was thought to be the fighter's capital. Indeed, it was not unusual for a comer to drop a few matches early on in his pro career (mostly against wily old trial horses) purely in the interest of acquiring it. Experience is still a valued commodity. But nowadays it must be smuggled in. For we are in the thick of the video era where image is everything and the illusion of unblemished innocence is what sells. The short of it is: Today's kid with a future can no longer afford to get his education in the pros, where he risks pulling the occasional bad grade (often by coast-to-coast cable hookup) and never graduating to Prime Time. As a result, a new sort of prospect has developed, one who lingers among the trophy fighters for half a dozen years or more—preferably until the camera shows it loves him like crazy at the Olympics and some high roller springs for him in a major way and promises him a title opportunity just a few clicks down the road. Then, and only then, will tomorrow's champion give up his pretensions to chastity and start hooking for pay.

Johnny Luna was not a prospect in this new mold, but a gym rat out of the old. The truth is, he was just another Latin kid who'd kicked around the cuchifrito circuit, around the New York gyms with a salsa beat, places with names like Solar and La Sombra, where the trainers used him as fresh meat to throw at their Big Top lions. That is, until one day an old fighter of Mickey's brought Johnny Luna by Casa Rosario and the trainer found out who Johnny's dad was and made him take the hunk of gold out of his ear and swear off the pack of no-goods he was running with in Union Square and the two of them got down to work.

Johnny Luna was not much to look at. Worse, it was getting so he could barely look at you. By this I mean, the kid was losing his eyesight (maybe from the abuse he'd taken in the gyms, maybe from the drugs Mickey did not yet know he was using, maybe from the blueprint they give you at birth). No matter. The trainer saw something in him, some trace of his old man beyond the name. Pretty soon everyone else saw it, too.

The kid's first pro fight took place at the Felt Forum nine months before this year's Golden Gloves got underway. He was paired with the Dominican kid who had stopped Smooth in the tournament a couple of years earlier and who had since become a prospect á la mode. Johnny Luna and the *platano* were matched in the "throwaway bout," or the initial four-rounder of the evening, which was staged while the fancy was still dribbling in from the saloons that ringed the Garden.

When Johnny, per his trainer's instruction, spent the better part of the first episode on the hoof, that portion of the crowd that had assuaged its bladders and found its seats was not at all pleased. Indeed, it was as if a covey of boo birds was released in the back of the arena and remorselessly winged forward. Yet by midway through the second stanza you could almost see the clamorous flock pick up from its perch on the ropes, bundle smartly above the ring, and make unambiguous undulations straight out of the building. Which is to say, a hush settled over the assembly, which seemed to recognize that it was witnessing something special.

What was curious about this was the trainer was still worried about the *platano*'s power and had his kid on a short leash. In the first round, Johnny Luna contented himself with moving in and out, feinting the Dominican out of his tube socks and dusting his puss with the jab. By the second round, Johnny had stopped moving altogether. He was standing right in front of the kid and, to the fans' increasing—it took them a while to get what he was doing—delight, was simply making him miss.

"Will ya look at that? I ain't seen that since Slapsie Maxie," said a natty old-timer just behind me. He had a stingy Thin Man moustache and a cap of lacquered black hair that glinted in the ring lights like an oriental bowl.

"Yeah, you can smell it from here," replied his equally venerable but more Lumpen buddy, who was holding his schnozz for emphasis. "This guy's strictly from Gorgonzola."

It was an old gag, and the two coots were clearly enjoying it. But it was also a tribute. "Slapsie" Maxie Rosenbloom was a pug from the thirties, a fight game character who became a character actor in the movies (most memorably, he played Big Julie in *Guys and Dolls*). As far as your average homocidal boxing fan was concerned, Rosenbloom was a figure of ridicule who fought pretty much the same lame way he talked. Which is to say, Maxie not only dealt in slug-nutty malaprops (he liked his steaks "well-to-do," for example), but he made "stinkin' " fights to boot (translation: all his bouts went the distance). A wag of the period went so far as to memorialize Maxie's odiferous talent in a ditty to be sung to "Love in Bloom":

> *Can it be ripe cheese that fills the breeze*
> *With rare and magic perfume?*
> *Ah, no! That isn't ripe cheese.*
> *It's Rosenbloom. . . .*

Naturally, the cognoscenti knew different. True, they said, Maxie had all the kick of a gelded poodle, and in either hand. But what did it matter, when you couldn't hit the guy, even though he stood square in front of you and seemed (in his own peculiar parlance) forever "on the brink of abcess"? And when, even as you were calling him a bum of the most fragrant kind, he was tinkling your ribs like a baby grand and stealing a decision?

"You know what made Maxie Rosenbloom great?" Cus D'Amato, the Nestor of our day, asked me one afternoon at his sprawling country house, appropriately located in Athens, New York.

No, I said. What?

"He was a master of himself."

Hmm, sounds like Zen.

"Well, you could call it that. When I say Maxie was a master of himself, I mean he was completely relaxed in the ring. He was in complete control of his emotions. Look, a relaxed fighter is like a man watching an accident who sees everything that happened and can tell you about it in exact detail. Yet the people who were in the accident, because of the excitement, the pressure, and everything else, you ask them what happened and if there's ten of them, you get ten different answers.

"See, it's all a matter of vision, of being able to see when you're under pressure. If I'm under pressure, if I'm emotional, to the extent that I'm emotional my emotionalism will limit my vision. If I'm relaxed, and I've got ring experience and know what to look for, I can see everything. I can see punches coming a split second before they are actually thrown. Sounds strange, doesn't it? But that's the way it has to be with a fighter. That's the way it was with Maxie Rosenbloom."

I don't want to anoint Johnny Luna here and now, to say he was a relaxed fighter on the order, even embryonically, of Slapsie Maxie. But on the night of his pro debut, when his stomach should have been a lepidopterist's field day, Johnny Luna appeared to be not in the slightest a-flutter. Indeed, so unburdened and at ease was he, it was as if he were not in the ring at all, but back, say, in Jefferson Park romping with Fleabag, the gym dog, or maybe curled up on the couch after dinner at Mickey and Negra's with *El Diario* in his lap and a cup of Colombian roasted in his hand.

Most young fighters, even good ones, tend to parry blows with their gloves, bounce them off their wrists the way Wonder Woman does bullets. Or they simply duck or lean away from punches and often into trouble. Not Johnny Luna. Somewhere along the way, probably during those long tête-à-têtes with

Mickey, he'd learned to slip and roll—which is to say, how to bob beneath the wide punches and how to move his head a serious millimeter or two this way or that to let the straight ones whistle by. Above all, he'd learned to feature on the muscles of the opponent's shoulder—the little ones that rise and inflate just as the other fellow starts his punch and betray thereby when that punch is coming and from what part of the country and enable you, if you're keen and step lively, to pack up and evacuate before it arrives. It is, admittedly, an odd thing to say about somebody who was going blind, but I'm going to say it anyway: *Johnny Luna appeared to see everything.*

By the third stanza, the *platano* would no doubt have rather been in Philadelphia. Johnny Luna was punching now, and he still would not stay in any one place long enough for his opponent to reach down and grab a piece of the floor and bring it tremendously up in the form of a hook. To the contrary, the little fellow with the rheumy eyes weaved in and out on the Dominican, as if he were a maypole and Johnny Luna a celebrant of the rites of spring.

Finally, perhaps from the sheer volume of crepe Johnny Luna had hung on him, the *platano* seemed ready to swoon. As Johnny went in after him, he presented the stationary target his opponent had been looking for all evening. The Dominican greeted Mickey's kid with a straight right hand that caused the crepe to briefly descend over his eyes as well.

"Hey, I got hit," Johnny Luna said in the corner.

"Of course you did, son." Mickey laughed. "Now you got to finish strong."

Which he did, and to sizeable ovation.

As Johnny Luna made his victory loop around the battle box, the trainer leaned toward his wife and said, "I think we got us a winner here."

"It meant for us to win," said she in all solemnity. "We got the power."

The trainer took this in without comment. Then leaned back

and whispered to me over his shoulder, "The only time I got the power is when I pay the bills, and that's when it always seem to desert me."

The next day there was a summit in Mickey's office occasioned by Negra's dream. I gathered that in this early morning vision Johnny Luna, the wretch, had left Mickey for another manager, a fellow named Mafoo who owned a candy store in the neighborhood and once handled Benny "Kid" Paret.

I could tell that Mickey only half-wanted the meeting. He was skeptical per usual about Negra's prophecy, but, well, what the hell, he had to live with her. Then, too, he was worried about Johnny Luna himself. Worried, among other things, about losing the kid to someone who might not do him any good.

"Look, Negra," said Mickey, "I got no contract with these kids. If they could do better with somebody else, then I want them to go."

"No, no," said Johnny Luna. "I'm leaving everything in you hands. All I going to do is fight. You do the rest."

"I know, I know," said Mickey.

"If I want to leave, I would leave a long time ago. What I told my old lady," said Johnny Luna, nodding toward his girl-friend who was tucked in the corner by the file cabinet, "was I hope you could get us a deal with the Garden or somebody, so we could move upstate."

I'd never seen Johnny Luna's girl before, but I knew the tree, all ripe and succulent, that she'd fallen from. By this I mean, she was patterned after the latest Puerto Rican Salome, the zaftig queen of swirling buttockry and bovine concupiscence known to fans of Latin TV as Iris Chacon. There was too much leg, too much breast, too much everything, and she knew it, and she knew you knew it and couldn't have cared less.

"Ask Ariel, man," said Johnny Luna. "He'll tell you. I ain't going with nobody but you."

Negra stood up and walked out of the office.

"All right," said Mickey, relieved, at least momentarily, "it's always good to get things out into the open."

"I hear you."

"Like I say, I got no papers on you. If you want to stay, fine—"

"I ain't going."

"I ain't apologizing for her. Negra's my brain. She's my light in the tunnel. She's my Prudential's rock. She's my—"

"I'm staying."

"All right. I'm just asking the question to satisfy her."

"I ain't taking no two weeks off neither. I'm training Saturday. Let me work out tonight."

"I don't want you to work out tonight. Now, listen—and I guess this is the main thing I got to tell you—there going to be a lot of people after you behind. They going to give you a lot of sweet talks—"

"I don't want to talk to nobody. I started with you. I'm happy with you."

Negra was back. "I spoke to Ariel. He say I was wrong."

"I'm telling you, Negra," said Johnny Luna, "you the last person I would lie to. I ain't doing a Billy Costello. Nothing like that. I been with you four years. You took me when nobody wanted me. You brought me up."

"I think you going to be better than Billy Costello," said Mickey. "You better already. You put up a performance last night like I never dreamed. But let's get one thing straight. I gave Billy Costello away. They didn't take him from me. You see, back then, I couldn't help Billy, because my whole love was amateurs. Now, since Mike and Tiburón and these others turned pro, we got us a squad. I can help you, if you will only help youself. You know what I'm talking about?"

Johnny Luna looked at him blankly.

"I'm talking about all these friends and cousins you got down in that park on Fourteenth Street. What I want from you is to start eliminating these people from you life. Don't fuck youself up, son. You got a future in front of you, I'm telling you."

"If I dreamed it," said Negra, "it going to come true sometime."

"Like I say, I ain't going nowhere," said Johnny Luna.

"See," said Mickey, "Billy Costello came to me. He said, 'Pop, I got this problem. I can't be fighting for trophies no more. I got kids. I got to make some money.' But I already knew it. Billy ate with me. He slept with me in my house. His children was my children."

"You know what got me up out of the dream?" asked Negra. "Bill. A phone call from Bill Plummer."

Negra looked at me, as if I were somehow complicit in her vision. So did everyone else. Even Johnny's girl roused briefly from her languor and took me in. Her mouth was full and damp, the lips slightly parted. Her eyes looked like cloudy hothouse grapes.

"What I want you to do," said Mickey, "is take off today and tomorrow." He paused. "Johnny, please, don't fuck up you life."

"No, no. I told you, I'm going to do it right."

"Let me tell you, I don't think you father did that good in his pro debut."

"They say I don't hit hard."

"But you were told not to go for the knockout. You were in there with a banger, right? You box a banger."

"I know. Next one is a six-rounder."

"No, we got to take it slow. When you got something good, you don't rush it. The only thing, you got too many cousins, too many friends and well-wishers. You got to work *en cuarto* —you got to stay to youself."

"Yeah," said Negra, "and don't be hanging out in Mafoo's candy store."

"I don't hang out there. You know, I got a cousin that look like me. He hangs there. Maybe that's who they meant."

"Ain't nobody told me nothing. I dreamed you was there. I ask Ariel and he say you don't have no conversation with Mafoo. I say to Ariel, 'Not yet. But in the future he will make that conversation.' "

"Negra," said Johnny Luna, shaking his head.

"No, I got to warn you ahead of time. I want you to know what I dream before you stick you feets in water and get wet."

"You are mine, son," said Mickey, heaving a sigh. "Yet you got a mind of you own."

Over the next six months Mickey managed to get three fights for Johnny Luna, two in Atlantic City and one in the Felt Forum. Yet on each occasion the opponent backed out at the last minute, claiming one excuse or another and leaving no time for the matchmaker, even if he were so inclined, to find a replacement. Professional boxing often seems like a combination of "Let's Make a Deal" and "Beat the Clock" (not to mention "Who Do You Trust?"). By this I mean, every card is in flux, each bout in danger of not coming off, right up to the moment the fighters get into the ring. Boxing is subject to the full sweep of life's vagaries. Things happen to fighters at a greater rate than they do to the rest of us, especially at the lowest levels of the game, where the life is most elemental. Fighters get sick, injured, arrested, fearful; and as there is seldom a clause in their contracts that requires them to perform, or show cause why they can't, they simply bow out of their obligations and vow to try again when they're feeling up to snuff. The veteran pug, after a few such disappointments, comes to see that fights are written on water. He learns to be philosophical about his profession, to fence his hopes for advancement, even for a payday, with skepticism. Johnny Luna, alas, was not so fortified. He trained for each fight as if his life depended on it, and more and more it was beginning to look as if it did.

After each nonevent the kid went on a binge. There'd be a

call from the constabulary down by Union Square, saying they had him under lock and key. He'd been causing a ruckus in the underground, or he'd been messing with the dealers in the park or with the sales girls in Mays, looking for trouble and mostly finding it, creating it himself when he couldn't.

I didn't get PCP at all. What was the attraction? It didn't make sex any better. It didn't make you feel heroic. It was mildly hallucinogenic but, from what I could learn, it didn't put a fist through the pasteboard mask and flush out Reality. On the street the stuff was known as "angel dust." It was also called "goon" and "wack wack" and "dummy dust," and for good reason. At one time it had been used to tranquilize circus animals. When it wasn't making your skin pucker with hostility, it was scaling you of any kind of affect at all.

Typically, after such a lapse, Johnny Luna would not be seen around the gym for a week or two. Eventually, he would straggle in, unshaved, his nappy hair raked into a lopsided bulb, his eyes thick with silt. He'd strip down to his red union suit and start hitting the bag, talking giddily to everyone around him.

"I'm clean, Mom," he would shout to Negra.

"That's what you always say," she'd toss back.

"I mean it, *limpio.*"

"Now, all you got to do is prove it."

"I'm serious."

"Me too."

Mickey finally made a fight for Johnny Luna that took. He and Mike, Jr. would be appearing on the same card, waging four-and six-rounders, respectively, at the Felt Forum a week before the Quarterfinals of the Golden Gloves. That afternoon I arrived at Casa Rosario expecting to find everyone in a buoyant mood. They were buoyant all right, even "chipper," if that word better conveys the trumped up quality of their gaiety.

I was given to understand, largely by head cheerleader Refugio, that Johnny Luna had hurt his hand. It was nothing, really, just a scratch. He had it in the bucket of ice water to bring down the swelling, which wasn't actually that great. Refugio, who was grinning for all he was worth, made me think of a Care Bear with a lobotomy.

And then I saw the hand. How do I describe it? For starters, it was a third again the size of its mate. It was pouched along the back like a frightened blowfish and tended toward blue in color. As for the "scratch," there was a series of yellow puss-filled holes along the knuckles, suggesting someone had tried acupuncture with an ice pick. The prevailing fiction was that Johnny Luna had injured the hand a couple of nights earlier during an after-hours session on the bag. My guess was somebody bit him.

I looked quickly and hard at Mickey and saw that he was returning my gaze with equal force. I knew what he was doing, knew that he was trying to temper my response. We were in that zone again, that stark laconic space where pain is the anthem men live by. I knew the drill. I said I don't remember what to Johnny Luna, something suitably innocuous and up-beat. I saved my barbs for his trainer.

I can't believe you're going through with this, I said, once the kid was out of earshot.

"I got no choice," said Mickey.

You mean you're worried the kid will think you can't get him fights and you'll lose him to somebody who can. Maybe this guy Mafoo, I sneered. And you say you always put the kid first.

I guess we all do it—every now and then we get so complacent or, by contrast, so screwed to the moment, that we forget where we are, or who we are with, and we act, or speak, totally without regard for our context and the potential therein for harm to our person. This is to say, it looked for a moment like the trainer was going to kill me. His eyes narrowed to little points. He tensed all over and actually took a short step toward me. Then, for whatever God-sent reason, he relaxed, decided to make do with a smile so cold it gave off steam.

"Look, Bill," said Negra, interposing, "what do you think you know about Johnny Luna?"

"Don't bother, Negra," said Mickey. "He been to college. He know everything."

"You know Johnny Luna never meet his mother or father since he's very little? You know the court take him and his brothers away from them because they's addicts and give them to the grandparents? You know this about Johnny?"

Still watching Mickey, I shook my head no.

"How about that he grow up in a abandoned building, six of them in one room with no heat or water, and the grandfather is a cripple that hop and Johnny Luna since he seven got to get up at five and take the cart out and sell food, *alcapurrias,* on the street so he can buy milk at school and have clothes? You know this about Johnny? Or you know he run with the gangs like Mickey, only he ain't so lucky, because he got no Eugene in his life and he almost kill a man and they send him to the bad boys' school for three years? You know this?"

I had to admit I didn't.

"You know Johnny Luna's got bad eyes, right? Everybody know that. But you know every time before he fight Mickey goes with him to the commission and they give Johnny Luna the eye test, and you know what Mickey do? He stand next to him and whisper what the chart say. You know why Mickey do this? Do you?"

No.

"Because the only thing Johnny Luna got going for him in his life is boxing. You seen this girl he got? Pretty, huh? She's a addict too. You know them three brothers I mention? Two of them's dead from drugs and alcohol, just like the father. You right, if Johnny Luna can't fight we going to lose him. But you know what, Mr. Smartypants? It ain't Mafoo we worried about. It's that little park down there on Fourteenth Street."

The kids from Casa Rosario were spear carriers for the principals of the evening, a local hero-type named Kevin "E.T." Moley and his designated punching bag, one Hernando "Pecho" Castillo. While Castillo had a robe advertising a San Juan car wash, Moley had an honest-to-God following. The band played Irish songs when he entered the arena, and one nut popped into the aisle and jigged. Several others stretched a banner across the mezzanine. E.T. IN 3, it said. CASTILLO PHONE HOME. The Moley fans looked like their idol, only bigger. Which is to say, like altar boys on steroids. For his part, Castillo looked recently exhumed, which of course he was, his alleged seventeen-and-nine record with thirteen kayos notwithstanding. It didn't last long. These things never do. Pecho—which means "breast" in Spanish and connotes courage, which the kid was not entirely without—should have worn the advertising on the bottoms of his shoes. That way everybody would have been sure to see it.

After the main event, the cable TV lights went dark and the band started packing up to go home, which seemed to be the signal for Mike, Jr. to come locomoting out behind his mom and pop. Mike was wearing a rose-colored robe with a pale blue sash over knee-length pants with his name in script on one thigh. His opponent was a tall black kid from Starrett City, the huge middle-class housing complex out near Kennedy Airport. When the announcer said Mike was from the Bronx, no one in the crowd got up to protest because, in contrast with Moley, Mike's faction was limited to the people in his corner and a lone scribe along the press rim.

The fight was dull, excruciatingly so, and before long the fans were letting the fighters know it. Both kids had fast hands and both were willing enough, but they were still caught in the amber of amateur ways. Which is to say, they had no appreciation of defense or sense of measure. Each round began with the two kids coming electrically together in the center of the ring and availing themselves of more leather in a handful of seconds than Thom McAn can in a month. The trouble was, the fusillade lasted little more than that handful of seconds. The rest was lunging, brawling, slow dancing in the Big City.

The officials gave the fight to the kid from Starrett City, which seemed to surprise the Rosarios. There was no doubt that the decision angered them, and I suspect that had the match taken place in the amateur venue, which is more overtly political, the pair would have made a stink about it. Yet it struck me that Mike's own body language was eloquent in its support of the verdict. With the final bell the kid had slunk back to his corner, eyes down, tail drawn up under him, as if he were a favorite pooch caught piddling on the rug. The kid from Starrett City, meanwhile, oblivious to the crowd's granite indifference, ran around the ring throwing kisses.

There could be no argument about Johnny Luna's verdict. Johnny was matched with a flaxen-haired Latino who had apparently caught the fancy of Vidal Sassoon (or such, at least, seemed to be the import of the hairdresser's logo, which was emblazoned on the kid's red trunks and robe, as well as on the matching ensemble of his corner). The kid was good, all supple shoulders and sculpted combinations, but there was no telling how good he was. For it gradually became apparent that he was in with a one-handed fighter.

Johnny Luna tried to conceal the injury. He threw both mitts, especially at the beginning, with apparent abandon. But the grimace that closely attended upon the landing of each right, combined with what was surely a lack of clout in that hand, had to give him away. Clearly, it did. For by the start of the second chapter the hairdresser's kid was moving exclusively to his own left. Which is to say, to Johnny Luna's right and away from his left, which the kid must have figured out was the only hand that could possibly hurt him.

"*Venga*, Johnny! *Como tu padre!* C'mon, Johnny. Do like your father!" exclaimed a small chestnut-colored man in the audience, no doubt one of those cruel admirers of Julio Leon who told Johnny Luna he didn't hit hard.

"*Apetito, hijo!* You must have appetite, son!" said another man, a fool, sitting not far from the chestnut-colored fellow.

The man was a fool because appetite was the one thing Johnny Luna clearly did not lack. The kid's desire was so radiant you could feel the heat at ringside. For three rounds Johnny

Luna persisted in trying to match his opponent, blow for blow, even though his ability to punch was so diminished it looked like he wasn't punching at all, but dabbing the other fellow with powder, as if he were a babe fresh from a bath. Johnny Luna's vaunted defense, his ability to see and evade punches before they were thrown, had utterly deserted him. Indeed, hardly a punch seemed to miss him, and when one did, he appeared to stick his head out to collect it, rather than let it buzz harmlessly by.

This latter was merely a grim piece of whimsy that passed through my brain as I watched Johnny Luna undergo his battering. And, then, as the fourth round came into view—and Johnny ceased trying to lead or counterpunch, and did not attempt to clutch or tie up his opponent or do anything to protect himself, much less win the fight—I realized it wasn't whimsy at all. It came to me—and I don't know if this was something I was impressing upon the spectacle, some unearned bit of melodrama, some construct to tidy up, to make sense of what was playing out before me—that Johnny Luna was now only superficially fighting the hairdresser's kid. His real opponent was Iron Necessity itself.

It struck me that Johnny Luna had been caught up in one of those inexplicable tragic actions where the sins, or merely the weaknesses, of the fathers are visited on the sons. He was being punished for something that we are taught in school to call "hubris," or pride, or overreaching, which, in his case, was just reaching at all, trying to make something of his life. And, in some part of his blasted soul, I realized, the kid knew it and was not going to play ball. This sticking his head out for further abuse, well, it was Promethean stuff he was up to.

By this I mean, Johnny Luna knew he'd already lost the bout with the kid from Sassoon, but he was damned if he was going to lose the other one too. He was determined to meet the Gray Ones head on and to thumb his nose at them at the same time ("I must accept my fate," said Aeschylus's Prometheus, "as lightly as I may"), to show them that, yes, he might be beaten, but, no, he wasn't about to go mewlingly into the tank, just because they had him shackled to a rock and the eagle was making tartare of his liver.

After each series of punches, the hairdresser's kid would step back, somewhat as a lumberjack might pull back from a tree to watch it fall. Only Johnny Luna didn't fall. Invisible wires, guy lines of character, were holding him up. . . .

An hour later we were still numb. We were downstairs, sitting beneath the fluorescent lights in different corners of the hospital-green dressing room. The corridor outside was silent. Everyone else who had taken part in the gala evening had long since gone home.

Finally, Johnny Luna stood up and started removing his gear, which, with one hand, was not easily done. I watched him struggle for a few seconds, then got up and helped him shed his trunks and his foulproof cup, which were thick with sweat. Pretty soon Mike, Jr. came over and started unlacing the kid's shoes and Mickey got to work unraveling his hands. In what was becoming a family effort, Negra picked up one of the torn Foodtown bags that served the kid as both bureau and luggage, and she began putting his things in it.

"Johnny," she said. "You should have told me."

The kid looked wearily over at her, his eyes soupier than ever.

"You could have used my shopping bag. You know, the big one from Gimbels I got in my closet."

Chapter 8

A NIAGARA OF NOISE

Madison Square Garden has had several glimmering incarnations. It was dreamed into being for the first time in 1874 by Phineas T. Barnum, who carved it out of an aged depot left to rot by the New York and Harlem Union Railroad. The old bunco artist seized the four-acre site at Madison and Twenty-sixth Street to create his Monster Classical and Geological Hippodrome, which he promptly filled with the scarlet toys of his cornball imagination: Roman chariots with busty showgirl drivers and naughty skits on the libidinal doings of Bluebeard the ogre, as well as Japanese acrobats and waltzing elephants and sideshow freaks galore.

Erected five years later in the traces of the original, the second Garden was a decidedly more lavish affair and the first to carry the MSG name. Designed by Stanford White and directed by Barnum and J. P. Morgan, among others, it was a confection of yellow brick and white Pompeiian terra-cotta complete with cupolas and Moorish arches. Its crowning glory was a tower copied from the Giralda in Seville, which was topped off by Augustus Saint-Gaudens's naked statue of Diana the Huntress. Revolving on ball bearings and spot-lit at night, the statue was known to the matrons of the City as "that undraped hussy."

This Garden became a national showplace, the scene of a bewildering array of events. It was the site of six-day go-as-you-please (walk, run, or crawl) races, of aquatic exhibitions in the mammoth pool, of Elks conventions and the first American automobile shows. Paderewski played here and Bernhardt acted. Teddy Roosevelt stumped for office and Carry Nation for temperance. Annie Oakley shot glass balls out of the air and one night, at a dinner for 900, Harry K. Thaw put three lead balls through the head of Stanford White two years after learning that the architect had drugged and deflowered Harry's wife, the angelic Evelyn Nesbit, when she was a mere sixteen.

The third Garden was built in 1925 on the grounds of an old trolley barn at Eighth Avenue and Forty-ninth Street. It was a more practical and even more flexible place of business, as is the "New Garden," which—put up for $116 million in 1968, rising thirteen stories and containing 20,000-odd seats—resembles a child's drum. Yet the Garden is the Garden for all that, something more than its passing aspect or the sum of its current set of parts. The *New York Times* called it "one of the great institutions of the town," and the *New York Herald* termed it, "not a building, but a state of mind." Going these two one better, O. Henry proclaimed it "the center of the Universe."

O. Henry must have been in his cups. And yet for years, as far as the pre-Copernican world of boxing was concerned, the Garden was precisely that: the hub of the empyrean. All the greatest stars eventually turned out there, beginning with the Boston Strong Boy, the great John L. Sullivan himself, who on July 17, 1882, staged a four-round exhibition with British heavyweight Tug Wilson. Wilson won $1,000 and half the gate merely by remaining perpendicular. In those days, boxing was illegal in New York. To get around the ban, Joseph Durso tells us in *Madison Square Garden: 100 Years of History,* the promoters would bill the fighters as "professors" and claim they were offering "illustrated lectures" in the science of pugilism.

After 1920 the ruse was no longer necessary. Boxing came in off the barges, bringing into the Garden such talents as Benny Leonard and Jack Dempsey. The Garden became the red-hot center of what Jimmy Cannon called the "red-light district of sports." It was in the Garden that Gene Tunney experienced his only loss to Harry Greb and that Willie Pep took his lone decision in four mix-ups with Sandy Saddler. It was in the Garden that Joe Louis conducted much of his "Bum of the Month" tour, defending his laurels eight times and finally losing them to Rocky Marciano. It was in the Garden that Muhammad Ali and Joe Frazier came together for the first time in a contest Ali likened to death.

Madison Square Garden meant boxing, and everyone in the world knew it. Even those only nominally in the world knew it. Harry Markson, the arena's boxing man during the sixties, told of going to Rome to sign newly annointed middleweight champ Nino Benvenuti for a sequel with Emile Griffith. While in Rome, Markson managed to wangle an audience with the Pope. "I was introduced to Pope Paul," he remembered, "as 'Harry Markson of the Garden.' And the Pope stepped back, his face lit up, and he sort of exclaimed, 'Ah, Madison Square Garden—*boxing*.' "

This was the sort of feeling, the reverence for the Garden as a *locus classicus* for the boxing idea, that Mickey was attempting to grapple with one morning toward the end of March. It was the day of the Gloves Finals, and the trainer had gathered on the floor of that hallowed place—even as the arena work force was busy slapping the ring together a few yards away—the three youngsters who would be competing for City-wide honors. The trainer had no doubt that his kids understood what it meant to be fighting in the Garden. Actually, he was worried that they understood it too well and were overawed by the occasion. His concern was to convince them that what lay before them was just another outing, except, that is, for the fans.

"Now, this the thing I got to tell you," he said, winding up, "especially you, Chino, and you, Nelson, because it you first time here. Jackson, I expect you know this already. Anyway, you going to experience something this night you never experience before. I'm talking about the crowd. There going to be a million locos out there tonight and every mother son of them going to know you name. Hear what I'm saying now. This is the killer—not you opponent, but the crowd. You cannot let the crowd get to you, because, you do, well, you might as well take off them little pants and go on home. You got to do what you been doing all along. You got to tell youself, 'Hey, this the same ring I been fighting in down in the Felt Forum—they just carry it upstairs.' " The trainer waited to let this sink in. "You got to carry you fight upstairs too."

We stood there quietly watching the Garden no-sweats batten down the canvas, each of us locked in the solitude of his own private compartment, until Chino finally flipped the latch on his and walked out. "After I waste this guy tonight," he said with his usual winsome arrogance, "who I fight next?"

"Chicago," said the trainer. "Then maybe England."

"England? Who we fight there?"

"You fight England. They ain't got no Ricans there, you know."

"Just guys from England?"

"Okay. You fight cockneys, limeys, Wales—"

"Whales?" interjected Nelson. He seemed genuinely perplexed, worried even, as if anything were possible, even squaring off with Leviathan, at this level of competition. He shot an anxious look at Refugio, but the assistant trainer just shrugged, as did Jackson. Then he turned to me, but I wasn't about to help him. I was too interested in seeing what came next.

It was at this point that Chino, whom I suspect was equally in the dark, attempted to allay the kid's fears.

"Hey, don't worry, man," he said, fondling Nelson's shoulder. "I hear they got a lot of blubber on them."

By the time the big night rolled around, Chino already knew his final adversary rather well. We all knew him. This was the aforementioned "Rat Lips," a high-yellow youngster with lozenge-shaped freckles, dozy-looking eyes, and a mouth that never let up.

We first met the kid—or, better, he first thrust his existence upon us—in Yonkers, the scene of the second round of Gloves preliminaries for the 147-pound Novice Class. We were sitting on a rolled-up wrestling mat in the high school gymnasium, waiting for the fights to begin, when this ambulatory event in human disguise broke upon our collective attention.

"Hector Camacho from your gym?" he said loudly to a trainer a few yards away from us.

"He been up there all right," said the trainer, a big, friendly black fellow who was mostly legs, six foot five or better.

"You handled him in the amateurs."

"Not me, my—"

"I'd like to get that Camacho. I'd smoke 'em."

The trainer had started to say that it wasn't he who had developed Camacho, but his partner. It was clear, however, that Rat Lips wasn't interested in the nicety. He merely wanted a chance to rooster around, and not for the tall trainer's edification, but for ours.

"You got three good boys fighting tonight," he was saying a beat later to Mickey. "I hate to see them lose."

"Ain't nobody here going to lose," Mickey replied.

"That's good," said Rat Lips, widening one of those dozy-looking orbs, "cause I got plans for them."

The next week the kid chased Chino Number Two all over the ring and, ignominy of ignominies, into premature retirement. By this I mean, Mickey's kid was disqualified midway through the going, in effect, for failure to engage the enemy—this even though he had assured me beforehand that Rat Lips didn't worry him in the least. "I ain't scared of nobody," he had said, rather specifically, "less he got three balls."

Afterwards, Rat Lips dropped by the Rosario dressing room to gloat, naturally, and to stick it to Reggie and Chino Number One. "One down," the kid winked at Mickey's remaining welter-warriors. "Two to go."

He beat Reggie in the Semis, took him out, for all intents and purposes, as I said, downstairs in the Gloves field command merely by throwing him an amused sidelong glance when they announced the pairing. For whatever reason, that night after he disposed of Reggie the kid chose to spare us his company. Yet here he was back to haunt us on this evening of Golden Gloves Finals. He was standing just inside the door of the Gold dressing room (in the Finals the kids are given either blue or gold shirts and are assigned to matching changing closets). He was waiting, no doubt, to confer with Chino Number One. But Chino did not see him, as he was busy regaling Nelson with a triumph recently achieved in an altogether different arena.

Chino was a Casanova of famous attainment. Yet I gathered that his latest conquest was inadvertent and maybe vexatious. She was a friend of his mother's—by his lights, an impossibly ancient crone carrying nearly thirty-five years on the planet. Seemed she'd seen the kid walking down the street in his shiny new black jacket, the one that bunched at his waist, neatly set off his buttocks and flattered his shoulders. The woman had known him for years—that was the puzzlement. No matter. The shiny black jacket tipped her over the edge of civility into the uncharted country of desire.

"It just come over her," explained Chino. "She don't want it, but what can she do about it?"

"What your mother think?" asked Nelson.

"My mom ask this lady how come she never be by to visit no more. This lady say she can't come to our house. She feel so much passion she say she can't tell how she going to act."

"Dag!" said Nelson.

"Forget about it, if I will let her, she will try to have a physical relationship with me."

"Dag!" said Nelson, still more vehemently.

"You know how I know?" Nelson didn't. Neither did the rest of us. "Because when I come out from work one day, she there waiting for me. She say she looking for her brother and don't know I work there. But when I leave, she walk with me. And, you know, she, how you call it? She do this to me."

Chino Number One took Nelson's hand in his. He placed

the tip of his long middle finger in the black fighter's soft pink-white palm and swirled it slowly and luxuriously around.

"Dag!" said Nelson, giving a little shiver.

I'll say this for Rat Lips: He waited until Chino was through before beginning his harangue. "When that bell ring, it's destruction and destroy," he started in on Mickey's kid. "That's when they hand me a license to fold, spindle, and mutilate. Fact is, you can't lose with the stuff I use. . . ."

The genial black trainer with the legs of a Tennessee Walker was also hunkered down in the Gold dressing closet, although not for long. "Man, that shit's deep," said the trainer, getting up to leave. "Should of worn my hip boots."

The Casa Rosario contingent stayed put and heard the kid out with a uniformly bored expression. After he left, Mickey took Chino aside and fashioned for him an impromptu bestiary, locating Rat Lips within it.

"What we got here," said the trainer, "is a frightened creature. You might not think so, because he talk so bold. But the skunk, see, he put out an odor when he get scared." The trainer held his nose, and I sensed that there would be slides with this lecture. "A porcupine going to shoot them prickers off his back. *Poosh!*" Here Mickey used his index fingers to show long pointed objects rocketing off into space. "The turtle"—he crossed his chest with his arms and scrunched down for this one—"he got his shell. But poor ol' Rat Lips"—the trainer inhaled dramatically and shook his head in mock sympathy—"all he got is them lips."

The kids trotted down the runway leading out from beneath the seats that banked up and back for maybe half-a-dozen stories. Accompanied by their trainers and seconds, they made their way to the corners in lighting that was dimmed to create a sort of artificial twilight; and by the time they hopped up the steps to the ring itself the arena had been plunged into obscurity.

They stood there in their corners, wrapped in sable; then, suddenly, they were suffused with light, as a beacon from somewhere up above poured down upon them, bathed each kid by
turn, and a voice, Matt Cusack's, heralded their names and
their gyms' names and the litany of their accomplishments: "In
the Gold corner . . . from the Centerreach Boxing Club . . .
with a record of two knockouts and three decisions . . ."

During the fights themselves, the ring was illuminated and
the rest of the house was somewhat darkened. Looking back
over my shoulder from my seat along the press rim, I did not
think the fighters would be able to distinguish faces in the crowd,
not, certainly, above the first ten rows, which were splashed by
the ring lights. Above that demarcation, the spectators seemed
to blend into the shadows and, as the evening wore on, to be
increasingly concealed by a canopy of cigarette and cigar smoke.

It struck me that the crowd for the Golden Gloves Finals was
probably not so very different from that which used to gather
for the illegal prizefights in Regency England. I don't mean to
suggest that there were swells parading to and from the concession stand, snuff-tippling gentlemen of fashion in white box
coats and pigtails. Nor that there were coal heavers, watermen,
and butcher's boys roiling about. I'm talking about the mix of
the fancy, which did break down, roughly (as in the chroniclers
William Hazlitt and Pierce Egan), into dandies and groundlings,
carriage-traveling toffs and foot-toddlers. The toffs would be
the merchants and moguls, the magnates and mongers, who
kept the *Daily News* fat with ad pages and thus were awarded
the best seats in the house, who rose up from ringside in a surge
of blue serge. Above them was the pasture of the common
herd, the fighters' folks and relations, their girlfriends and
schoolmates, fight fans of modest means and various description. Down in the runway, meanwhile, were the milling and
flash coves, the kids from the clubs and their coaches whose
dreams of owning the City had been deferred for another year,
and the professional sharpers, managers, and promoters, the

patrons and parasites of the game, sweeping in and out of the arena, undulant as the tide.

The noise from the crowd was thunderous, as advertised. Yet it had the virtue, I thought, of being impersonal. I remembered one of Joyce's stories, how the snow was described as being "general" over Ireland. The clamor in the building seemed to be like that, comprehensive but indifferent. I remembered, too, Sugar Ray Robinson likening fighting in a major arena to being under a waterfall, a Niagara of noise, and that also seemed to be about right.

Yet even as I was thinking this, a handful of voices, apparently right behind me, began to insist on its particularity. The owners of the voices were getting some raffish mileage out of a kid from the islands whose hair seemed to geyser up through his headgear. "Hey, look, a Rastus-afarian." "No, it's a cone-head." "Who's got the smoke, or EXCUSE ME, the ganja?" "Hey, Sweeney"—this was said to the kid's opponent—"make him a bleeder. I never seen one of them bleed before."

This last voice was female. I know because I turned around and saw her. She was nothing, really, a pallid trifle with a red gash for a mouth and a pair of those boots Nancy Sinatra said were made for walking. Her companions were more interesting. Older than the girl, and no doubt deeper into the sauce than lobster in Newburg, they were both ensconced in wheelchairs and sporting customized gim'me hats, one of which identified the eminence underneath as HARRY THE HUMPER.

None of this, I was certain, would so much as put a crease in Chino. Chino was a tough kid, surely the toughest in the gym, Johnny Luna's recent heroics notwithstanding. He was someone, I fancied, who, even were he given notice of the sadness to come, might still have joined Leonidas' bunch at Thermopylae or Custer's at Little Big Horn. I don't mean to suggest that Chino was just another ghetto mouth-breather. For the kid had other suits as well, notably, a sparkling sense of humor, including about himself, which is not usual even among us less bellicose and "better-balanced" sorts. Plus, and this was the thing that finally got me: He was extremely affectionate, always touching you, fingering your shirtsleeve, saying your name (as if he savored it), and asking after your family (although he did not know them), whenever you conversed with him.

Chino was a bit of a puzzle to me, not the Gordian knot, perhaps, or something the Sphinx might waylay you with on the road to Thebes. But he was unlike anyone I'd ever met before on my shuttle through this vale—a quantum yoking together of innocence and violence. Thus, a few days before the Finals, I had gotten into my car and driven up to the South Bronx to try to unravel him. The plan was for the two of us to spend the afternoon together, for me to meet his mother and get some idea of what and where he came from—in short, to try to figure out why he was so different from me.

The kid's mother worked for one of those high-profile slum-town priests who do something more than make the daily lap around the rosary. This one was a durable old pol in clerical attire who puffed cigars, took the odd meal with the local power brokers, and put up housing for the poor. Chino and his mother and his three brothers had just moved into spanking new digs on Simpson Street. You could hear the sirens of police cars dispatched from the precinct house a mile or so up the road and, with the wind blowing in from the East River, you could learn more than you might care to know about the Hunt's Point Market. The view from Chino's balcony was limited, however, to other spanking new buildings and, in the gaps between them, to the Bruckner Elevated Expressway. As the kid's mother was held up indefinitely at work, I suggested a drive over to his old neighborhood.

It seems incredible, but the South Bronx was once a region of dairy farms and country estates, a landscape of rolling hills populated by gentlemen farmers who educated their sons at Princeton and Yale and abroad. So Arcadian a spot was it in the early nineteenth century that a poet named Joseph Rodman

Drake was capable of writing with his tongue nowhere near his cheek:

> *Yet I will look upon thy face again,*
> *My own romantic Bronx, and it will be*
> *A face more pleasant than the face of men.*

The Irish were the first of the white trash to descend upon the place in any number. They swarmed in late in the century to lay the ties for the Harlem Union Railroad and dig out the Croton Aqueduct. A stream of German farmers meandered in as well. Yet it was the subway that permanently altered the face of the Bronx. With its construction, everything changed. Between 1850 and 1900 the population grew from 8,000 to 200,000. By the late thirties, with the extension of the IRT, the body count had ballooned to 600,000. The quiet country town turned into a metropolis. Speculators threw up row after row of tenement housing. The Morrises, Freemans, Simpsons, *et al.*, the grandees of the borough's salad days, became the proprietors of sweatshops that put the Jews in harness. Later, in the forties and fifties, the Jews themselves took over and hitched up the Puerto Ricans.

It was sometime after the Second World War that the South Bronx began to take on its peculiar postapocalyptic aspect. Many blame rent control, which was instituted with the best intentions: to protect the immigrant from rent-gouging landlords. But when the men of property discovered they couldn't turn a profit, they started neglecting their buildings; and the whites, who were already afoot, stepped up their exodus to the Grand Concourse and Pelham Parkway, to Scarsdale and Rye beyond. Pressed by the City for back taxes, the landlords abandoned their holdings and/or prayed for a miracle, which generally arrived in the form of "Jewish lightning." Which is to say, they torched their buildings for the insurance.

Chino and I rode up into the area between Boston Post Road and the Bronx River. The streets were named for poets (Bryant and Longfellow), and they recalled the borough's agrarian past (West Farms and Hoe), but what I saw with Chino as my Virgil was hardly the stuff of urban pastoral. We plowed through a sea of run-down and nuked-out tenements and, as we did, the kid pointed out the shooting galleries, crash pads, and numbers drops, which did not disclose themselves to the untutored eye. We also passed several institutions of learning that Chino had attended and that sang their way back into memory purely in terms of fist-play on asphalt playgrounds. After one especially gory retelling ("This guy look like he been hit with a truck. Forget about it, Bill, even I got to feel sorry for this guy"), I broached the topic of my inquiry.

"Chino, you know what I don't understand? You're such a warm and affectionate person—"

"That's because you so cute, Bill."

"No, no, I mean it."

"So do I."

"Okay. Why do you think you fight so much?"

"I don't fight so much, you know. Not any more, now that I got Mickey and the gym."

"What about last week with Los Muchos?"

"That's different. I got jumped. You got to fight when you get jumped. But you know why I start fighting, I mean when I'm small?"

"No. Tell me."

"Because of my name."

"Your name?"

"Sure. You know my real name, right?"

"No."

"You don't think my mother name me Chino, do you?"

"No, I guess not."

"I will tell you my real name," said the kid, leaning across the car seat and lowering his voice. "But you don't got to tell the guys in the gym, right?"

"Fair enough."

"Wilmer."

"What's wrong with Wilmer?"

"I know—it's the name of the guy that build the airplane, right? But the kids would pronounce it 'Wil-MA.' "

"Like a girl?"

"Bill, every time they call me Wilma Flintstone, I got no choice, I got to hit them. Remember, we go by P.S. One-fifty? Forget about it, they's dying for me to get out of that school. To make a point, they don't leave me back, even if I can't read."

"But that was when you were small. What about when you got older? You kept fighting, right?"

"We used to fight because we have to."

"Why did you have to?"

"Because the guys we used to fight, they's like bullies. And you don't take care of it now, you got to in the future. Better to take care of it now."

"You never started fights yourself?"

"Sometimes."

"Maybe people thought you were a bully."

"Maybe they did. Maybe they was right." Chino smiled at this, a modest smile, not his famous one. "What about you, Bill? You don't fight when you's a kid? What, it so long ago they don't invent fighting yet?"

"Thanks a lot. It was around. But nobody I knew did it, not really, not the way you and your buddies did."

"So what'd you do for, how you call it, recreation?"

I looked at him. I assumed he was still jerking me. But he wasn't, he was serious. He really wanted to know what kids from my tax bracket and with my color skin did with their excess energy and animus, how they amused themselves, if not by standing toe-to-toe and trying to take each other's head off.

It was one of those strange and disquieting moments—and there'd been any number of them with Mickey—when I abruptly realized that I was every bit as exotic to my partner in conversation as he was to me. When I realized that the cliché was even less serviceable than I had thought. People were *not* "all alike beneath the skin."

I told Chino that my friends and I used to do things, sports mostly, in season. That we played tennis, swam at the local country club during the summer. That, with the onset of winter, we got out our hockey stuff and went over to the rink or river, switched from tennis to squash. ("Squash?" It's a little like tennis, only indoors. "They build a tennis court indoors?" Well, sort of, actually a whole string of them.)

Chino was awestruck by this, by this what? This Fitzgerald short story or Currier & Ives print come to life, this glimpse of what was to him an impossibly privileged childhood. Yet he was no more amazed than I was, when, a few minutes later, he told me we'd reached our destination.

"This is it," he said, "where I grew up."

Where? This building right here?

"Yes."

Jesus, what happened to it?

I was incredulous. Nobody could have lived here. Chino's family seat was the only building still upright on its block. It was a squat, gray five-story structure whose windows had been boarded over. The boards themselves were adorned with vinyl decals complete with a floral pattern, which were supposed to do what? I wondered. Make poverty more appealing?

"My mom was the super," Chino explained. "Everyone know and respect her. But when she leave, the people don't take care of the building no more. You heard about the lady that got killed last week when she walking with her two kids?"

No, I didn't.

"She walking right over there, down West Farms Road, going to a bingo game. A sniper got her."

Did you know the woman?

"No, but my mom did. Bill, you asking why I always fighting when I'm a kid. Forget about it, over here everybody fight with everybody. Over here's the hardest the South Bronx was. You seen that movie, *Fort Apache?* That's this district. You seen the part where they throw the kid off the roof? Well, it's like that too. See, there's a club over there?" Chino pointed across a broad rubble-strewn lot with a broken-down bandbox in the middle of it. "See that blue door? That used to be a hangout for the Seven Immortals. They was a gang. The detecs used to come and rumble with them."

The detecs?

"Cops. You used to see kids up on the roof, kids from every-where, from here, from there, from where I live, from across the street. And all you see coming down is rocks, bottles, gar-bage, on the detecs. Maybe fifty or a hundred kids is up there on them roofs. And you don't see nobody on the street. Just the people the detecs is having problems with. Hey, we got time, right? Let me take you around the corner to Hoe Avenue where I used to play each day, and you could see where I start my career."

What career is that?

"My career as a jaw-breaker, what else?" said Chino.

This time he smiled his famous smile, tilted back his head in silent laughter, and raised the curtain on a maharajah's ransom in ivory.

There were times when I believed that boxing was solely about fear. Show me a boxer, I thought, and I will show you fear in a handful of dust. I believed this, to an extent, even before I got into the ring and knew it, in my case at least, to be true.

I got confirmation in this belief from a strange quarter. I say "strange" because I quickly discovered that nobody in the game would allow that a pugilist of quality, a Tommy Hearns, say, or an Alexis Arguello, could possibly fight scared. Nobody would allow this, that is, but Constantine "Cus" D'Amato, who insisted upon it.

D'Amato was different from other people in the fight racket, or anywhere else, for that matter. He was an eccentric legend in the sport, the type of integrity in a game where that virtue does not exactly abound, a species of knight-bachelor who gained his reputation by standing up to the boxing monopolists of the fifties and almost single-handedly bringing them down. For the rest, I discovered, he was something more rare and quirky: an American original. By this I mean, he was completely self-taught, in a sense, self-created—a high school dropout from the Bronx (which lay across his voice like gravel across a dirt road) who regarded the prejudices of the day, or even the accumulated wisdom of the ages, as the merest hearsay, as, at most, a kicking-off point for his own investigations.

I visited D'Amato, at Mushy's suggestion, shortly after beginning my own training. I journeyed up to the old man's redoubt in upstate New York, high above the Hudson River at its most lordly, and fenced with him for the better part of a day before he finally warmed to me and granted me access to the particulars of his life.

D'Amato told me that, as a kid, he'd had an unshakable "preoccupation with death." On where this preoccupation came from, however—whether it was caused by his mother dying when he was just four, or by the fact that three of his seven brothers were already gone the dusty way by the time he came along, or simply by his coming of age in a neighborhood that gave rise to Dutch Schultz and Frankie Carbo and other leading men whose pictures hung in the post office, a neighborhood where death was a way of life—he did not care to speculate. All he chose to reveal was that he used to watch funerals go by with a perverse desire to change places with the fellow in the box, and that, for a time, he thought about becoming a priest, presumably a Jesuit.

The obsession with death led him to experiment. One day he sealed off the kitchen in his family's Frog Hollow apartment, put his head in the oven, and turned on the gas. He managed to save himself at the last minute by staggering to the window, somehow jimmying it up, and draping himself over the sill for the better part of an hour. "I don't know how I got the window open," he said. "Next thing I did was try hanging. Sounds crazy, but I was damn curious, curious about dying."

D'Amato was curious about everything. He read Einstein and a pamphlet on astrology with equal interest, always looking for something he could use, secrete into his own cosmos. Yet he was especially curious, I think, about the things he feared, or that society believed any man in his right mind should fear. And, being a person of extraordinary fiber, he was determined to confront those fears, even egg them on. Thus, his taking on the International Boxing Club. Thus, I suspect, his interest in boxing in the first place.

When it came to handling youngsters, D'Amato was not simply a manager and a trainer, but a teacher whose curriculum was premised upon fear itself. Before his kids even clapped eye on the gym, he would sit them down in his parlor for days, sometimes for weeks on end, and attempt to tease out their private doubts and insecurities. Once he had these little fears out in the open and, therefore—he was a Freudian in this respect—shorn of their menace, he would move onto the big fear, the one that undergirded the pastime itself. The old man would tell his youngsters that fear was the fight game's dirty little secret. He would tell his kids that, when it came time to climb into the ring, they would experience a rumbling down below such as they had never felt before; that when they actually did get between the twine and started fielding punches, they would be as helpless and timorous as a newborn babe; and that there was no shame in it, for every fighter, whether he is willing to admit it or not, discovers terror in the ring.

"What is the difference between a hero and a coward?" the old courage-teacher would ask his charges. "Nothing," he would say. "Both experience fear. Except the hero dominates his fear and the coward lets his dominate him.

"Fear is like a fire. If you control it, as we do when we heat our houses, it is a friend. When you don't control it, it consumes you and everything around you.

"See, Nature is smarter than anyone knows. She gives us fear for a reason. I want you to imagine a deer crossing an open field. He's approaching the forest when his instinct tells him, 'Think! There may be a mountain lion in the trees.' The moment that happens, Nature starts the survival process, which is injecting adrenaline into the bloodstream, which causes the heart to beat faster and enables the deer to perform extraordinary feats of strength and agility. Normally a deer can jump five or ten feet. With adrenaline he can jump fifteen or twenty, enough to get away from immediate danger. Fear, you see, is Nature's way of preparing us for a struggle. Without it, we'd die. . . ."

I have shanghaied Cus D'Amato and dragged him back into this chronicle, not just because he was such a singular mind and presence, but because Mickey was worried about Chino. Because, from what he knew of him, and from what he could see on this night of Golden Gloves Finals, the youngster had no fear of his opponent whatsoever. Because, given his slender talent as a boxer, he certainly should have.

In my conversations with him, D'Amato could remember just two kids who were completely fearless. Both of these youngsters were deaf and thus were impervious to the anxiety that sliced through a dressing room before a fight, that could be felt in the passages of silence between the japes and the horseplay that often served as emotional camouflage. D'Amato said the deaf kids were a danger to themselves because they had no fear, because they thought themselves, like the mythical salamander, capable of inhabiting fire without getting burned.

If the scuffle with Rat Lips turned out to be an altogether different affair from the one I'd expected, it was not Chino's doing. For the youngster comported himself pretty much the way I thought he would, especially as the contest wore on and Mickey was persuaded to toss out his prefight strategy.

But let me back up some and fill. Let me start by saying that Chino was the kind of fighter boxing people call a "zebra." In other words, much as he might have looked like the other ponies in his trainer's stable, he was not like them in one vital respect: He was an unmitigated hardhead, essentially untrainable, just like that striped critter of the African veldt.

Now, Mickey knew this, of course, better than anyone. And yet, for reasons that I initially found hard to understand, he still tried to make Chino bring a fight that wasn't in him. He told the kid during their prefight get-together that he could not just breeze out there, per usual, and expect to find a permanent resting place for the straight left hand. Rather, he had to bring a more considered attack. He had to go in under cover of the jab, which, in Chino's case, as he was a southpaw, meant the right hand.

Such was the kid's trust in the trainer that he did not balk at the directive but did his best to carry it out. Chino did make his first sally under cover of the jab. The trouble was, Chino's right hand was a rather skimpy piece of business, which, for all the cover it provided, might have been designed by Frederick's of Hollywood. After several forays conducted behind this jab proved unavailing, the kid began, rather fitfully, to revert back to his old ways. Notably, he threw two absolutely barbarous left hands, which you could have probably seen coming all the way from West Farms Road.

No, it was not Mickey's kid, but his kid's opponent who surprised me. I'd been misled by the kid's devastating victories over Reggie and Chino Number Two, fooled into thinking him a two-fisted *pistolero,* when what he had been in those fights, against two youngsters he had completely cowed and half put away already with rhetoric alone, was merely opportunistic.

Far from being a slugger, Rat Lips showed himself to be that sweetest of fistic varieties: the counterpuncher. By this, however, I don't mean to confuse the kid with the tribe of Chino Number Two. He was not *that* sort of "counterpuncher," not the kind who is just in there to survive, to engage in round upon round of after-you-dear-Alphonse, the kind known to the cognoscenti as the "agony fighter." Quite to the contrary, Rat Lips was the sort of counterpuncher who was always open to the main chance, even creating it after a fashion. He was the kind who would go so far as to offer his opponent a little piece of himself, who would take the other fellow's specialty punch, but as lightly as possible, or who would throw some purposely half-ass punches and let the opponent stop them, purely to give him the feeling he was getting something done, and then quickly smack him three good ones of his own.

All of this—having his left hand stapled to his side, even as he was getting cuffed about by his unfettered opponent—had Chino in a terrible funk. And returning to home base after the first lamentable go-round, he made no effort to hide it, but plunked down heavily on the stool and, head bent, elbows on knees, stared morosely at the patch of canvas between his feet.

"Something wrong?" said Mickey, as he extracted the kid's gumshield and Negra reached in with the water.

By way of answer, the youngster merely shifted on the stool.

"Don't tell me," said the trainer. "Let me guess—you want to fight this fellow. Am I right?"

This time Chino lifted his head and glowered at the trainer, then shrugged. "You the boss."

"You got *that* right." The trainer paused a moment. "Okay, I'm going to let you fight him. Only you can't just fight this kid. You got to rough him up. Understand?"

Chino nodded.

"You got to steal that desire from him. You got to make him wish he stood in bed or took up another line of work. Understand?"

Chino nodded again.

"Okay, so how we going to do this?"

"Body."

"Right, we got to light him up with body shots. Let's see what this Rat Lips got inside."

If the two kids had been gladiators courting the favor of Rome, Chino would have been the thickly muscled brute with the sword and suit of armor, and Rat Lips the skinny fellow with the fisherman's net, the one who waited for his opponent's misstep so to put the trident to him. Rat Lips was shrewd, patient, wonderfully resourceful, a bit like Smooth only smoother, more fully evolved. He was someone, to paraphrase Archie Moore, to whom you could give 200 pounds of steel wool, then sit back and watch him knit you a stove. Where Chino knew but one thing—to keep coming forward and flail that left arm and take no prisoners—Rat Lips knew a bunch of things and put most of them to use. He played the fox to Chino's hedgehog.

Toward the end of the second round, the kid hit Chino with a combination that had more tiers than a fancy wedding cake. It was clear, to me, at least, that Chino wasn't hurt, merely bewildered. But so spectacular was the combination, the referee felt compelled to give him a standing eight-count anyway. Worse, when Chino came back to the corner at round's end, you could see that he was incubating an egg over the right eye. One well-placed dart and the thing would surely spew its contents all over the place, and the referee would be forced to call matters to a halt, if for no other reason than to save the folks at ringside from nausea.

I was beginning to see why Mickey had sought to throw a blanket over his kid, why he'd wanted him to just box this fellow, even if it cost him the fight. As old Mush might have said of the spectacle before us, it was like watching hamburger slug it out with a meat grinder.

And yet a boxing match, even one between laymen, is never merely a spectacle. Nor is it a simple narrative. It is a story constructed before our eyes. It is a run of seemingly casual events straining toward meaning, searching for a way to cohere in a plot (complete with beginning, middle, and end), so to illuminate character, usually one character in particular, that of the hero. It seemed, for a time, that the elements in front of us were determined to fuse in a fairly straightforward tale with little in the way of complication: that Rat Lips would be consecrated the hero; that the turning point would prove to have been the raising of the goiterlike growth over Chino's right eye; that from that moment forward the action would plunge toward a resolution that would seem to have been inevitable from the moment the principals tied on the gloves.

There is, however, another kind of story—a detective or mystery story, if you will—one where you, the reader, think you are paying strict attention to the text before you, sorting out the details and assigning them their proper formal and hierarchical meanings. But you are not, you are mistaken. You are possessed by the false story that has taken insidious shape in your mind, and you don't see the real clues that sail, unweighted, innocuously, by, like leaves on a rushing stream.

What I hadn't noticed was that Rat Lips's tactic of taking Chino's specialty punch—in however small a quantity, in however inoffensive a place (the shoulder, arms, and so on)—was beginning to cost him, as was his hauteur. I didn't notice this until Chino buggy-whipped a fairly ordinary left hand into his opponent's hip, and the kid's eyes, well, the way they lit up, they made me think of a raccoon discovered by flashlight in the middle of the night.

Rat Lips's arrogance consisted of this: his belief that skill would always out. Yet, as old Nestor, Cus D'Amato, liked to say, boxing is 75 percent mental and emotional, and only 25 percent physical. A boxing match is not primarily a contest of skill, but a test of wills. "Any fighter that fought Muhammad Ali," D'Amato told me, "was intimidated by him. You see, Ali's secret weapon was a tremendous will to win, an ability to take his own fear and project it as an irresistible force, which immediately tended to inhibit the ability of his opponent to execute what he knew."

Rat Lips did not fall apart, not completely. He was too experienced, too slick, for that. But he did seem to forget most of what he knew. Where only moments before he had been hooking off the jab—or inducing Mickey's kid to lead, then stepping inside the arc of his punch and beating him with a short, crisp left hand—he was now unabashedly on the lam, putting down his felony shoes, one in front of the other, as fast as he could pick them up.

None of this was lost, of course, on the gentle folk behind me. "Hey, Sambo," bellowed Harry the Humper at Rat Lips, who, I suddenly realized, had his hair done up in corn rows for the occasion. "Better watch your black ass. It's harvest time."

And Nancy Sinatra: "C'mon, greaser. Fuck 'em up!"

Alas, a boxing match is a story told in time. And time, as they say, was passing like greased Purina through a short dog. In the end, Chino could only add a twist to the plot. He could not make himself the hero.

To understand what happened next, to get a line, I mean, on the crazy business with Nelson and Nelson's father and the Garden rent-a-cops, it may help to know something about Negra's current state of mind. People, events, just plain things were starting to crowd her, to push her to a place where she would not allow for coincidence, for the merely random or simply fluky. Everywhere she looked she saw pattern and design and nasty intent. It was just a matter of time, I thought, before she lost it completely.

The day before the Finals we were sitting, Negra and I, in the Delightful Restaurant. I was hunched over coffee and my usual pineapple cheesecake, and she was sluicing down Coca-Cola. (Have I mentioned that Negra wouldn't drink water—for roughly the same reason W.C. Fields supposedly said he never did, which was that fish did their business in it—but knocked back five or six family-sized bottles of Coke a day?) She was briefing me on the latest sequence of treachery and misadventure to befall her and Mickey and the gym.

A kid named Sapo, or Toad, whom the Rosarios had taken into their home, had gone down to New Orleans to live with another ex-am of theirs who was campaigning, among the money fighters, as a middleweight. By way of parting shot, the little reptile lifted ten pairs of Negra's jeans, which, as I'd never seen her in skirts, had to make up the better part of her wardrobe.

Then there was Markie, a sad-eyed waif who hung out at the gym but had little stomach for fighting and none at all for training. Markie had been arrested for, of all things, belting a teacher. Also busted, apparently for letting his fingers do the walking in a midtown department store, was a kid named Madero. Madero was missing for days ("This kid's mother lose so much weight she look like a concentration camp."), until Mickey called in a chit and a cop he knew dug Madero out of the Tombs.

Most distressing of all, the Boxing Commission had hauled in Johnny Luna, ostensibly to take a look at his hand. While he was in there, they sprung an eye test on him, only this time Mickey was made to cool his heels in another room. The commission found the kid to be legally blind and told him he could never box again, not in the state of New York or anywhere else its findings held sway. ("The doctor who do this is a black man," said Negra. "But he ain't from here. He don't know he giving Johnny Luna a death sentence. Bill, why these people got to mess with things they don't understand?")

The rehearsing of the calamities had a curious effect on Negra. They caused her to grow moist around the eyes and soft all over, to visibly pine for the kids of the past, who, as she spoke, seemed to come before us in cameo. There was Tommy Flores, who used to tie her braids to the seat when they would take the bus to the Ohio State Fair and all the kids would see him doing it and wait for her to get up, then laugh like crazy; and there was Tito, who had a plate in his head from the war and could feel the weather like Negra herself could; and this other kid Salina, who used to go to the Feast of Saint Carmen with her, the one where they would carry the saint down First Avenue and all these people would walk behind it, dressed in white and barefoot and crying out for forgiveness. . . . Above all, there was Robert Rodriquez, the youngster she and Mickey inherited from the "Little Man," a trainer from Castle Hill who gave up on the kid because he was so wild and dared Mickey to do anything with him. Robert ended up winning the Gloves for the Rosarios, which did not mean they succeeded in taming him. Far from it—Mickey would toss the kid out of the gym once a month, and each time he would go and bat his baby browns at Negra, who would say to him, "Robert, you want back in the gym? Well, you go tell Mr. Rosario you not his fighter. You *my* fighter. And I ain't thrown you out yet."

The dilatation on Robert summoned the shade of another lovable con man, a skyscraper of a Jamaican heavyweight named Pete Minott. Pete Minott had never met Robert Rodriquez, who preceded him at the gym by a couple of years, but he was nevertheless heaped by him—obsessed by the kid's memory, especially as it continued to live and breathe in the Rosarios' daily conversation. One Mother's Day, Pete called up Negra and asked her what booty she had received. When she laughed and said none, he arrived at the door with two packages, one bigger than the other, both wrapped in the Sunday funnies. When Negra opened the smaller package and found an eight-ounce bottle of Joy, she thanked the youngster for his thoughtfulness. When she opened the second package and discovered a color TV, she said, "Peter, Peter, why do you do this?" Answered Peter, "Because I want you to love me more than him." A year later, intent upon discovering just who this Robert Rodriquez was and in what exactly consisted his preferment, Pete followed the kid into the Marines, pursued him to Camp Lejeune, where they both figured on the boxing team. Shortly thereafter, Negra received a phone call from Robert, saying, "Mom, there's some nut down here named Pete Mi-nutt. And he's following me everywhere." "Quiet, Robert," shushed Negra. "He's jealous about you."

Negra's memories seemed to have a life and logic of their own, and she was, more, I think, than anyone I had ever known, a prisoner of their whimsy. Before long she was skittering back and forth between nostalgia and anguish: One moment she was warm and toasty and fond, the archetypal grandmother of the fairy tale; the next moment she was drawn and fierce and bereft, Rachel from the Bible weeping for her lost children.

She started telling me about these three brothers, kids from the gym she got involved with and wanted to take into her home but didn't because they had a home of their own. She used to tell them that if they won a fight she would bake them a cake and decorate it with flowers and put their names on it; and she did, she baked them many a cake. Emilio was the older brother, the one with the mole on his cheek. Esteban was the middle one, and then there was Ernesto, who was also called "Cat's Eye." "He was the same age as Mike Jr.," Negra remembered. "He was like my own. Anything I would buy for Mike, I would buy for him. When they get a kick from roller skating, I buy skates for Mike and I buy for Cat's Eye too. Then the mother get jealous of me and take Cat's Eye away. She tell me she don't want her son with me and Mickey because we teaching him such a rude sport. I will never forget, she come up to me and she say, 'How you could let you son get beat up like that, and you just look at it?' This lady's name was Fernanda and I say to her, 'Let me tell you something, Nanda. I rather see my son doing this than see him out on the street shooting some dope into his vein.'

"One day me and Mickey come back from a show, and a girl tells me, 'There's a lady out on the street screaming you name.' And it Cat's Eye's mother. Cat's Eye had got caught with some drugs and they have him in jail. 'See, Nanda,' I say to her, 'you get so jealous because you think I'm going to take you son from you. You take you son back from us, and this is where you send him.' Mickey go over to the Juvenile Hall and get Cat's Eye out, and Cat's Eye stay with us and later in life we get him into the National Guard. Esteban turn out to be a lawyer in the downtown courts—can you imagine that? His brother, Emilio, go to Puerto Rico and gets married. He become a kick boxer and gets very good at it.

"You meet Clemente, right? Mike, Jr.'s other best friend is a kid named Baby. For some reason, I been thinking a lot about

Baby. I don't know why—maybe because of all these bad things that been happening to us. Baby would come and live with us a month at a time. He got a mother that I never meet. Baby's a good mechanic. He's a kid that own the streets, like Clemente or Chino Number One. But he always so afraid of dying. He would call me in the middle of the night. 'Negra?' he would say. 'What?' 'I'm scared. I'm here all alone.' 'Where are you, Baby?' 'Come get me.' 'Tell me, what you scared of?' 'I'm scared of dying.' It's two or three in the morning and I would wake Mickey and send him across the street to the project, and Mickey would bring Baby back and he would stay in Mike's twin bed, the bed Ralphie now got. Baby's a white-skinned, freckle-faced, red-haired Puerto Rican, and I would sit next to him and joke with him, and he would tell me over and over he's ascared of dying. 'Why you always thinking about that? You just a kid. You not going to die for a long long time.'

"A week before school open, Baby's thirteen. It's raining and he come up to our house and he and Mike go downstairs with Mike's bike. Mickey tell them they got to be careful with the bike, it slippery out. When I go downstairs I ask Mike where the bike at, and he tell me he lends it to Baby to go over to One hundred twenty-eighth Street. I ask him what Baby wants over there? There's buses there. Then, all of a sudden, this man is coming round with Mike's bike. It don't look like nothing hit the bike. It look good—maybe the sissy pole's a little bit bended. Mickey run to where the man say Baby is, but Mike is there first and Baby is talking to him. He saying, 'Mike, don't let me die. Please, don't let me die. I can't breathe. Please Mike.' My Mikie tells him, 'No, Baby, I ain't going to let you die. My pop going to be here soon.' And Mickey get there and start to giving him the mouth-to-mouth so he could breathe, and the ambulance come and they put the mask on so he could keep on breathing. The next day I call the hospital to see how Baby's doing and they say, 'Oh, he took his last breath this morning.'

"You know, Bill, they's all babies, really. And sometimes I

think they just ain't got a chance. Another kid, Berto, they shoot him in the head three times—that must have been five– six years ago. He's mistaken for his brother on One hundred nineteenth, right near Patsy's Restaurant. His brother was into dealing. I remember we was in Ohio at the state fair and we was all going into a restaurant, and Mickey say, 'Ain't you coming in?' I say, 'No, I don't feel so good for my head. I want to be left alone.' I keep wondering why Berto would be coming into my mind in Ohio. He so far away. Then, all of a sudden, I feel something that go *pow!* in the top of my skull.

"But let me tell you about Berto. Berto had come from Puerto Rico. When he come to the gym he's wearing a girl's coat. The kids are laughing at him. Now, Clemente, he's a pitiful guy—he feel for everybody. He buy Berto a jacket. But first I got to look at these kids and say, 'How you like somebody to laugh at you? No? Then wipe them smiles and introduce youself to the kid and shake hands with him. Tell them you name, boy.' Berto get attached to us and everywhere we go, Berto go too. We used to call him 'Bro' because we would go to a show and he would see a fighter about his size and he would say, 'Hey, bro, how much you weigh?' Then he would say, 'You want to fight me, bro?' That's all he knew in English. He was a good little fighter. He wore an Afro and he believed in witchcraft and he died when he was about seventeen years old. Once when a bird flew into my house he worried about the bad luck. I went to his funeral all four days just to be with him. I get up early on the fifth day, and I go down there and I find out they already send him back to Puerto Rico.

"We had a lot of nice kids. We had bad times, we had good times, we had suffering times. And when something happen to one of them kids, Mickey cry like a baby. He don't want to sleep. He start to walking the street all through the night. He just can't accept they have to die. Sometimes, Bill, you give so much, you just give and you give and you give, and you wonder for what you are giving, because they take it all away from you. And you get all twisted up inside. . . ."

*   *   *

For the better part of a round, Nelson didn't do too badly against a more seasoned kid from the Jerome B. C. Nelson had a stiff, upright style with no bend to it, but he showed he could punch a little, even if he didn't know how to elude the return fire. Then, suddenly, for no apparent reason, he started wobbling all over the ring, as if his legs had a private agenda, which did not include standing up to the kid from Jerome.

In the corner between stanzas, Refugio went at Nelson's left leg with both hands, as if he were wringing a towel, pausing now and then to finger the *collares* beneath his shirt and look up toward the heavens and yammer something, a prayer, I guess, to his gods. Mickey, meanwhile, was directing his entreaties to the kid himself, telling him he needed to invest more heavily in lateral movement and flurry his fanny off, if he truly wanted to win. "You want fame?" asked the trainer. "You want success, you want to be known as a finisher?"

These were all, surely, worthy goals. But seconds later, the efforts of Nelson's corner, both sacred and profane, went for naught, when the kid stood up to re-engage and abruptly pitched backwards into the turnbuckle. The two cornermen had assumed the youngster was suffering a cramp, when his trouble was more radical. Apparently—and we did not learn this until later—the kid from Jerome had stepped on Nelson's foot in the initial episode; when Nelson attempted to pull free, he shattered at the ankle in several tiny places.

Stranger business by far was going on in the runway.

If Negra is to be believed—and she has to be, up to a point, since I have little else but her testimony to go on—she and Ralphie were standing in the passage between the dressing corridor and the arena, watching Nelson's fight, when a ruckus developed in front of them. A squad of Garden security cops had formed a flying wedge and was plowing its way through the congested multitude, dragging behind it a human form that turned out to be Nelson's father. We later found out that Nelson *père,* in an understandable but imprudent attempt to get a snapshot of his son *in flagrante bello,* had breeched the barrier that protected the press from contamination by the working stiffs at ringside. Negra, of course, was in the dark as to the nature and magnitude of the older Nelson's transgression. Yet, given her mind-set at the time, I suspect that she would not have cared to be enlightened. Which is to say: All Negra could see, in her "twisted" state, as she watched the Garden militia strong-arm Nelson's father, was that "they" were once again hurting one of her own.

What exactly the lady did next is open to argument, and speculation. According to one of the Garden's finest, whom I overheard maybe ten minutes later when I finally arrived upon the scene, Negra came flying out of nowhere, dived upon the cohort of blue shirts, teeth bared, talons unfurled, as if she were a Harpy determined to make a meal of them. ("Is that the one who kicked Smitty in the balls?" were the actual words I heard outside the cell on the dressing-room corridor where, by that time, they had Negra and her younger son incarcerated. "Yeah, that's the bitch," came the reply. "She ain't gettin' out, either.")

Yet according to the malfeasor herself, whom I interviewed some days later upon her return from the hospital, she was substantially more sinned against than sinning. "It all happen," she told me, "like the dream I have the night before, where I see me and Ralphie in a room with these men in blue. I'm watching Nelson's fight and my son is next to me. All of a sudden, they forcing this man inside, and I hear a voice, 'Negra, help me! Help me, Negra!' Then this big fat man is shoving me against the wall. He's grabbing my hand and bending it behind my back and saying, 'You started the whole thing. I'll break you arm, bitch!' Ralphie seen this and he try to come to my rescue, but this other man in blue with the salt and pepper hair—like you hair, Bill—he get hold of him, and the two mens push us inside a room. And, you know, Ralphie's so skinny, the other man take him and use his head like a ram into the wall. I get free of the fat man and I grab the salt and pepper's arm and I say, 'Let go my son!' Then the fat man got me again and he go like this to me with his knee.''

What, he kneed you in the stomach? I asked.

"Kneed me in my operation, where they take the ovary. That's why I go to the hospital.''

Where was Nelson's father at this point?

"They give him over to the City cops, and I hear from the mother they take him down to to the tunnel, you know, where they keep the horses, and they whip the living days out of him. The mother say they put him unconscious.''

I heard one of them say you kicked them?

"Ha, that's a lie. You know the other guy, the salt and pepper, after he beat up Ralphie, you know what he do? He take a cigarette into his mouth like a movie star.'' Negra leaned back against the wall, put her fingers to her lips, pretended to inhale deeply and blew imaginary smoke rings. "I see him doing this and I say, 'That make you a big shot, don't it, man—to beat up a scrawny little kid that's half you size? You think you a big star, right? You must watch a lot of TV.' ''

Anyway, the short of it is, I ended up having to fish out, not just Negra and Ralphie, but Mickey too. For, naturally, when he and I arrived on the scene, and he saw that the Garden S.S. had his wife and son in their hairy mitts, the trainer didn't stop to sort things out, but jumped right in, paying no mind to the fact that, by this time, there must have been twenty blue shirts of various affiliation cruising the dressing-room corridor, each of them massaging his night stick with lubricious anticipation. Fortunately, before he sank from view, the trainer yelled at me to run and get a friend of his, a cop, not a rent-a-cop, but a real one, a full-fledged inspector on the NYPD, who was sitting ringside.

It turned out that the inspector was less than thrilled by the opportunity to extract the Rosarios from this latest spot of trouble ("What?" he said. "Them again? Jesus, these people should have me on retainer.''). But he did it—he came and cajoled his fellow defenders of the peace to let Mickey out of the makeshift hoosegow, to parole him long enough to see Jackson through the Finals, even as Negra, accompanied by Ralphie, was whisked off to the hospital to check on her complaint about pains in her middle.

Walking over to the dressing room to meet up with Jackson, I noticed that Mickey was strangely elated. What's up? I asked.

"This could be the biggest break we been looking for."

How's that?

"Suing the Garden. You can't tell me that turkey can get away with kicking Negra in the ovary." The trainer was practically crowing. "Hey, I don't want no food concession neither. *I want the whole store!*"

Have I mentioned that Mickey was also litigious?

It was a hook that nearly turned Jackson into a still life. It came during the waning seconds of the opening stanza, and its source was one Horatio Horn. Jackson was shook up bad, but he did not altogether crumble. He made a pass at the canvas with one knee before regaining his footing, which suggested that he'd picked up on the punch sometime before it arrived and had at least partly prepared his mind to receive it. No matter, not to Horn, who raced to the neutral corner and vaulted onto the ropes, from whence he essayed to whip the fancy into a frenzy.

Horn must have been waiting for this moment, and what it portended, all year long. He was one of the brothers who'd improvised Jackson's portrait, so to task it, on the heavy bag at the Bedford-Stuyvesant club. Horatio was the older brother. The younger one was named Marcellus (suggesting that in her search for suitable appellation their mother had dipped into *Hamlet* I,i.). In addition to being younger, Marcellus was the smaller and better-looking sibling (indeed, so ill-favored was Horatio that, upon spotting him earlier in the evening, Mickey had felt compelled to apologize to his kid: "Man, I'm sorry— I thought *you* was ugly until I seen this Horn."). Marcellus was, finally, the one said to be able to box. Not that the kid had gotten a chance to show it against Jackson at the previous week's cotillion.

What transpired between the two young men bore only a passing resemblance to boxing as we know it, and may actually have been closer to the event in the Greek games known as the pankration. This latter was an "all-in" form of fighting that frowned only on biting and gouging and might well have brought professional wrestling to mind, that is (*pace* Ariel's father), were it for real. Pausanias gives us a taste of it in his *Guide to Greece*, where he treats of an Arcadian pankratist named Arrachion going for his third Olympic victory. "He was fighting his last opponent for the wild olive," Pausanias tells us, "when the opponent, whoever he was, caught Arrachion and held him with a scissors grip and at the same time throttled him with his hands; so Arrachion broke one of the man's toes. Arrachion died of strangling, and at the same time the strangler gave in from the pain to his toe." A problem for the judges? Not at all. According to Pausanias, "The Eleans crowned the dead body of Arrachion with the wreath and proclaimed it as the winner."

Jackson did not, strictly speaking, attempt to strangle the younger Horn during their time together. Nor did he break any of the kid's toes (largely, I suspect, because he was wearing gloves and he couldn't get at them). But he did, at one point, while tripping over his own size fifteens and crashing to the deck, throw his legs up and around the astonished Marcellus to complete a version (doubtless by way of Antonino Rocca) of the scissors hold. The short of it was, Jackson was simply not going to let the kid box. Hell, he was not going to let him get off at all.

To this end, the big galoot—who was twenty-five to his opponent's sixteen, and 240 to the kid's maybe 190—was all over the youngster like a shower of molasses. With the start of each round, Jackson would rush the kid and the kid would how-do-you-do him with a jab. Jackson would almost literally "eat" the jab. By this I mean, the kid's fist and arm would vanish into Jackson, who would proceed to envelope the kid himself with wide, oleaginous swings at his shoulders, kidneys, back of the head. It was truly weird. The more Marcellus struggled, the more he fought Jackson, the deeper he seemed to disappear into the older kid's grasp; and when the referee stepped in, as he did repeatedly, and tried to separate them, you could almost see the long strands of viscosity begrudging their separation.

It occurred to me that this must have been what it was like for Brer Rabbit to fight the Tar Baby, although Jackson was not of course so passive-aggressive and, in the end, when he had the kid completely wasted, he did manage to sledge him to the floor. . . . Anyway, something like this tableau, in less agreeable colors, surely, must have painted itself upon the consciousness of the elder Horn, as he exulted from his perch upon the ring ropes. In his mind, Horatio must have been getting Jackson back for what he did to Little Brother.

Naturally, the crowd was ecstatic. Harry the Humper and Nancy Sinatra, I'm sure, had many clever and learned things to say about the mastodonic contest that was heating up before them, but I couldn't hear them above the delirium. Nor could I catch what Mickey was saying to his kid between cantos. So I moved still closer to the corner. I was actually sitting on the steps leading up to the ring when Jackson got popped again.

This time, after the eight-count was tolled, the big lug was led back to the corner by the referee. The punch had apparently done more than alter his perspective. It had unbuckled his headgear. I watched as Mickey reached up to fix the thing, listened as the trainer made a futile attempt to establish verbal contact with his kid, whose eyes were slipping back and forth in their sockets rather like the bubble in a surveyor's level.

It developed—rather mysteriously, I remember thinking at the time—that the strap of the headgear was not merely undone, as the referee had thought, but broken. Indeed, Mickey held up the evidence for the official to see.

"Tape," said the ref. "You got any?"

"Sure, always got tape," said the trainer, even as he reached back and stopped his assistant from extracting from his pocket what I later figured out was a roll of same.

Mickey made a great show of checking his own pockets, then his aluminum case at the base of the steps.

"I don't know, man," he said to the official, his face radiating sincerity. "Always got tape with me. I know—why didn't I think of it? Negra's got it with her."

As the third-man-in hurried across the canvas to seek tape in the enemy camp, Refugio was dousing Jackson with water, which, as there were chunks of ice floating in the bucket and the assistant trainer was pouring the fluid down the front of the kid's trunks, seemed to do wonders for his attention. Mickey, meanwhile, was talking to the kid, breaking out every appeal in his repertoire. For starters, he brought up Negra, shared with the kid her alleged last words before she was carted off to the hospital.

"Mickey," he said she had told him, "don't worry about me. Go out there and stay with Jackson, no matter what. Because this is Jackson's night. This the night he going to make up for all them years of bad luck, all them years watching the Mitch Greens and the Carl 'The Truth' Williams walk away with what should have been his." The trainer paused a moment, then flirted with eternal damnation. "May I rot in hell," he said, "if she don't tell me this. But—but I don't want you thinking too much about Negra."

"Okay," said Jackson, who was still a little woozy.

"I don't want you thinking about how Negra been working you corner all these years, how she been looking out for you like you was her own son. I don't want you thinking about Negra being all alone by herself with nobody around in a cold hospital bed."

"You right," said the kid, tilting his head and shaking it, as if to get water out of his ear. "I'm putting Negra out of my mind right now."

This threw the trainer, but only for a moment. By this time the referee had come back with the adhesive, and as he taped the headgear together, the trainer tried a different tack. "Yes sir, I don't want you thinking about nothing but this fellow Horn, and how you going to get back into this fight and beat him—"

"That's what I'm studying on."

"I don't even want you thinking about the things he been saying about you, about—"

"Wait a minute. Horn been saying things about me?"

"That's what I hear."

"Like what?"

Mickey shrugged. "Oh, nothing much. Just that you punch like a girl—"

"Punch like a girl!" This was so incredibly lame I couldn't believe Mickey was saying it. But he clearly knew his kid a lot better than I did. For a scowl overtook Jackson's immense physiognomy, caved it in like a beanbag chair.

"What else he been saying?"

"That you about as smart as them retards you always working with."

"Retards! He called them *retards?*" This was insupportable to a humanist such as Jackson. Outrage bumped irritation off his pan. "He got anymore to say?"

"Let me see if I can remember." The trainer appeared to ransack his mind. "Oh, yeah—he was going to teach you a lesson, bust you up for putting you weight on Marcellus."

"Okay," said Jackson, his voice pouring out warm and thick, like syrup into a bucket, "I think I'm ready now."

Jackson *was* ready and, curiously, Horn was not. Or, rather, he was beyond ready. You could see him over there, pacing back and forth like some enormous jungle cat. He was wrapped so tight he couldn't sit down, not that his trainer wanted him to. Mickey would say later that, the whole time he was going through the charade of the tape, he was watching George Washington across the way, noticing that the opposing trainer was busy souping his kid up, which, Mickey felt, was counterindicated because the kid was sky-high already. What Washington should have been doing, said Mickey, was bringing his kid down to a governable idle, getting him to relax and think about how he was going to take Jackson out. "I knew," said the trainer, "soon as I seen my kid go out there and cock his fist, that punch lands it's all over."

Now, Jackson was slower than a federal tax refund, but he was stronger than ten acres of garlic. And he didn't much need speed, anyway, for Horn provided enough of that commodity for both of them. Mickey was right. Horn was about as composed as a runaway freight train with the engineer, a heart attack victim, slumped over the throttle. All it took to derail him was a series of prodigious Jackson right hands.

I suspect that no one who saw this fight will ever forget how it ended. For after the last right hand, Horn did not simply go down. Rather, he went for a stroll. He picked his pickled way across the canvas, starting from Jackson's corner, where he'd received his walking papers, his head slouched back on his shoulders, his mouth wide open and his great brown jowls swaying to and fro and making a vaguely obscene noise, as his breath coursed roughly through them. Finally, he came to a halt among his own people, turned, and plumped down heavily on the floor, slowly drooping forward until his head kissed the canvas.

The whole while this was happening, the entire arena watched virtually without a sound, as if transfixed. When the kid finally completed his peregrination, the place exploded. The crowd seemed to pour down to the ring, over the barrier that kept the press inviolate, until it was lapping at Jackson's feet.

The heavyweight was bleeding from the ear, but he didn't seem to notice. He was, curiously, a little miffed.

"Think back to the first round," he yelled at these newfound votaries. "How many of you thought I was going to lose? Be honest now. Raise your hand."

Not one of them did.

Chapter 9

SALON DES REFUSÉS

After the Gloves, I did as most of the kids did. I went on hiatus. Stayed away from Casa Rosario for about three weeks.

I returned one April afternoon just as day was beginning to call it a night, pushed open the heavy metal doors, and was greeted by a pungent, decidedly invasive aroma that I suspect will always make me think of Negra. Odor of Verbena. And there was the lady herself, down the hall at her desk, guarding the entrance to the gym proper. Apparently recovered from the blow to her "ovary," she was on the horn, riffing away no doubt at one of her sisters.

Stepping to the the edge of the training floor, I sensed that the gym had recaptured its immemorial rhythms. Not only were all the bags under heavy siege, and the kids in triplicate before the mirrors, but the radio was blasting forth some of the most lachrymose, goober-bunting stuff you'd ever want to hear.

In the *mis-en-scène,* the usual talent was variously deployed— arranged, it struck me, in virtual John Rogers Groups. By this I mean, the kids were grouped upon the floor as if they were plaster figurines set out to illustrate a proverb. Milton and Luke were drubbing adjacent sacks under the pensive gaze of Refugio, even as Smooth was over on the calisthenic mat with a collection of urchins, breaking off the steps that had made him famous in the long-ago with the Rocksteady Crew. Mickey was posted by the sparring ring, where Ralphie and a kid named Pepsi (so named because his father was out getting one for his mother when she decided to bring him into the world) were enjoying a respite from the exchange of fistic ideas. It was the lull between rounds, and the trainer was conversing with one of several youngsters queued up and awaiting an audience, in a *tableau vivante* that might have been titled, "A Mentor's Guidance."

You would never know from the cozy picture before me that the gym had sustained further attrition in the handful of days just since the Gloves closed down. You'd never suspect that Jackson had decamped for Gleason's, where he expected to turn money fighter with a professional manager who'd vamped him into thinking he was the next George Foreman. Or that Johnny Luna had not been manifest since the Boxing Commission took his occupation away. Or that Chino Number One had gotten into a wrangle on West Farms Road and been shot in the stomach and hied to Puerto Rico to get a handle on his need for wild justice and recuperate.

The news—especially the part about Chino, which I'd gleaned from Mickey over the phone—was disturbing. Disturbing, that is, to me and, naturally, to the trainer, but not somehow to the gym itself. Not really. A rock had been dropped in a pond and, for a few furious seconds, the water ringed away. Then, well . . . nothing. The wound covered over, and pretty soon the water bugs were back skimming the veneer. The gym had its own protective placidity, its own claustral imperturbability and insularity from the outside world.

You'd never know either, to look at the picture before me, that, to quote old Mush, "the wowsers were at it again." Which is to say, that the fine, upstanding citizens of America were trying once more to kill boxing in this country.

In the past, the abolitionists had had their best innings during eras of confidence in America. They'd done best of all at the turn of the century, back when such as James J. Jeffries and Tommy Burns were throwing haymakers and were limited, by popular outcry, to throwing them overseas and in obscure corners of the American West. The early 1900s was a period of "Uplift," a time when Americans, encouraged by philosopher Herbert Spencer's rosy take on Darwin, believed in the March of Progress and the Perfectability of Man. Boxing was perceived as an atavism, an unseemly throwback to the days when men lived in caves, an ugly blot on the developing scheme of things, which, according to the new mandate, was getting better and better with each passing hour. "Two things revived boxing [during this period]," says Randy Roberts, a professor from Texas who has written well about the pastime. "The first was Jack Johnson, who took the heavyweight crown from Burns in Sydney, Australia, in 1908. Johnson was black and arrogant, and even reformers agreed that he needed a good beating." The second was World War One. "Next to the carnage of Verdun and the Sommes, a cut eye or a bruised lip seemed tame stuff indeed. All the reformers' thrilling talk about a finer world and a better people now seemed chimerical."

In recent years the drill has changed, thanks again to boxing's inconstant bedfellow: TV. Nowadays, all it takes to get the abolitionists stirred up—and taken seriously—is the telecasting of a series of matches the general public considers particularly brutal, or of a fatality. Some months before the Gloves there had been three such matches. The first was a contest between Alexis Arguello and Aaron Pryor, which contained much of what was exhilarating and terrifying about boxing. It paired a younger and stronger man, a romantic stylist (and certifiable flake said to be a heavy cocaine user) who swooped into combat from all angles, against the old master, a three-times world champion who was seeking an unprecedented fourth set of laurels, a figure of heart-warming dignity and classic abilities who advanced with cool assuredness behind the jab and iced his confections with the straight right hand. Pryor simply wore Arguello down, as if he were offering a seminar in geologic time, finished him with a torrent of blows.

The second match was between Larry Holmes and Randy

"Tex" Cobb. Cobb failed to win a single round, but was simply there for Holmes for upwards of an hour. The fight was called a "massacre" in the press and was generally regarded as an "indictment" of boxing. It was not very pretty. And yet, Holmes versus Cobb was a recognizable entity—a staple, in fact, of the Cauliflower Industry. It was a species of club fight that is not meant for general consumption, but for the fascination of a select audience of unregenerate fight bugs in an appropriate setting, say, in L.A.'s Olympic Auditorium. There have always been fighters like Cobb (the stalwart of my grandfather's youth was aptly named Joe Grimm), white fighters, by and large, who achieve a certain nutsy renown for their ability to sponge up punishment. The beatings, in the eyes of the fancy, become *sui generis,* beautiful in their own grotesque way, *fleurs du mal.* The problem with the Cobb fight was not so much that it was made (the critique of "mismatch" is foolish, even disingenuous, as everyone knew from the start what Cobb's role was), but that it was aired on network TV during prime viewing hours with a rabid Howard Cosell applying the commentary.

These two fights sandwiched a third, which trained back and forth on them like a spotlight from hell, making the darkness at the root of boxing visible. In this third fight Ray "Boom Boom" Mancini killed Duk Koo Kim, ruptured a blood vessel, apparently, in the oriental warrior's brain in the penultimate round of their charmless brawl for the Lightweight marbles. The Kim fight became a *cause célèbre.* It was not necessary to know anything about boxing—or about the men who professed it and the world they came from—to take a shot at it. It was open season on the pastime, as Mushy said, for any "sob sister" with a voice box.

Then, in January, just as this year's Gloves was getting underway, the American Medical Association's Advisory Panel on Brain Injury in Boxing issued a much-awaited report. The report was extraordinary, as much for its tone, which was moderate and considered throughout, as for its findings. The bad news for the ostriches in the proboxing camp was that the panel found brain damage ("as evidenced by dementia, memory loss, slurred speech, tremor, and abnormal gait") to be an authentic hazard of the sport, present in "perhaps 15% of professional boxers." The good news was that the panel counted ringside physicians, as well as neurologists, in its expert company. Thus boxing was viewed in the round: Its ravages were seen against its benefits and against the ravages of other sports.

The panel noted that, in the thirty-five-year period between 1945 and 1979, 335 deaths had occurred in boxing worldwide (both amateur and professional). This factored out as 0.13 deaths per 1,000 participants, which meant that boxing was nowhere near as lethal as most people thought. In fact, its fatality rate compared favorably with the rates for college football, 0.3; motorcycle racing, 0.7; scuba diving, 1.1; mountaineering, 5.1; hang-gliding, 5.6; sky-diving, 12.3; and horse racing, 12.8. As for brain injury, as I said, the panel found it to be a real and present danger; yet it also observed in passing that brain damage was not peculiar to boxing—that a recent British study had discovered "conditions resembling the punch-drunk state in rugby football players, professional wrestlers, a parachute jumper, and steeplechase jockeys." It observed as well that "many boxing physicians feel that the incidence of the punch-drunk syndrome has been sharply reduced because of increased medical supervision." In their thoughtful concluding portion, the experts stated, "Some would favor banning boxing completely, but this is not a realistic solution to the problem of brain injury in boxing. Moreover, the sport does not seem any more dangerous than other sports presently accepted by society."

One might have expected the report to dampen the reformers' ardor. It didn't, largely because it was accompanied in the *Journal of the American Medical Association* by a pair of incendiary editorials that got more media attention than the report itself. In one, George D. Lundberg, M.D. pretended to see the virtues of boxing, but asked whether the sport was worth the price of "chronic brain damage." He declared his true feelings in his last paragraph: "This editor personally believes that boxing is wrong at its base. . . . Boxing seems to me to be less of a sport than is cock-fighting; boxing is an obscenity."

In the companion editorial, someone named Maurice W. Van Allen, M.D. showed himself to be a complete hysteric. Van Allen did not pretend to pull his punches, but flailed wildly at anyone and anything in our society that made light of head injury. Van Allen was scandalized by the world of boxing. And no wonder. I would be too had the real world of boxing borne a resemblance to the one he trumped up. It was a nightmare world ruled by cold-eyed Fagins in the business of "the recruitment of children"—of "minority youth" no less—who were sacrificed "for the profit and delectation of self-styled sportsmen." A place utterly devoid of human feeling, where "the punch-drunk fighter is an amusing oddity, seldom the object of pity and not, it seems, a catalyst of guilt." In Van Allen's view, boxing was a "basic degradation" that soiled all those "who fight for the entertainment of others even when victorious." It was not just "savagery." It was—are you ready?—"sin" itself.

As I stood on the fringe of the training floor and watched Casa Rosario take up its immutable rhythms, I thought about how little of this debate, and the hot air it swirled in, had pierced the gym's protective carapace. I wondered what the kids would make of Lundberg and Van Allen, whether they could possibly understand what was really eating them. I have no doubt that the two men were genuinely concerned about the health of fighters (in the abstract, at least), about the increasingly disturbing news about the effect of boxing, over time, on the fighter's brain. Yet one had only to attend the language of their complaint to recognize that their real objection was not medical, but ethical. Lundberg objected to boxing rather than, say, to football or horse racing (whose fatality rate is higher and whose incidence of brain injury might well be comparable) because in those two sports brain injury is only the "by-product" of the activity. This is to say, what distressed Lundberg and Van Allen was the sight of two half-naked men in a ring with their dukes up being egged on by a supposedly bloodthirsty mob on the other side of the twine. What distressed the good doctors, and what continues to bother reformers around the globe, was what this "public spectacle of brutality" averred about the human species—how little distance we've come since we dropped from the trees.

Lundberg and Van Allen were "humanists" in the sense that Camus uses the phrase. They were men "blinded by narrow certainties." They were ethicists uninterested in the ethics (or ethos) of others, specifically of those human beings they would purportedly help. They did not care that Ariel—himself, with any luck, a future physician—treasured boxing because it enabled him "to express a side of me that I've never been able to express, a part of me, believe it or not, that is creative." They did not care because their "morals" made them indifferent to the beauty and artistry of boxing. They did not see the fighting-ring canvas as a "blazing white island" (to use James Dickey's figure for the unprinted page), awaiting population by the boxer's creations. They did not see this because when they looked at the boxer through the lens of righteousness they did not see an artist at work, but only a brute in harness.

What, I wondered, would they have made of literary critic Ronald Levao's notion that a boxer's work merits the same kind of attention we lavish on a dancer's or a sculptor's—his assertion that "the fighter creates a style in a world of risk and opportunity," that a great fighter, like a great artist, "redefines the possible"? Or Levao's assertion (seconded inadvertently by Smooth) that the symbiosis between the fighter and the fancy is much healthier, certainly more complex, than the reformers would allow—his observation that the crowd at a fight (such dim bulbs as Nancy Sinatra Boots and her wheel-chair cowboys notwithstanding) is not there to witness a bloodletting, but to feel throbbingly alive. That it is not a massacre the crowd hopes for, but an even-handed contest (indeed, at most fights, when one fellow begins to overwhelm the other you hear the cry "Stop the fight!" carry through the multitude). One where the outcome is always in question and "character" (that wonderful boxing word) is continually on display. One where the tension is thick as a nun's ankle and excursions into pity and fear are tied up close by, ready to shove off at a moment's notice. (Or to quote Smooth, "I don't believe all this jive about people going to the fights thinking, 'Hey, this guy might die, let's go see it.' No, the people go to see the skill and the actual fight. They go because a fight's like life, only more so.")

What, I wondered, would Van Allen *et al.* have made of Chino's saying he fought for "recreation"? It's a startling idea to us housebroken gringos who last raised our hands in grade school, and then only to indicate we needed to go to the bathroom. In a famous conversation with Hemingway, Scott Fitzgerald is said to have remarked, "Let me tell you about the very rich. They are different from you and me." Well, let me tell you about the very poor. They are too. They are closer to their emotions than we are, and these emotions are relatively uncooked. For the most part, they have not learned—or, more to the point, they have not seized or been afforded the opportunity—to sublimate their more primal feelings. Which is to say, unlike their "betters," they have not learned to divert their hatred and envy to socially acceptable ends, say, to screwing their peers in business deals. Not only are their feelings more raw and accessible than ours, they are apparently more elastic as well. In any case, they permitted Bobby Chacon (who gets my vote for pugilistic ideal), when he was just a teen-ager, to spend the night at an amateur tournament in the same cot as his buddy, Danny "Little Red" Lopez, and then go out the next day and, with no remorse whatsoever, deposit Danny among the sugar-plum fairies. Some years later they also permitted Bobby to name one of his kids "Alexis"—this in homage to Alexis Arguello, shortly after he was eclipsed by the master in their battle for the Junior Lightweight title.

What the good doctors didn't see—couldn't see, I suppose, looking down upon the ghetto from the heights of privilege—was that, for a kid like Chino, stepping into the ring was like spending a day at the beach. At least in boxing there were rules and a third-man-in to see that they were upheld, and nobody was grabbing a bottle when things started to get rough, or pulling a knife or, as somebody apparently recently did with the kid, a gun. What the reformers didn't seem to realize is that, for some people, the world is full of danger. They didn't understand that most of the youngsters in the gym had already had a brush (or two or three) with violent death, and that, to their mind, the least of their worries was sustaining brain injury from boxing (which, admittedly, most of them could not fully comprehend—this, in great part, because, despite the popular belief, one doesn't see punch-drunk fighters anymore). The reformers didn't understand that most of these kids looked at life as a lottery, as a gun held up to the head with one of the chambers loaded.

"In anything there's a danger," Vince Shomo, the comptroller of *Ring* magazine and four-times New York Golden Gloves winner, told me one day over lunch. We were talking about Mancini-Kim and the latest findings on brain injury, and he proceeded to furnish me with an *exemplum* that neatly points up the boxer's attitude toward the hazards of his craft and life itself. "Let me tell you," he said, "about this neighborhood drunk we used to have, name of Van Puddin' that had a little dog called Sonny. Now, Van Puddin' used to get plastered and walk around the street. One summer night, I'll never forget, it rained cats and dogs. I mean, it *poured*. Van Puddin' started out for the liquor store, which is still on the corner of One hundred forty-third Street and Seventh Avenue. He began that long walk from his house by the fire station in the Two hundred block, and he went to cross over to buy his bottle, when this car, going sixty-five, came racing down Seventh Avenue. It never stopped. It hit Van Puddin' and knocked him on the other side of the street, knocked him right out of his shoes!

"You know, there's a saying: If a car hits you and knocks your shoes off, you're supposed to be dead. Well, the ambulance came and took Van Puddin' and Sonny, because the little dog wouldn't let him go by himself, took them to Harlem Hospital. I saw Van Puddin' three days later with a broken arm—that's all that happened to him. Come winter time, Van Puddin' is walking down the sidewalk from that same liquor store with his bottle of Tokay. He slips on some ice and busts his brains open. Kills himself right out on the street. You hear what I'm saying? When it's your time, it's your time. If it's meant for you, you could be in the shower."

The kids in the gym, boxers in general, I found, regarded the future with a kind of cheerful fatalism that was almost classically Greek. It was the present that engaged their hopes and fears. And what they feared most of all, I discovered, was aimlessness, social impotence, invisibility, or the wrong kind of visibility—getting caught up in the cycle of violence that only gets you dead (it's a well-known fact that homicide is the number-one killer of young males in the ghetto) or time in the slammer. What the kids feared was the kind of "brain damage" that is born of despair (what one does see in the ghetto is crazy people, which is to say, people punchy from life). What Van Allen & Co. didn't realize was that most of the kids in the gym had never done anything with their lives before, never given themselves over totally to something, pursued it with the passion of an anchorite, denied themselves easy pleasures in quest of something bright and austere and symbolic of heroic endeavor: miniature gloves, say, made of gold to be worn on a chain around the neck.

It occurred to me, as I watched the kids on the training floor begin to draw near and cluster around Mickey, that the reformers did not get boxing at all. And not getting it—and fearing, I suspected, what it whispered to them about their own darker side—they reduced it to a lurid cartoon. It occurred to me that these men had missed the central paradox of the gym, one which underlies the game. Which is to say, they failed to see that the gym, boxing itself, was the place, strange as it may seem, where the youngsters of the ghetto, or at least the harder cases among them, went to be safe. They failed to see that the gym was a sort of *salon des refusés,* a place, in Nietzsche's phrase, where "combat is salvation" and "every talent unfolds itself in fighting." A place where, when you had to go there the people there felt compelled—on their terms, of course—to take you in. In short, the gym was a home.

It's funny. During the past year, people, friends, had asked me why I was doing this, hanging out at a boxing gym, mixing it up some. I told them, well, a variety of things, whatever I thought they'd like—or, in some cases, not like—to hear. The truth was, I really didn't know why. All I knew was that I took my pulse one day and boxing was what made it flutter. It was the thing, I suppose, I could least imagine myself doing and was therefore the most intriguing. I see now that what I wanted to do was to cut loose from the familiar, to voyage forth, enter another world. I had contracted a mild case of what Baudelaire calls, "the great malady: horror of one's home." Which is to say, a revulsion of the known, of a life not fully explored and spent, of the dull drizzle in my soul. The irony is, of course, that what I ended up doing was entering another man's home, sojourning among his extended family.

I was thinking these things as I moved out onto the training floor and gravitated toward the sparring ring, where Mickey was holding forth among the ephebes like the *gymnastai* of old. I quickly gathered that the focus of the assemblage was on the Book of Holy Writ, swaddled in red leather, that Reggie had tucked in his trunks. Reggie was saying he'd gotten the book from his uncle and had started reading it, but he didn't know too much about it. He wondered what Mickey thought of it.

The trainer took the Bible from the kid and began to thumb through it, then stopped and gave it back to him. "It's very exciting to start reading about David and Jehovah and all them names, but," he said with emphasis, "you can't let youself get too involved with it. Because you do and you mind it's going to—" Here Mickey made a snapping noise with his fingers.

What? I said. You go crazy?

"Cuckoo, like a clock."

"If you read the Bible too much? Are you serious?"

"Truthfully," said the trainer, ignoring me as best he could, so as to get on with the excursus, "the Bible is just a code of rules men must go by. It begin with the beginning of time."

"What about the stories?" I insisted. "What about the people in the Bible and all they go through?"

"Oh, it's nice and all. The Bible talk about Ham and Jehovah and all them. It say we was created in seven days, whatever. But you know what the scientists say, right?" The trainer had turned back to the ephebes. He was moving among them with his eyes. "They say a long time ago, millions of years ago, really, the sun explode and the pieces float around. Then all these steams surround the clouds for a while, blah, blah, blah. And the world fly to a cool atmosphere. And when it turn around, it face the sun—that's how come we got the summertime. Anyway, in the beginning, there's all this water all over the place, and lands grow out of it. Then comes what they call the 'evolution.' Bugs was first—"

"Bugs was first!" I said. I couldn't help myself. I was enchanted by the trainer's cosmology, which struck me as the Big Bang theory strained through Thales, one of the "seven wise men" of ancient Greece. But "bugs" was too much. It was bad enough that we came from fish.

"That's right—*bugs,*" said the trainer, looking at me sharply. "You know why?" He was addressing the kids again. "Because sometime you leave a bottle of water in a warm place and you come back later and what do you see? All these little animals jumping up and down. From *nowhere!*"

This was great stuff—I had no idea that Mickey was a man of science—and I would have loved to have pursued it. But the lady of the house was beckoning from across the training floor. And we all went over, the whole gym, it seemed, en masse.

Standing next to Negra was a kid who'd been sent round by Hector "Macho" Camacho, the celebrated barrio bad boy Mickey had introduced to boxing maybe a decade earlier. The kid was fourteen or so trying to pass for twenty and, apparently, was not doing such a hot job of it. He was dressed for the part, certainly—his hair was swabbed with about a quart of crank oil, and his shirt was split to the navel, revealing, atop a chest innocent of foliage, the requisite nest of gold chains. But his eyes betrayed him: Where there should have been fire, there was only frailty.

"I got this problem, Mick," came this little voice.

"Shoot," said the trainer.

"Well, it's like this, I—I—" the kid began to stammer, then pumped it all out in a rush, "I got this girl pregnant. I don't know what to do. Macho say I should talk—"

"Hell, that's nothing." Mickey threw up his hands histrionically and smiled. "Whew! You know, son, for a minute there you have me worried. I thought you say you got a problem?"

The kid looked at the trainer, mystified. "Yeah, but my mother—"

"You love this girl?" asked the trainer.

The kid nodded. "I think so."

"You got a phone in you house?"

The kid nodded again.

"Good. Give me the number, because I'm going to call you mother, and me and her we going to sit down and have us a chat. This ain't the end of the world, you know."

"But all these people, this priest in the church and my mother, they keep saying . . . You going to call my mom tonight?"

"Listen, son," said the trainer, taking the kid's face in his hands and looking deep into his eyes, "let me tell you something. If it wasn't for what you got hanging, and that soft place a girl got, wouldn't none of us be here. You wouldn't be here. Bill here wouldn't be here. Hell, I wouldn't even be here. And you know what that mean, right?"

The kid shook his head.

"Wouldn't nobody be here to get you ready for next year's Gloves."

This said, the trainer turned the kid around and marched him toward the office, where he would get his Juan Hancock on a piece of ABF parchment and, with any luck, indenture him for life. Mickey paused only, in the midst of these maneuvers, to give me a wink and Negra a chance to reach up and pop the gold stud from the youngster's ear.